THE COGNITION OF GEOGRAPHIC SPACE

This book is dedicated to Reg Golledge.
A good friend and colleague

THE COGNITION OF GEOGRAPHIC SPACE

Rob Kitchin

*Department of Geography, National University of Ireland,
Maynooth, County Kildare, Ireland*

and

Mark Blades

*Department of Psychology, University of Sheffield,
Sheffield, UK*

I.B.Tauris *Publishers*
LONDON • NEW YORK

Published in 2002 by I.B.Tauris & Co Ltd
6 Salem Road, London W2 4BU
175 Fifth Avenue, New York NY 10010
Website: http://www.ibtauris.com

In the United States and Canada distributed by St. Martin's Press
175 Fifth Avenue, New York NY 10010

ISBN 1 86064 704 9 hardback
     1 86064 705 7 paperback

A full CIP record for this book is available from the British Library
A full CIP record for this book is available from the Library of Congress

Library of Congress catalog card: available

Typeset in Baskerville 11/12pt by Q3 Bookwork, Loughborough
Printed and bound in Great Britain by MPGBooks Ltd, Bodmin, Cornwall

Contents

Figures and Tables

Tables

Preface

Over the last 40 years, researchers from a number of disciplines – including psychology, geography, planning, anthropology, computer science, and cognitive science – have sought to understand how we think about and behave in geographic space. They have been particularly interested in analyzing the cognitive maps and spatial cognition of people, and sometimes other animals. That is, analyzing what people know about spatial relationships at the geographic scale and how they learn and use this knowledge in everyday spatial behavior and decision making.

To date, there has been little attempt to draw together theory and practice from across and within disciplines and to critically assess the 'state of play' beyond edited collections, and theses concerning specific populations such as children. As a consequence, this book has three principal aims. First, to draw together the findings of empirical research so far conducted and the theories that have been developed, comparing and contrasting different positions to provide a synthesis of knowledge. Second, to provide a reflexive, critical appraisal of the field, charting the development of study across disciplines and assessing contemporary theory and practice. Third, to forward new ideas and theories concerning cognitive mapping and to outline a future agenda for research which might guide subsequent studies.

Rob Kitchin and Mark Blades

CHAPTER 1

Introducing Cognitive Mapping

Our lives comprise a myriad of spatial behaviors; movements across
and within spaces. From crawling across a playroom, to traveling to
school, to driving to work, to flying great distances for business
meetings or a holiday, our daily lives involve hundreds of complex
spatial choices and spatial decisions that have to be successfully
negotiated. In the vast majority of cases, in order to undertake such
complex spatial choices and decisions we rely not on external references such as maps but on a previously acquired spatial understanding of the world in which we live; our ability to remember and
think about spatial relations at the geographic scale. Indeed, spatial
behavior would be limited or impossible without at least some
knowledge of the environment (or the ability to learn about a new
environment). As a consequence, any research that has as its aim the
study of behavior has to take into account the knowledge that an
organism has of its environment. *Cognitive map* is a term which refers
to an individual's knowledge of spatial and environmental relations,
and the cognitive processes associated with the encoding and retrieval of the information from which it is composed.

1.1 Definition of Cognitive Maps

As with so much terminology, the phrase 'cognitive map' is a useful
shorthand phrase, but it can also be misleading, partly because of the
emphasis on the word 'map' and partly because the term has been
used in different ways since it was first used by Tolman (1948). Other
terms that have been used to describe cognitive maps include:
abstract maps (Hernandez, 1991), cognitive configurations (Golledge,
1977), cognitive images (Lloyd, 1982), cognitive representations
(Downs and Stea, 1973a), cognitive schemata (Lee, 1968), cognitive
space (Montello, 1989), cognitive systems (Canter, 1977), conceptual
representations (Stea, 1969), configurational representations (Kirasic,
1991), environmental images (Lynch, 1960), mental images (Pocock,
1973), mental maps (Gould and White, 1974), mental representations

(Gale, 1982), orientating schemata (Neisser, 1976), place schemata (Axia *et al.*, 1991), spatial representations (Allen *et al.*, 1978), spatial schemata (Lee, 1968), topological representations (Shemyakin, 1962), topological schemata (Griffin, 1948), and world graphs (Lieblich and Arbib, 1982).

To a large extent these terms are interchangeable, but we will persevere with the term 'cognitive map'. Indeed, it should be borne in mind that the term itself is little more than a useful umbrella term under which to group a selection of the research into people's spatial, geographical and environmental knowledge. This research includes, for example, investigations into how people learn new environments; how they find their way through familiar environments; how they draw sketch maps from memory; or how they give verbal route directions; or how they use their representation of the environment to make decisions about where to live, where to work, or where to travel.

As such, the term 'cognitive map' does not imply that an individual has a cartographic or any other type of map 'in the head', because the word 'map' is simply a convenient label to summarize the information encoded in a person's cognitive representation of the environment (Kuipers, 1982; Newcombe, 1985). However, one advantage of using the term 'map' is to emphasize that the representations we are discussing are representations of space, and spatial relationships. In other words, we distinguish between knowledge, beliefs, and behaviors that are based on representations of space and other types of knowledge or beliefs that might be represented spatially but which do not necessarily depend on a spatial representation. For instance, some early research, referred to at the time as the study of 'mental maps', included investigations of people's attitudes to places (e.g., Gould and White, 1974). In these studies, people judged how much they liked, for example, different areas of their country. The preferences for different areas could then be plotted as contours on a cartographic map to show areas of high and low desirability. This research is related to the study of cognitive maps, but in this case people's preferences need not have been derived from a spatial representation of the country.

Irrespective of the particular terminology used by a researcher, the aim of most cognitive map research is to identify an individual's cognitive representation of the environment, and this includes:

> the awareness, impressions, information, images, and beliefs that people
> have about environments... it implies not only that individuals and groups

2

have information and images about the existence of these environments and of their constituent elements, but also that they have impressions about their character, function, dynamics, and structural inter-relatedness, and that they imbue them with meaning, significance, and mythical-symbolic properties (Moore and Golledge, 1976: p. xii).

Although the content of cognitive maps includes all the aspects listed by Moore and Golledge, most of the research into cognitive maps has, however, concentrated on the geographical and spatial elements of the representation (Kitchin, 1994). As such, there are a large number of studies that have investigated people's knowledge of places, routes, distances, directions, and other spatial relationships, but there are only a comparatively small number of studies that have attempted to link this spatial knowledge to the attitudes, beliefs, and feelings that people have about an environment (e.g., Wood and Beck, 1976, 1989).

The diversity of the terms used to describe essentially the same aspect of cognition arises because the centrality of cognitive maps to spatial behavior has been recognized by researchers in many disciplines, including geography, planning, psychology, anthropology, computer science, cognitive science, and neuroscience. This mix of interested parties has been both an advantage and a disadvantage in the development of cognitive mapping research. It has been an advantage because the field of cognitive mapping has attracted many different approaches, and stimulated many ideas. It has been a disadvantage because the diversity of approaches has sometimes resulted in a fragmented approach to study. In the course of this book we detail some of the approaches that have been used in the investigation of cognitive maps, charting their connections and divergences, and give examples of some of the empirical research findings. We adopt a rather critical position in relation to some of this research, and point out that there has been comparatively little progress in developing a unified theory of cognitive mapping that can effectively incorporate all the research findings. In adopting this critical approach, we hope to highlight the research areas and methodologies that may offer the best way forward.

1.2 The Origins of Cognitive Map Research

The first research into cognitive maps was with animals, and the first theories of route learning were derived from studies of rats running mazes. Hull (1943) described route learning in terms of stimulus–response behaviors, which were reinforced by a successful

outcome. In other words, an animal learning a route from a starting box to a food box in a maze would recognize a choice point
(the stimulus) and make an appropriate response (e.g., turn left)
because on a previous occasion such behavior had resulted in
finding the food. Longer and longer routes could be built up as
each individual stimulus–response was linked with another to form
a chain of behaviors that created a successful route through the
maze.

Tolman and Honzik (1930) suggested that rats learning a route
learnt more than just a series of stimulus–response connections.
They pointed out that if a rat had learnt a specific route through a
maze to a food box, and then part of the route was blocked off,
the rats would be able to find an alternative route to the food box,
even if the alternative route involved moving through novel parts
of the maze. Tolman (1948) argued that rats could do this because
when learning the route they internalized more information about
the maze than just the choices at each junction along a specific
route. He suggested that rats had learnt, for example, the relationship between the start of the maze and the food box, and this
allowed the potential for overcoming blocked pathways without
getting lost, or the ability to take short cuts. Tolman took this latter
achievement as evidence that rats had an understanding of the
configuration of the maze, rather than just a specific route through
it, and referred to this configurational knowledge as a cognitive
map.

Later experiments demonstrated that whether rats learnt a maze
as a series of stimulus–response actions or as a cognitive map
depended on several factors, including the age of the animal, its
experience in the specific maze, and the type of environment
(McDonald and Pellegrino, 1993). For instance, in mazes with
many cues and landmarks that are external to the maze itself (such
as a light source), rats may develop cognitive maps, but in mazes
with few cues rats may rely on learning a series of turns along a
route.

It is from this early research that the studies of human cognitive
maps developed (see Chapter 2), and many of the issues raised in
the original studies (e.g., the difference between route and configurational knowledge) are still being debated with reference to
human cognitive maps (see Chapter 4). There is now also a well
established tradition of research into the spatial abilities and cognitive maps of non-human species, but this research will not be considered in this book (see Gallistel, 1993; Golledge, 1999).

1.3 Definitions of space

The central role of cognitive maps is to manage knowledge of, and behavior in, space. But what is space? Like the term 'cognitive map', *space* is a poorly defined concept and various categorizations have been forwarded (for a review, see Freundschuh, 2000). Some researchers have categorized space using a dichotomous classification in which space has been referred to as either small-scale (table-top) or large-scale space (e.g., Ittleson, 1973; Canter, 1977; Downs and Stea, 1977). Small-scale space would typically be space that can be seen from a single viewpoint, and large-scale space would require movement to perceive it completely. Other researchers have used three categories of space (e.g., Gärling and Golledge, 1989), four (e.g., Zubin, 1989; Montello, 1993) or five (e.g., Couclelis and Gale, 1986). Based on these classifications, Freundschuh and Egenhofer (1997) proposed six categories of space:

(1) *Manipulable object space.* These are small spaces that would not require movement to experience them because they can be seen from one viewpoint, and are made up of objects that are smaller than the human body.
(2) *Non-manipulable object space.* These are small spaces that are not manipulable and do require movement to experience them, because they cannot be seen from one viewpoint. These spaces would include features larger than the human body, but would usually be smaller than house-size spaces (trees for example, or cars).
(3) *Environmental space.* These are large spaces that are not manipulable and cannot be viewed from a single viewpoint and therefore require movement to experience them (for example, the inside of houses, neighborhoods, and city-size spaces).
(4) *Geographical space.* This is very large space that is not manipulable, and which, due to practical limitations, cannot be directly experienced by movement. This includes spaces larger than cities (for example, regions, countries and the world).
(5) *Panoramic space.* These are small or large spaces that are not manipulable and that do not require movement to be experienced, and include views of a room, across a field, or from a hill.
(6) *Map space.* These are small or large spaces that are manipulable, such as maps or models.

Most spaces, both real and virtual (computer) could be included in the categories described by Freundschuh and Egenhofer (1997). The category scheme emphasizes different possible spaces, but most cognitive map researchers have considered spaces that would be included in the category of 'environmental space'. There have also been several studies of 'manipulable object space' and a few of 'geographical space'. The other categories of space have, so far, hardly been considered.

As a consequence, studies have investigated the cognitive maps of rooms, buildings, college campuses, neighborhoods, city centers, regions, countries, and the world, as well as toy landscapes (which can be seen as a whole), model towns (which can be walked through), and computer simulations. The vast bulk of research has concentrated on the first four. Route knowledge has been investigated using real routes in the environment, films of real routes, slides of real routes, and invented routes (shown as slide sequences or via computer-generated images). Some of these environments have been chosen for specific reasons, but it is rare for researchers to explicitly justify the choice of environments that they have used, and therefore it might be suspected that environments have sometimes been chosen for convenience rather than for any other reason. There is certainly a great deal of research into the cognitive maps of college campuses. If researchers believe that the processes which contribute to the development of cognitive maps are common to all environments then the choice of environment may not be of great importance, because the issue is one related to the processing of environmental knowledge, whatever the specific components of that knowledge. However, some theories of cognitive mapping conflate cognitive processes with the environment itself (for example, by discussing types of 'landmark knowledge') and the type of landmark offered by one environment might be different from the type available in another environment.

In addition, the inseparable relationship between environment and behavior and the fact that researchers are using different test environments means that research concerning cognitive maps is hindered by the difficulty of replicating results. Even if the definition of a cognitive map is only considered, rather simplistically, to refer to a cognitive representation of the physical environment, there are a very large number of different physical contexts. The researcher who studies, for example, memory for faces might assume that the way an individual encodes and recalls one face may be very similar to the way the same individual encodes and recalls a different face. Despite the variation in faces across the world, there is a sense in which all faces have features in common. This is not true for environments.

To take a commonly used example, the way that Europeans learn their way round a typical European city with an irregular street pattern may be very different from the way a person in North America learns a city based on a regular grid pattern. As researchers have tested participants in quite different environments it is often difficult to make comparisons and generalize from the variety of different physical contexts that have been used. On the one hand, this makes the study of cognitive maps difficult; on the other hand, it makes the study of cognitive maps an intriguing challenge. Findings that are 'environment dependent' (i.e., they only apply to a specific or a narrow range of physical environments) may not be of great interest. What is needed is an understanding of the underlying processes of spatial and geographical reasoning which operate across many different environments.

On the one hand, the focus of research on environmental spaces may not have introduced any bias into the literature, if the theories that have been developed from results in environmental space also apply to other categories of space. On the other hand, if the processes contributing to the development of cognitive maps are different in different spaces, this is something we will not discover until there are more studies that include the same participants being tested in more than one type of environment.

1.4 Why Study Cognitive Maps?

As already noted, the central reason for studying cognitive maps is to find out more about the cognitive processes underlying people's ability to learn about their environments and the relationship between cognitive map and behavior. The study of cognitive maps also has several applied implications (Kitchin, 1994; Jackson and Kitchin, 1998).

1.4.1 Predicting spatial behavior

Cognitive maps provide insights into the relationship between people's environmental representation and their behavior in the environment. People can only operate on the basis of their own knowledge, and their plans and decisions will be based on their cognitive maps. Cadwallader (1976) suggested that cognitive maps affect at least three types of spatial decisions: first, the decision to stay or go: second, the decision of where to go, and third, the decision of which route to take. Gärling et al. (1985) added a further decision to this list; how to get there (i.e., the choice of transport). These planning decisions will be based on the individual's cognitive map which may or may not include the ideal information for the decision (Gärling and Golledge, in press), and the inherent structure of cognitive maps could bias behavior (Timmermans, 1993). To give just one example, cognitive maps may have a hierarchical structure (e.g., Golledge, 1978; McNamara, 1986; see Chapter 4) and places may be grouped in relation to salient landmarks or distinctive regions. In which case, decision making may be influenced by the perceived proximity of places (rather than their actual proximity).

Researchers have considered the relationship between the cognitive map and behavior for a variety of spatial activities that include, for example, consumer behavior (Coshall, 1985), residential and business location (Pacione, 1982), movement patterns within an urban area (Briggs, 1973a), and recreational and leisure destinations (Golledge and Timmermanns, 1990). Other researchers have pointed out that predicting behavior can be important for many reasons. For example, Canter and Larkin (1993) investigated the spatial distribution of crimes committed by serial rapists in order to predict their future behavior, and similar studies have been carried out to predict the pattern of burglaries and other crimes (e.g., Brantingham and Brantingham, 1981). More recently, Heth and Cornell (1998) pointed out that understanding the errors people make during wayfinding can contribute to planning search strategies to find lost people.

1.4.2   Other applied issues

Investigating cognitive maps is one way to identify the most effective strategies that people use to learn about the environment, and once the strategies are identified they can be taught as a way to help people improve their cognitive mapping skills. For example, learning these skills might be beneficial in helping children develop their cognitive maps (e.g., Spencer et al., 1989; Matthews, 1992). They may be particularly important for people who have not had the opportunity to develop them fully. For example, some mobility training courses for people with visual impairments incorporate strategies that can help them generate effective cognitive maps (e.g., Espinosa et al., 1998).

Research into cognitive maps is also important for some aspects of geographical work. For example, understanding more about how people integrate existing environmental information with map-based information should lead to better ways to teach geographical skills (MacEachren, 1991), and cognitive map research could improve our understanding of how people interpret remotely sensed data images (Edwards, 1991). Cognitive map research is also important in the development of GISs. Medyckyj-Scott and Blades (1992) pointed out some of the limitations in the usability of GIS, including the difficulty of comprehending some systems, and the ease with which data may be misinterpreted. One way to reduce these is to design systems that take into account the typical ways that people process geographical information, so that the GIS complements, rather than conflicts with, the cognitive processes of the users (Mark and Gould, 1991). Jacobson and Kitchin (1997) extend these ideas to the design of systems for users with visual impairments.

Successful wayfinding is one aspect of cognitive maps and a better appreciation of how people find and encode routes may be beneficial in designing in-car navigation systems which help drivers to select routes (Bonsall, 1992). At present, the content and the form of geographical information provided by these systems is usually based on designers' intuition of what might be appropriate to give to drivers, and with a few exceptions (e.g., Jackson, 1999) there has been little research into the suitability of the information provided. Wayfinding is also necessary in computer environments (such as hypertext environments, games-spaces, virtual reality) and a greater awareness of route finding processes should lead to the better design of such environments.

It may be easier to form a cognitive map of some environments than others (Abu-Obeid, 1998) and this is a factor that could be taken into consideration when designing new environments. Gärling and Golledge (1989) argued that the more we know about cognitive maps the easier it will be to plan and build environments that people can learn and navigate successfully. Other researchers have pointed out that when people find it difficult to learn existing environments, the addition of landmarks, signs, and maps can improve wayfinding if they are provided in ways that contribute to people's cognitive maps (e.g., Carpman et al., 1985; Passini, 1992).

1.4.3 Summary

In conclusion, the study of cognitive maps is important for three reasons. First, it is of intrinsic interest to understand how the human cognitive system processes spatial and geographical information and how this processing develops over the lifespan. Second, many aspects of a person's spatial behavior are based on his or her cognitive map, and understanding cognitive map processes can lead to the explanation and prediction of behavior. Third, the study of cognitive maps has many applied implications, and these include issues related to environmental planning, the design of wayfinding systems, and the education and training of skills to children and adults who can benefit from the improvement of their cognitive map abilities.

1.5   Research into Cognitive Maps

Since Hull and Tolman's experiments with rats there has been a wealth of studies in relation to the human cognition of environments—how people learn, encode, process, and use cognitive maps. In the subsequent chapters we describe in detail contemporary cognitive mapping research, outlining the central theories and findings of empirical research. We start by considering conceptual models of cognitive mapping (Chapter 2). These are very general models designed to place the processes of cognitive maps within a broad context. In the following chapters we concentrate upon specific processes, such as learning spatial information from primary experience (e.g., walking through a city) and from secondary sources (e.g., maps) (Chapter 3); how information is structured within memory (Chapter 4) and how cognitive maps develop over the lifespan (Chapter 5); and on making comparisons between the cognitive maps of individuals and groups (Chapters 6 and 7). In Chapter 8 we change the tone slightly to discuss how the evidence for theories reported in Chapters 2 through 7 is generated, examining methods of data collection and analysis and issues such as validity and reliability. In each of these chapters we adopt a critical perspective, critically appraising theories and suggesting new avenues for research. In the final two chapters of the book we detail our own conceptual model of cognitive mapping, linking a number of specific theories into a single model, and outline an agenda for future research.

CHAPTER 2

Models of Cognitive Mapping

There have been many attempts to conceptualize the process of interacting with an environment and the role of cognitive maps in determining spatial behaviors. These have ranged from fairly brief outlines to comparatively complex theories drawing on and integrating earlier proposals. An effective theory of cognitive mapping will offer some integration of the processes, concepts, and relationships involved in the formation and use of a cognitive map, and will include predictions that can be tested in empirical research. That is, the theory will go beyond the descriptive and generate hypotheses. As we will point out with reference to some of the theories summarized in this chapter, some models have not been put forward in a way that makes it possible to derive testable hypotheses from them, and although they have been important for continuing the tradition of theorizing about cognitive maps they have not always generated much empirical research.

Most, but not all, of the theories in this chapter have their basis in geographical research. In Chapters 5 and 7 we will discuss other theories of cognitive mapping which had their origin in psychological theories. This is, of course, an artificial distinction, especially with regard to the more recent theories that incorporate both geographical and psychological traditions. Nonetheless, the distinction is convenient because the varying emphases of the different theories is easier to explain in the context of their origins. Also, the theories summarized in Chapters 5 and 7 have generated rather more empirical research and are best assessed in relation to that research. A discussion of the related research will reflect on the usefulness of all the theories and highlight those issues that still need to be addressed for a fuller understanding of cognitive maps.

The models described in this chapter are divided, for convenience, into several categories: perceptual (Gibsonian), information processing, transactional, computational process models (CPM), connectionist (neural networks) and inter-representational networks

(IRN). We discuss each in turn. A new conceptual model of cognitive mapping linking elements from informational processing and trans-actionalism (with elements of connectionist and IRN ideas) is discussed in Chapter 9. This theory aims to marry general conceptual ideas (as detailed below) and specific theories (as detailed in subsequent chapters) to provide a new set of hypotheses to guide future research.

2.1 Perceptual (Gibsonian) Schemata of Spatial Behavior

With one exception, all the theories of human spatial behavior described in this chapter focus on cognition. The one exception is the theory put forward by Gibson (1979), who developed a theory that focused on perception and argued that environmental features are perceived directly with little intervention of cognitive processes. Gibson pointed out that as people travel through an environment they experience a continuous flow of perceptual information, and that this in itself is sufficient to encode environmental information without additional cognitive processing. For example, a person in the environment will have a view, or 'vista', that is immediately available and which is seen from one perspective. As they move through the environment their perspective on this vista will change, and changes in perspective provide information about movement. However, some aspects of the vista will not change. For example, the view of a building will alter depending on the person's perspective, but the building itself will be an invariant feature of the vista. As movement takes place one vista will be over-taken by a new vista (e.g., when turning a street corner, or reaching the crest of a hill), and where one vista turns into another can be noted as a point of transition. During travel, transitions provide important information about the sequence of the most important changes along a route and may be the basis for successful wayfind-ing. For example, Heft (1983) found that people learnt a route better if they viewed slides showing the sequence of transitions along the route, rather than slides showing a sequence of vistas along the same route.

Heft (1996), following Gibson, argued that every route will be uniquely specified by the order of vistas and transitions, and that retracing a familiar route consists of recreating the flow of information along it. People recreate the flow by action (i.e., by moving along the route) and that action generates the subsequent vista, which guides further action. In Heft's words, there is an:

on-going, reciprocal interaction between perceiver and environmental structure. It is not the case that actions precede the information, nor that the information elicits the action... What is being described here is a continuous loop of perceiving and acting (1996: 122).

Heft (1996) also pointed out that a route through the environment has a hierarchical structure, and gave the example of walking from a house to a post office along a route that was made up of paths between salient points (e.g., from house to newsstand, from newsstand to post office, and so on). Each path might include transitions, and these in turn would each include several vistas, and Heft suggested that this hierarchical structure helps people to anticipate changes in the flow of environmental information.

Gibson's (1979) theory has often been cited but has rarely generated empirical research into cognitive maps (although see Cornell and Hay, 1984; Heft, 1996). Nonetheless, Gibson's emphasis on the importance of the environment has been echoed in transactional and inter-representational network theories (discussed below), and Gibson's work provides a counterbalance to those theories of cognitive mapping that have focused mainly or only on the internal cognitive processing of environmental information, to the exclusion of any interaction between the individual and the environment.

2.2 Early Theories of Cognitive Mapping (Information Processing)

One of the first models of spatial behavior was put forward by Kirk (1963), a geographer, who made a distinction between the objective and behavioral environment (see Figure 2.1). The objective environment refers to the physical world around us and the behavioral environment was the 'psycho-physical field in which phenomenal facts are arranged into patterns or structures and acquire values in cultural contexts' (Kirk, 1963: 366). Kirk believed that the behavioral environment was the basis for rational human behavior and, as such, he combined two earlier theoretical traditions: that of rational decision making in geography, and the idea of perceptual principles from gestalt psychology (Gold, 1980). Kirk's model was, however, limited because of his belief that decision making was based upon a rational appraisal of a total situation, and it did not allow for individual idiosyncrasies (Gold 1980).

Kirk's model was rejected by behavioral geographers as researchers sought to provide more psychologically sophisticated models centered on the cognitive processes of information (Gold, 1980).

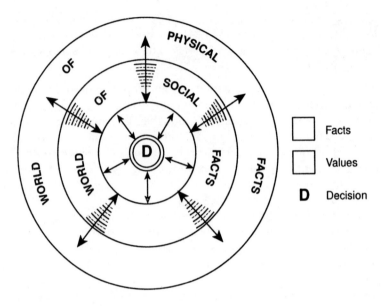

Figure 2.1. Kirk's (1963) model of the behavioral environment of the decision maker

The most important conceptual model after Kirk's (1963) was that proposed by Downs (1970), as shown in Figure 2.2. The boxes represent concepts and the arrows represent the link between those concepts. The starting point for the model is taken as the real world, which is the source of information. This information is filtered through a system of perceptual receptors which are essentially the five main senses. Meaning is given to the information through an interaction between the individual's value system and his or her stored 'image' or cognitive map of the real world. The filtered information is then used to update the cognitive map and to formulate a behavior decision. This decision leads to a reiteration of the whole process, creating another search for information from the real world until sufficient information has been acquired, or to time/cost limitation acts to constrain the search, or to overt behavior. As a result of the latter, the real world undergoes a change, new information becomes available, and the whole process begins again.

In Downs' (1970) model, behavior is a function of the real world and the decision making process is a dynamic one, constantly changing with the receipt of new information. The role of the individual was recognized in several ways, for example, it was the individual

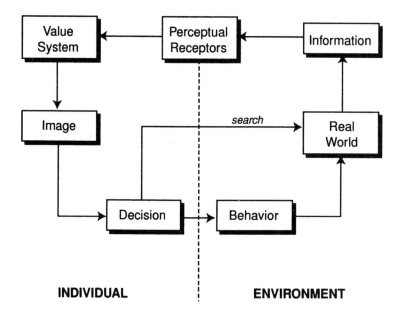

Figure 2.2. Downs' (1970) model of cognitive mapping

who filtered the environmental information, and it was decisions by the individual that might result in the search for further external information. Downs's model was an advance because it made explicit the relationships between people, place, and decision/choice making, which had mainly been discussed only conceptually in earlier work, and it did so by placing importance on the individual as a rational being capable of independent decision making, although the individual was seen mainly as a passive receiver of environmental information. As Downs himself acknowledged, it was oversimplified and did not lead directly to testable hypotheses.

Pocock's (1973) model was an elaboration of the proposal put forward by Downs. It was divided into three main sections, each consisting of inter-related components (Figure 2.3). The first section was the environment and comprised three sets of stimuli: previous information, present context, and the actual environment. The selection from these sources influenced the information reaching the second, perceiver, stage, which included four sets of factors: basic physiological make-up, basic psychological organization, cultural characteristics, and the current state of the individual. These factors, in combination, acted as filters—selecting which aspects of received

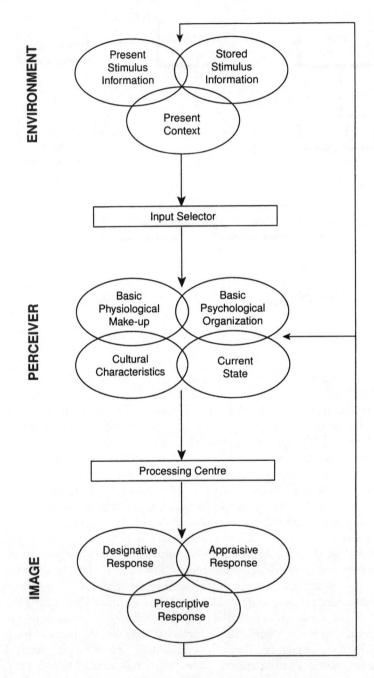

Figure 2.3. Pocock's (1973) model of cognitive mapping

information were processed—and the output from this processing contributed to the 'image'.

There were three inter-related types of responses: the designative response, concerned with description and classification; the appraisive emotional response, concerned with feeling, value, and meaning; and the prescriptive response, which refers to the inferences that can be made from the information encoded in the image. Feedback could be distributed back from the image to the environment and perceiver in a cyclical system. Pocock's (1973) theory represented an improvement upon Downs' (1970) model, because the individual was no longer seen a passive receiver but had an active role in selecting and processing information.

Lloyd (1976) and Pacione (1978) also added to Downs' original model by emphasizing the role of the individual in selecting the information that was processed. Lloyd's complex model emphasized the role of preferences in affecting individual behavior within the environment (Figure 2.4). Pacione added two stages to Downs' original model (Figure 2.5), and suggested that the perceptual filters interact with the incoming stimuli through physiological, social, and cultural factors. He also incorporated 'constraints', which were an

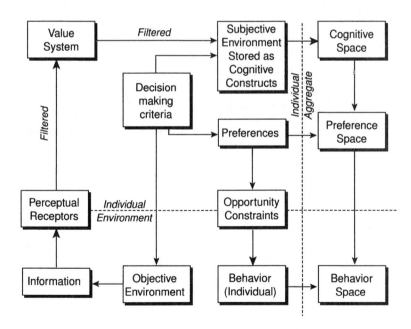

Figure 2.4. Lloyd's (1976) model of cognitive mapping

explicit recognition that an individual's choice was limited by internal and external factors related to the cost of any behavior.

These models all emphasized that human behavior was best understood by examining the thoughts, knowledge, and decisions which influenced that behavior, rather than by studying the behavior itself (Golledge and Rushton, 1984). However, little immediate progress was made in either developing or testing these models, and the models themselves were criticized for being psychologically naïve. Given the rather general descriptions of human reasoning and behavior provided by these models it has been impossible to prove them incorrect, and as a consequence they did not establish a firm base for new research.

Nonetheless, further extensions of these models were proposed. For example, Gold (1980) produced a more complex model which was further refined by Golledge and Stimson (1987) (Figure 2.6). Like Kirk (1963), they suggested that an individual is simultaneously part of both objective and behavioral environments, receiving locational and attributive information from the latter and making decisions based on this information which may affect both environments.

Passini (1992) also adapted earlier models with a theory of 'matched feedback' to emphasize the dynamic nature of decision making during wayfinding (Figure 2.7). Passini suggested that people

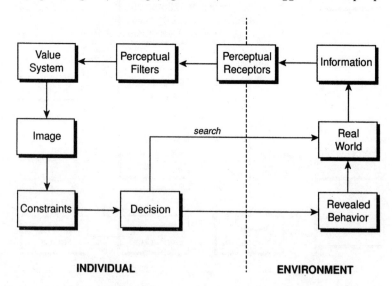

Figure 2.5. Pacione's (1978) model of cognitive mapping

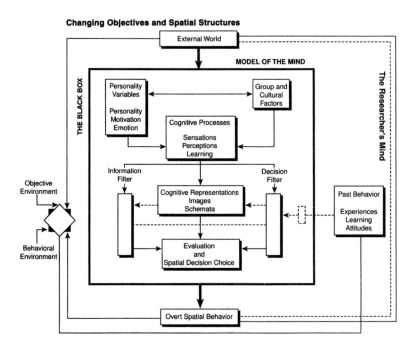

Figure 2.6. Gold's (1980) model of cognitive mapping

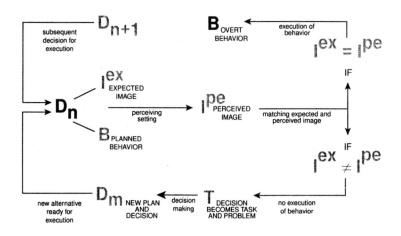

Figure 2.7. Passini's (1992) model of cognitive mapping

cycle through a set of decisions using a process of 'matchmaking' to evaluate a decision and determine behavior. In a familiar environment, a person recalls what should be sensed at a location and this is checked against what is actually sensed. If there is a match then a planned behavior is executed. If the two do not match, the decision making becomes a problem solving task, and a new plan is formulated and a decision based on the new plan is assessed for its viability. This process continues until a match is made and a decision executed.

The matchmaking model put forward by Passini (1992) and the other elaborations of the earlier models did little to revive behavioral research in geography, which by the late 1970s was falling out of favor as a viable approach despite continued widespread use. Although the later models provided a better reflection of the complexity of decision making, they went no further than the original models in providing the sort of hypotheses that would stimulate research. In contrast, some of the early theories, which focused more on the structure and content of the cognitive map did result in the generation of new research and these are described in Chapters 5 and 7.

2.3 Transactional Schema

In the mid-1970s, cognitive psychologists such as Neisser (1976) challenged the successive, processing models put forward by behavioral geographers. Neisser suggested that an individual actively and selectively searches the environment to gain information that is relevant to his or her immediate needs (Figure 2.8). He suggested that individuals use an 'anticipatory schema' that structures which information is acquired from the environment. This schema will have been developed from past experiences—not necessarily specific past experience in the same environment—but rather the anticipatory schema is made up of assumptions, beliefs, and predictions derived from environmental experience in general. This schema will guide behavior depending on the aims of the individual, by searching out relevant environmental information that is needed to fulfil the behavior. In the process of searching for information and carrying out behavior the individual will be constantly updating, altering, and adjusting the schema in the light of new information from the environment.

The important point here is that an individual's interaction with the environment will be determined by his or her aims and the need to seek out appropriate information for those aims. In other words,

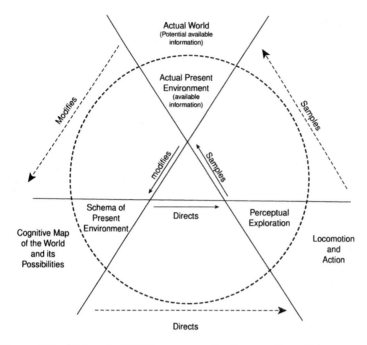

Figure 2.8. Neisser's (1976) conceptual schema of cognitive mapping

individuals will be active selectors of only the information that is relevant to their immediate needs. This approach to understanding cognitive maps is usually referred to as a 'transactional' perspective, because the environment and the individual are not separate entities, as the former is only selected and interpreted as far as it contributes to the individual's plans for action.

According to Neisser (1976), several schema may be active at any one time. Neisser used the example of a room and a lamp: an individual will have a cognitive map schema of the room and they will also have a schema for the lamp. Both can be simultaneously active, with the lamp schema embedded in the room schema, and Neisser explained that:

> each is a phase of a cyclic interaction with the environment; both interactions occur continuously. They cannot comfortably be separated. I could view the lamp without a surrounding room, but my perception will always be guided by some general cognitive map as well as a specific perceptual schema... [Thus] actions are hierarchically embedded in more extensive actions and motivated by anticipated consequences at various levels of schematic organization (1976: 113).

Although Neisser described cognitive map schema in terms of information gained while people are interacting directly with the environment, others have pointed out that the concept of anticipation schema may also apply to the acquisition of spatial information from indirect sources, for example, when a person searches out environmental information from a cartographic map as a way to plan behavior (Lloyd, 1993). Information from several sources (e.g., from direct experience, from maps, and from written descriptions) are thus incorporated into ever more comprehensive schema.

The transactional perspective has influenced several descriptions of environment–behavior interaction, both within geography (e.g. Aitken and Bjorklund, 1988; Aitken, 1991, 1992; Sell *et al.*, 1984), and in psychology (e.g., Altman and Rogoff 1987). Aitken and Bjorklund developed two related transactional models. They argued that environments are dynamic and variable systems and that people seek to maintain an acceptable level of homeostasis within them. To do this people can change their behavior, restructuring themselves relative to an event, and this involves changes from habitual behavior to purposeful behavior, or vice versa. Figure 2.9 summarizes four modes of possible person/environment relations put forward by Aitken and Bjorklund, who argued that, depending on the degree of environmental stress, individuals can change model to cope with different situations.

Aitken and Bjorklund's (1988) second model described human behavior as it mediates change (Figure 2.10). In this model, change prompts an individual to search for and select information, and to

ENVIRONMENT		
EVENTS	**Ordinary**	**Extraordinary**
Ordinary	Habitual behavior applied to ordinary events	Habitual behavior applied to extraordinary events
Extraordinary	Purposive behavior applied to ordinary events	Purposive behavior applied to extraordinary events

Figure 2.9. Aitken and Bjorklund's (1988) model of behavior/environment transaction and transformation

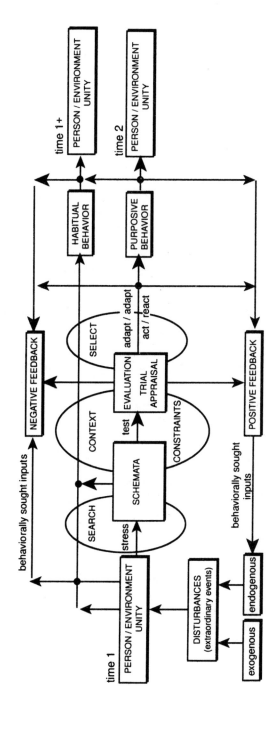

Figure 2.10. Aitken and Bjorklund's (1988) model of human behavior at the person/environment interface

try and anticipate and evaluate behavior in a new context. Once again, the intention is to maintain equilibrium and to reduce stress, using either negative feedback (by seeking stability) or positive feedback (by seeking change and adapting to a new equilibrium level). Aitken and Bjorklund did not, however, describe the mental processes used to process such information beyond describing the use of schema.

Some researchers have been positive about the advantages of the transactional perspective, arguing that this perspective might provide the basis for a rejuvenation of behavioral approaches and ideas, leading to the production of geographies of everyday life which fully acknowledge the changing contexts within which people operate (e.g., Aitken, 1992). Others have been more cautious, for example, Altman and Rogoff pointed out that:

> The lure of the transactional approach is simultaneously coupled with a sense of uncertainty. How does one build a theory of holistic, changing phenomena? What methods can we use to study phenomena at a holistic level? How do we incorporate change and temporal factors as part of psychological phenomena? (1987: 37).

2.4 Computational Process Models (CPMs) of Spatial Behavior

During the 1980s, several computational process models (CPMs) of spatial behavior were developed. A number of formal computational process models were proposed and in most instances coded into computer programs. Most of these consisted of a behavioral module and an objective task environment in which it operated. Typically, the behavioral module would consist of three inter-related entities: (a) a knowledge structure that specifies the manner in which information is represented symbolically; (b) the processes by which the knowledge structure is accessed and modified; and (c) a 'cognitive architecture' that organizes and controls information processing (Miller, 1992). The task environment is held in a symbolic format within the knowledge structure, and the behavioral module simulates behavior by processing decisions through a 'test–action–test' cycle where different actions are simulated within the task environment and evaluated for appropriate outcomes (e.g., Smith *et al.*, 1982).

An early example of a CPM is Kuipers' (1978) TOUR. This was designed to simulate navigation through an environment, even when information about that environment was limited. TOUR's spatial database (i.e., cognitive map) included three separate components:

(1) sensorimotor procedures, which were a knowledge of the sequences of actions required for travel. Movement instructions consisted of linked turn (intersection decision points) and go-to (linking paired places) statements which could be sequenced to create a route, which was learnt as a whole.

(2) topological relations, which included knowledge of non-metric spatial relations in the environment such as containment, connectivity, and order.

(3) metrical relations, which were knowledge of and the ability to manipulate magnitudes such as distance, direction, and relative position.

In contrast to the neutral environment used by Kuipers (1978), some researchers simulated route planning and execution through dynamic environments. For example, McCalla *et al.*'s (1982) ELMER program was designed to find routes through an urban environment that included information about pedestrian flows, traffic levels, and traffic lights. ELMER consisted of three major components:

(a) The *Map* consisted of a spatial database of information gained from successfully navigated routes (in contrast to the topological information included in TOUR).

(b) The *Planner* generated a travel plan using inferences about route knowledge derived from the Map.

(c) The *Executor* combined the travel plan with sensory data obtained from the simulated environment, and augmented the plan with behavioral information (e.g., how to stop at a red light), and then executed the amended plan.

If the plan was successful the map was updated with new route information. In contrast to TOUR, the routes in ELMER were not learnt as a whole but were made up of a series of hierarchically ordered sub-plans along parts of the route. Put another way, in ELMER each route could be made up of sub-routes, and those in turn could also consist of sub-routes, and so on. This organization meant that the same sub-route could be incorporated in different routes, allowing for the flexible learning of new routes and reducing the duplication of information that would be required if all routes were encoded as a whole.

CPMs like TOUR and ELMER were based on route learning, but other researchers used CPMs to simulate not only route learning but also the development of configurational knowledge (i.e., the

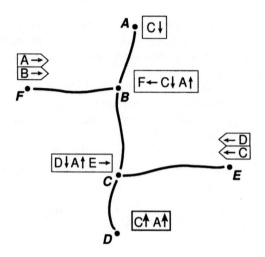

Figure 2.11. The spatial data format of TRAVELLER
Source: Leiser (1987: p. 99)

spatial relationships between places not connected by a direct route—see Chapter 5). An example of such a CPM is TRA-VELLER (Leiser, 1987; Leiser and Zilbershatz, 1989). The knowledge that TRAVELLER builds is equivalent to road signs at intersections (Figure 2.11) and is stored using an action table (Table 2.1).

In one version, TRAVELLER scanned all the nodes that were accessible from the origin, and if they included the goal the route was found. If not, it scanned the nodes that were accessible from each available node and so on until the goal was found. The found

Table 2.1. An action table for Figure 2.11

	A	B	C	D	E	F
A			↓			
B	↑		↓			←
C	↑			↓	→	
D	↑		↑			
E			←	←		
F	→		→			

Source: Leiser (1987: p. 99)

route was then encoded in memory as a series of production rules (e.g., if at node 4 then go to node 7). Routes are not separate from the representation of the nodes, and therefore routes only exist when they are enacted out.

In a second version of TRAVELLER some nodes were more recognizable than others, and these were labeled 'centroids'. Once the links or sub-routes between centroids were known, routes could be planned by focusing on these. For example, if centroid 1 is near the starting point of a route and centroid 2 is near the goal, the route finding task became three sub-tasks of traveling from the start to centroid 1, then between centroid 1 and 2, and then from centroid 2 to the goal. Using salient nodes, especially as the routes between these become known, made the routefinding task easier than planning a route through a large number of undifferentiated nodes, it reduced the demands on memory, and it generated configurational knowledge about the centroids (Leiser and Zilbershatz, 1989). Some of the components in TRAVELLER reflected beliefs about human cognitive maps, for example, the concept of a hierarchy of nodes or landmarks has been put forward by many researchers investigating human behavior in the environment (e.g., Golledge, 1978; see Chapter 5). However, other aspects of TRAVELLER, such as its broad scanning searches, did not reflect human processes or travel behavior.

Other CPMs have been designed as simulations of human wayfinding and for making comparisons between the CPM and human performance. For example, Gopal and Smith (1990) designed NAVIGATOR, based on principles derived from human wayfinding. The simulated environment was a network of horizontal and vertical streets, with information about different locations in the network and possible points where a wayfinding decision could be made. Perceptual processes selected the most salient information and these were encoded in working memory where the information was either lost (due to decay or interference) or transferred to long term memory. Long term memory included nodes that represented locations, sub-nodes to represent objects at locations and their saliency, and links between nodes.

Information was derived from traveling through the environment, but the stored information in long term memory might be incomplete or inaccurate depending on how well the perceived information was selected and encoded or whether it had decayed. Routefinding could be based on retrieving a complete route, or if the route information was incomplete, by searching the environment for cues to recognize and move between locations, or failing this, by using heuristic rules (such as moving in a constant orientation) until the end point of the route was reached or until failure occurred.

An important aspect of Gopal and Smith's (1990) research was to analyze the errors made by NAVIGATOR and compare these with the types of errors made during human wayfinding. Several of the errors made by NAVIGATOR reflected ones noted in empirical studies, and Gopal and Smith suggested that 'error analysis in NAVIGATOR compares quite favorably with the results obtained in previous empirical studies' (1990: p. 185). However, the level of error analysis in human studies is often superficial (usually depending on experimenters' subjective interpretation of participants' errors) and the fact that a CPM makes the same types of errors as humans does not mean that the errors are the result of the same processes. Nonetheless, CPMs like NAVIGATOR could highlight some of the cognitive processes that might be involved in wayfinding, and these could then become the focus of further empirical studies, though it is rare to find studies with human participants based on hypotheses derived from simulations.

In summary, the performance of CPMs was justified by comparing them to the known performance of humans in wayfinding tasks, but the CPMs only had a limited influence on stimulating research into real-world wayfinding.

2.5 Connectionist (Neural Network) Schema of Spatial Behavior

From the late 1980s, CPMs based on models of information storage and retrieval have been replaced with connectionist models based upon neural networks. In contrast to CPMs that processed symbolic information in a serial manner, connectionist models are large networks of interconnected computational units running in parallel. The models can be thought of as directed topological graphs consisting of nodes (or processing elements) connected by directed links (unidirectional signal channels) that carry weighted numeric, rather than symbolic, signals (Gopal, 1996).

As with biological neurons, computer-generated neurons can represent conceptual objects such as places or words, or abstract elements, and receive and output signals to other neurons (Lloyd, 1997). Groups of neurons in categorical pools are defined by a common theme with each pool linked by conceptual identifiers.

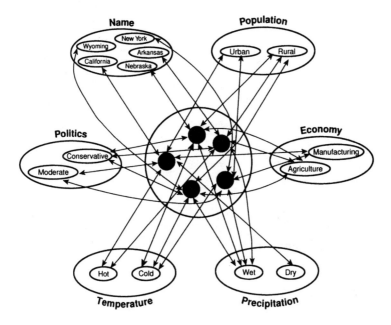

Figure 2.12. Cammack and Lloyd's (1993) neural network model for storing knowledge about a place

Consequently, information on any related topic can be retrieved from different pools and synthesized together. For example, Figure 2.12 shows the categorical pools and their links for Cammack and Lloyd's (1993) neural network model of a simple cognitive map of five states. The information encoded in the network is related to population, economy, politics, and so on. When a particular neuron is activated (e.g. hot temperature) there will be spreading activation throughout the network to activate the neurons in other categories that are associated with this characteristic. Other neural networks have been designed to model the identification of landmarks (e.g., Lloyd, 1997)—see Figure 2.13.

Schmajuk and Thieme (1992) proposed a real-time, biologically plausible neural network model to explain purposive behavior and cognitive mapping. Their model consisted of two main parts: (a) an action system, consisting of a goal-seeking neural mechanism controlled by a motivational system; and (b) a cognitive system, consulting neurally-based cognitive map knowledge (see Figure 2.14).

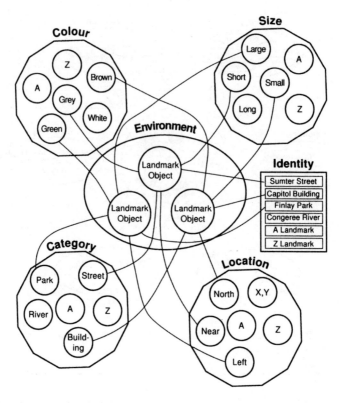

Figure 2.13: Lloyd's (1997) neural network model for identifying landmarks

The model worked through the goal-seeking mechanism displaying exploratory behavior until either the goal was found or an adequate prediction of the goal could be generated. Determining whether the goal was reached was carried out by a comparator which compared predicted views and the goal, and modified the cognitive map if a mismatch was detected. The cognitive map that was built by the neural network to aid navigation was topological, providing relative rather than absolute spatial information, and was interrogated by a relatively simple set of neural activities (e.g., the detection of synapse firing, or the excitement of certain cells). This map could be interrogated without modification and can be used in advance of behavior to aid prediction and planning. Although Schmajuk and Thieme used their model to explain the learning and spatial behavior of rats it could also have relevance to humans.

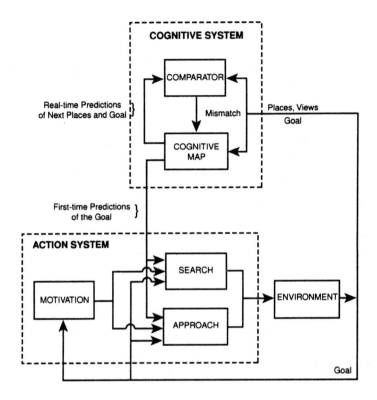

Figure 2.14. A biologically-based neural network model of spatial thought
Adapted from Schmajuk and Thieme (1992)

2.6 Inter-Representational Network (IRN)

A more recent theory of cognitive mapping is Haken and Portugali's
(1996) inter-representational network (IRN). Just as connectionist
models extended information processing models, IRN extended
transactionalist models by emphasizing the interdependence of internal (cognitive) representations and external (environmental) representations. Portugali (1996) described the IRN as a mixture of
Gibson's (1979) perceptual theory, information processing theories
and experiental realism. By the last phrase, Portugali meant that
patterns of internal processing are derived from the experience of an
individual in the environment.

Portugali (1996) gave the example of an experiment in which a
large group of people were each asked to make scale models of
buildings and were then asked to place their own building on the

floor of a large room. There were no rules for this activity, but as more buildings were placed on the floor, the more likely it was that later buildings were placed in spatial orders relative to the first buildings (e.g., in lines, blocks, or groupings of similar buildings). Portugali explained the creation of such a 'town' in terms of the later buildings being 'enslaved' by the emerging pattern created by the earlier buildings. He suggested that, in an analogous way, as a person experiences a new environment there will be an interaction between internally stored representations derived from previous environments (e.g., information about potential patterns of streets, houses, traffic, and so on) and the perception of external patterns in the new environment. These internal and external inputs will create a cognitive map, which may be incomplete after the initial experience but will form the basis for and partially determine further environmental exploration, and this further exploration will add more information to the cognitive map. While the cognitive map is developing there may be several ways to order and pattern the information it contains, but there will come a point when one particular pattern becomes dominant and any additional internal and external information is incorporated into this pattern, and the cognitive map will remain stable. Portugali's theory is of interest because it incorporates something of the dynamic nature of cognitive map formation, but as yet IRN have not generated much empirical research.

2.7 Conclusions

Many of the theories outlined in this chapter about how people think about and behave in geographic space are frequently cited. However, they have only had a limited effect on stimulating and shaping empirical research and we suggest that a more fruitful route to future research is through the further integration of theory and practice from the parent disciplines of geography and psychology. This integration needs to draw together theories that have concentrated on specific features of cognitive maps, which due to their specificity have been more successful in generating empirical research and theory making. In Chapter 9, we attempt such a marriage of broad conceptual ideas with specific theories through the development of a model which aims to advance transactionalism by including a number of theories concerning the underlying mental processes that govern spatial thought and behavior. We next turn to work that has concentrated on investigating precise aspects of cognitive mapping.

CHAPTER 3

Learning and Acquisition of Cognitive Maps

The diversity of natural, built, social and cultural environments to which a person is exposed and the variety of media sources which portray spatial relations mean that there are many factors that influence, or can potentially influence, the acquisition and development of cognitive map knowledge. In this chapter, strategies of learning spatial information and the factors that affect the acquisition of knowledge are examined. Further discussion of these issues, with reference to the development of children's cognitive maps, is included in Chapter 5.

3.1 Learning and Acquisition

Both Goodey (1971) and Liben (1981) produced conceptual models of the sources that can affect cognitive maps. Goodey (1971; see Figure 3.1) developed what he termed 'man's simplified perceptual map', which detailed the social and physical environments with which individuals interact and from which they learn. The model details how individuals encounter a range of knowledge through either direct interaction or passive reception.

Burnett and Briggs (1975) pointed out that the factors that affect the acquisition of cognitive maps are either stimulus-centered, in which cognition is a function of environmental features; subject-centered, in which cognition is a function of the individual; or subject/stimulus centered, in which cognition is a function of the interactions between an individual and environmental features. Liben (1981) extended this categorization, producing a conceptual model (Figure 3.2) of how these factors are inter-related. Liben also added a reference to cultural factors and the individual's history to illustrate how past experience and socio-cultural factors, such as expected behavior, may contribute to the cognitive map. Liben's model thus hypothesizes that an individual's spatial activity, and

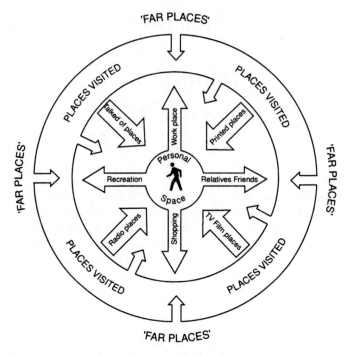

Figure 3.1: Goodey's model of cognitive map knowledge acquisition

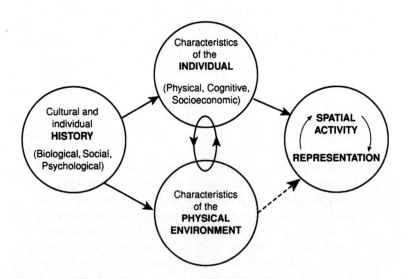

Figure 3.2: Liben's model of cognitive map knowledge acquisition

their associated cognitive map knowledge, is grounded in their cultural and individual history, their personal characteristics, and the type of environment experienced.

Like the conceptual models outlined in Chapter 2, Goodey's (1971) and Liben's (1981) models are oversimplified, with many factors that affect the acquisition and learning of cognitive maps, and their inter-relationships, not explicitly detailed. The model described in Figure 3.3 is an attempt to include other sources of information that may be salient in the formation of cognitive maps. This model recognizes that there are a series of mediating factors which in themselves do not directly provide spatial information but may influence the uptake and use of both primary and secondary sources of information. This model does not provide specific details of spatial learning, which is described in more depth in Chapter 9. Each of the variables within the model, and the debates to their significance, is discussed in turn. While each factor is outlined separately, many of these will be interdependent and therefore affect one another.

3.2 Primary Learning

Primary learning is navigation-based, with the collection and processing of spatial information explicitly linked to an individual's interaction with an environment through spatial activity. There are three main theories about how we learn an environment through primary interaction. In the first theory environmental cues, such as landmarks, are seen as the fundamental building blocks and framework of knowledge to which subsequent information, such as paths, is added. The second theory hypothesizes that path-based information forms the initial framework of knowledge and that landmarks and other information are then placed in relation to this. Both these theories imply that environmental features contribute to the formation of a spatial database, but in contrast to these a third theory emphasizes that wayfinding can be dependent on memorizing a series of vistas. In other words, in its initial development a cognitive map can be made up of ordered views or scenes rather than landmarks and paths.

Siegel and White (1975), as detailed in Chapter 5, suggested that cognitive map knowledge is hierarchically organized into three different levels: landmark, route, and configurational. Siegel (1977) suggested that there is a set pattern of development. Initially, an individual notes and remembers landmarks, and once landmarks are established an individual can 'attach' actions to these, so that the

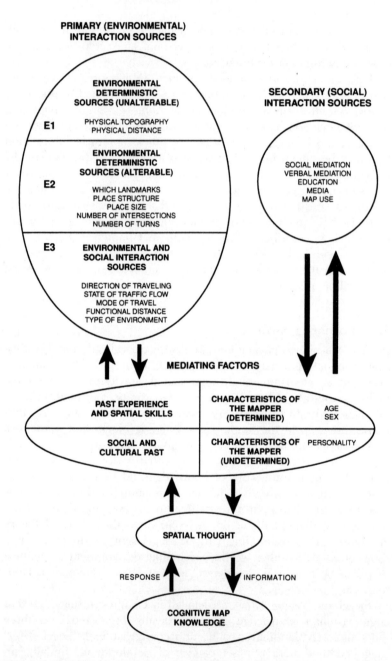

Figure 3.3. A new model of acquisition
Source: Kitchin (1995)

pattern of landmarks and actions is encoded as a route. Clusters of landmarks and routes form 'minimaps' in which the relationships between places are well understood. Several minimaps might be formed but need not be coherently related to one another. Only when the information in each minimap can be accurately related to information in other minimaps does the individual achieve a 'survey' or configurational representation of the environment. At this stage, an individual will have an objective frame of reference and will be able to estimate directions and distances between all places in the environment. Siegel and White's theory has been very influential in cognitive map research, especially as a framework for examining the abilities of adults, and there is evidence from many studies that route knowledge is a stage before configurational knowledge (e.g., Golledge et al., 1993). However, some researchers have found that adults can gain configurational knowledge very rapidly and this would not support the distinct stages of learning put forward by Siegel and White (see Chapter 5 for a discussion). Siegel and White's theory was based directly on an earlier theory by Piaget that was put forward to describe the development of cognitive maps in children (Piaget and Inhelder, 1956; Piaget et al., 1960). As Piaget's theory has not been applied outside the research into children's development, a comparison of Piaget's theory and Siegel and White's theory, and an assessment of the relative merits of these two theories, will be left to Chapter 5.

Closely related to Siegel and White's theory of learning is Golledge's (1978) anchor-point theory, which also emphasized the role of landmarks in the learning process. Golledge suggested that different places have different salience to individuals and become hierarchically structured in the cognitive map. Primary landmarks or 'nodes' become anchors to which spatial information, including other landmarks and paths, are linked. The primary nodes also act as mnemonics, increasing the probability of recognizing or knowing the position of landmarks and paths associated with that node. For most people, the most important primary nodes are likely to be home, workplace, and familiar shopping places, and people will know a comparatively large amount about these areas, and the main routes between these nodes. There will also be secondary, tertiary, and lower level nodes. For example, secondary nodes might include major junctions or frequently visited places and tertiary nodes might be minor junctions and places that are only visited occasionally. A number of researchers have found support for a hierarchical organization of knowledge based on landmarks (e.g., Golledge et al., 1985;

Ferguson and Hegarty, 1994). In one of the few longitudinal studies of cognitive maps, Evans *et al.* (1982) asked a group of students to draw sketch maps of a city two weeks and ten months after arriving there. Evans *et al.* found that the number of landmarks in the sketch maps did not increase, but the longer the students were in the city, the more elaborate was the network of routes between the landmarks.

Golledge (1991a) argued that, because of their importance, the choice and availability of suitable landmarks within an environment will be critical to both learning and structuring cognitive maps. On the one hand, this would imply that environments with differentiated landmarks and landscapes should be easier to remember, and ones with few landmarks should be harder to learn. On the other hand, Golledge suggested that in environments with too many potential landmarks, the number might place too many demands on processing and lead to confusion. Therefore environments that are optimal for learning are ones with landmarks that are easily differentiated and that can be grouped into a hierarchical structure.

In contrast to theories that have emphasized landmarks, Gärling *et al.* (1981) argued that routes are learnt before landmarks, because they provide a framework for the accurate recall of landmarks. As Gärling *et al.* pointed out, landmarks can only be encountered as parts of routes. They had participants travel through an unfamiliar suburban area, along a route that included six target landmarks, and they found that after just one experience of the route the participants were able to recall the order of the landmarks. Gärling *et al.* argued that encoding the order of the landmarks was equivalent to route knowledge, and that therefore routes are learned before or together with landmarks. This would not directly support either Golledge's (1978) theory or Siegel and White's (1975) theory of cognitive map development. Gärling *et al.*'s finding suggests that people can encode comparatively short routes very quickly, and other researchers have found the same effect (see Chapter 7). If this is the case it may not be possible to identify distinct stages of landmark and route learning in the small environments used in empirical studies (and there are no studies of people learning large, complex, unfamiliar environments).

Some researchers have placed less emphasis on a distinction between landmark and route learning. Couclelis *et al.* (1987) extended Golledge's (1978) anchor-point theory by suggesting that nodes within the hierarchy may not just represent landmarks, but could include any feature that acts as a cue or anchor. For example, a length of main road may act as an primary anchor. Gärling *et al.* (1986b) also suggested that it might be more useful to think of anchor nodes not as points but as areal extents and that these areas act as anchors for the rest of the cognitive map. As such, key land-marks, linear and areal features 'individually and jointly 'anchor' sub-regions of space and hierarchically link together environmental information' (Lee and Schmidt, 1988: p. 340).

Couclelis *et al.* (1987) argued that, if knowledge is encoded using a hierarchically ordered set of anchor-points, it might be subject to three types of distortion (Figure 3.4). The 'tectonic plates' distortion refers to spatial information linked to a particular anchor-point being displaced in the same direction as the anchor. In other words, the spatial relationships between all the features in the region asso-ciated with an anchor will be retained, but the region as a whole will be displaced in relation to the regions round other anchor-points. The 'magnifying glass' distortion refers to information around an anchor being displaced outward. Couclelis *et al.* suggested that the areas round a major anchor-point will be well known and therefore to accommodate the detailed knowledge of these areas the cognitive map will be 'stretched out' at these points. The 'magnet' distortion is

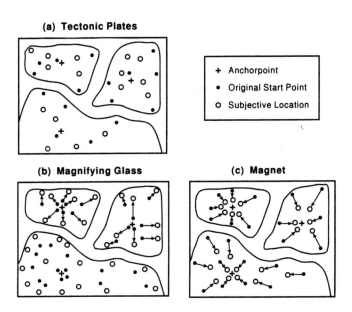

Figure 3.4. Types of anchor-point distortion
Source: Golledge and Stimson (1997)

39

the opposite of the 'magnifying glass' distortion and implies that the anchor-point attracts spatial information toward itself, because the relationship between features and their anchor-point will be subject to the clustering effects that are commonly noted in the recall of spatial information.

In contrast to both landmark-based and route-based learning, Cornell and Hay (1984) argued that the initial learning of an environment consists of recognizing vistas and learning the sequence of scenes along a route. This suggests that initial navigation is not based on a framework of landmarks or paths, but on being able to recall the order of views. With greater experience, the information gained from these ordered sequences can be translated into metric information and configurational knowledge. However, this approach to learning new environments has received less attention and support than the theories that have emphasized the role of landmarks and routes in the development of cognitive maps.

A number of factors have been found to contribute to the initial development of a cognitive map through primary learning, and these can be roughly divided into ones relating to the characteristics of the environment itself, and ones relating to the type of experience in the environment. We first discuss the effects of environmental characteristics upon primary learning, returning to mediating factors later in the chapter.

3.2.1 *Environmental characteristics*

The physical geography and characteristics of an environment can influence the development of cognitive maps. For example, geographical features that are barriers to movement may lead to increased distance estimations between places on different sides of the barrier. Several researchers have found that people overestimate distances between places that are on different sides of a river (Canter, 1977; Kitchin, 1990). Cohen *et al.* (1978) found that distances between places separated by hills and trees were overestimated, and in contrast, distances between places in areas that were flat and devoid of features were underestimated. Cohen *et al.* suggested that people overcompensated on the basis of the difficulty of traversing hilly routes. But barrier effects are not limited to the physical world, because they can also be demonstrated in small space and during map learning. For example, McNamara (1986) asked participants to learn the layout of objects in a room and the layout of object names on a map. The objects in the room and the names on the maps were divided into areas by barriers, and McNamara found that distances between objects within an area were under-estimated relative to objects in different areas.

In addition, Okabe *et al.* (1986) found that the slope of a route could have an effect on recall of the route. They found that uphill and downhill walking led to the overestimation of distance, and they suggested that this was due to physical effort in walking uphill and taking care (or possibly deceleration) walking downhill. It follows from Okabe *et al.*'s results that hilly environments that are learnt by direct experience might be represented as being larger than flat environments of the same area.

City layout, structure, and size have all been found to affect the cognitive maps of urban areas. For example, Antes *et al.* (1988) found that cities with a regular layout made the city more 'legible'. They investigated the building of a new traffic route that lessened travel distances of commuters by two miles, and found that the introduction of the more direct route led to more accurate dis-tance estimates. Lloyd (1989a) argued that cities producing over-estimates of distances tend to have more confusing layouts. Lloyd found that it took a longer time to estimate distances within a city than in a rural area, and he attributed this to the 'clutter' in urban areas. Clutter refers to the density of buildings and the complexity of the route network. It also refers to the hierarchy of the routes in the network, which will determine the routes that are most sensible to take, and these in turn will influence estimates of functional distance, the distance actually traveled between two places (rather than the straight-line, crow-flight distance). Many researchers (e.g., Cohen *et al.* 1978; Montello, 1991a) have argued that functional distance may be of particular importance to the spatial metrics of cognitive maps, because if two places are very close together in straight-line distance but functionally far apart then the straight-line distance may be encoded as being longer than it is in reality. This is similar to the barrier effect discussed above.

Some researchers have found that, as the number of turns or intersections along a route increases, the more likely it is that dis-tances will be overestimated (e.g., Staplin and Sadalla, 1981; Kahl *et al.*, 1984). For example, Sadalla and Staplin (1980a) found that participants who were asked to estimate two routes through a shop-ping mall overestimated the route with more segments. Downs and Stea (1973b) explained such overestimations by suggesting that when a route is traveled it is segmented to aid recall, and that small distances may be overestimated so that if they are added together to estimate the overall distance this produces a cumulative overestimation. Sadalla and Staplin (1980a) and Kahl *et al.* (1984), however, explained the overestimations as the result of routes containing more information requiring more encoding space and therefore being thought of as longer. Similarly, Milgram (1973) argued that areas of greater physical complexity are thought to be larger than areas with a simpler geography. If an environment is barren with few features, a journey through it will have less visual stimuli and, as a result, distances may be thought of as shorter than they actually are. In contrast, if an environment is complex and full of visual stimuli the journey may seem short and the distances may be underestimated. Some researchers have, however, found that the number of turns and intersections had no effect upon distance estimates (e.g., Okabe *et al.*, 1986). The differences in these findings may be the result of environmental factors (such as urban structure) or mediating factors (such as the mode of travel) and there is a need for more research to establish the effects of turns and intersections on estimates of route distance.

Evans *et al.* (1984) proposed that distortions are greater in cognitive maps of complex environments because more alignment and rotation heuristics have to be used when encoding such environments, and Matthews (1985) suggested that distortions are more likely in complex environments because people are likely to rely on frames of reference that are simpler than the environment itself. As a result, gradually curving routes in the environment might be represented as straight routes in the cognitive map, routes crossing at angles may be represented as ones crossing at right angles, and roads that are not aligned might be encoded as parallel ones. In contrast to complex environments that may be simplified in the cognitive map, homogeneous environments with little differentiation may have to have a structure imposed on them. For example, Berry (1971) reported that Canadian Eskimos must learn to pick out seemingly minor variations from monotonous, barren landscapes to aid their spatial learning.

Appleyard (1969) suggested that a number of factors can make specific locations easier to remember. How well a landmark or feature will be recalled will depend on how much it contrasts with its surroundings, and both Appleyard (1970) and Evans *et al.* (1982) found that a feature with a distinctive form was recalled with greater ease. Such features may become important cues or landmarks in the formation of cognitive maps. Kaplan (1976) suggested that there were two types of physical distinctiveness. The first relates to the physical distinctiveness of the feature itself which makes it stand out from other features because it is different in shape or form, and the second refers to inferred distinctiveness. In the latter case, a feature is only distinctive because it is different from the background, for example, an oak tree in a maple forest stands out because of its darker leaves, rather than its size or shape.

Evans *et al.* (1982) investigated why buildings become salient landmarks, and they found that there were 11 characteristics related to recall. These were the number of persons moving in or around the building; the clarity of building contour; the vertical height of the building; the complexity of its shape; the extent of building use; the uniqueness of its function; the extent of the building's cultural importance; the amount of physical maintenance; the texture and color of the building; the naturalness of the landscaping of the building; access to the building; and its distinctiveness compared to other structures. In contrast, other factors (for example, the building's proximity to a major road or the length of its frontage) did not have an effect on recall. Golledge (1991a) noted that distinctiveness may be related not just to physical features, but also to the type of personal or emotional attachment that people feel toward a place. These might include social, cultural, economic, political, religious, historical, or personal attitudes toward places, and it is likely that places with more functional or cultural significance will have more salience attached to them (e.g., churches or hospitals). In addition, if a feature is particularly visible, or is associated with a decision point such as a junction, it may be important for wayfinding and be better recalled than a similar feature that is located at a less significant place (Golledge *et al.*, 1985).

As discussed above, some urban spaces may be more legible, and therefore easier to learn. Greene (1992) outlined four principles that contribute to legibility and these relate to usability, understandability, distinctiveness, and appeal (Table 3.1). If an environment fulfils these principles it is more likely to be recalled effectively, because it will include factors that contribute to the formation of cognitive maps. Such principles provide a link between cognitive mapping and planning, because cognitive map researchers can help to identify and distinguish places that are easier or more difficult to learn, or where spatial behavior is more or less easy to carry out. Thinking about environments in terms of their legibility should contribute to the design of new environments or the improvement of existing ones.

Table 3.1. City structure factors that could affect cognitive map knowledge

Factors	Qualities
Function The area should be usable by all	Linkage Security Comfort Diversity
Order The area should be easily understood	Coherence Clarity Continuity Balance
Identity The area should be distinctive and recognizable	Focus Unity Character Specialness
Appeal Area should be pleasing and attractive	Scale Appropriateness Vitality Harmony

Source: Greene (1992)

3.3 Secondary Learning

In contrast to primary learning, secondary learning (e.g., from maps or books) allows the construction of a cognitive map without having to directly experience the environment. Secondary learning is a useful supplement to direct experience, and is the only source of information about environments at scales that cannot be experienced directly, such as countries or continents. Saarinen *et al.* (1988) asked people to indicate which secondary sources of information they thought had been important in contributing to their geographic knowledge, and found that the greatest influences were said to be school and travel experience. Other sources, listed in order of importance, included television, books, newspapers, atlases, magazines, movies, talking to others, games, and hobbies. Saarinen *et al.* found a positive correlation between those who drew the best world maps and those who used atlases and books and thought school experience had been important. In contrast, the poorest maps were drawn by those who thought that television, travel, and talking to others were important.

It is often suggested that media coverage of a place, either directly through a news item or indirectly as background information to a program, enhances people's cognitive map of that place (e.g., Golledge, 1976; MacEachren, 1991; Spencer *et al.*, 1989). Walmsley (1982) suggested that the more frequently a place appears in the media, the more likely it is that information about that place will be encoded in a person's cognitive map. However, Gilmartin (1985) found that cognitive maps of a place were not enhanced by media coverage, even when the place was the central focus of the news coverage.

3.3.1 Map use

The use of maps is thought to have two effects upon cognitive maps. First, training in map use can provide guidance in how to process and comprehend spatial information. As Liben (1991) noted, most maps are not 'transparent', but are complex models of spatial information that require specific skills and strategies. This implies that novices will not learn from a cartographic map unless they know how the map represents an area. For example, Butler *et al.* (1993) found that participants with little map training needed several minutes to discover and memorize a path in a complex building from a map of the building, and even then some respondents still had difficulty navigating the path. Nonetheless, when people have had experience of using maps they can be an important influence on cognitive maps, and Walmsley *et al.* (1990) argued that the content and structure of cognitive maps in map-using societies might reflect, in part, the skills acquired during map learning.

Second, studying a map can lead to greater knowledge of an area by revealing real world spatial relationships. Several researchers have demonstrated that spatial information derived from maps can often be different from the information derived by direct experience (Evans and Pedzek, 1980; Thorndyke and Hayes-Roth, 1982; Lloyd, 1993; MacEachren, 1992). This is because configurational knowledge is given directly by a map. In other words, maps show the spatial relationships between all the places represented on the map, but when an area is learnt from direct experience this knowledge has to be constructed gradually. Lloyd (1989a) argued that configurational knowledge learnt from a map may often be more accurate than configurational knowledge constructed from direct experience. Moeser (1988) demonstrated this by comparing how two groups of people developed cognitive maps of the same building. One group had learnt the building from two years' experience of working in it, and the other group learnt the building from floor plans. The latter group were able to make better distance and direction estimates between places in the building than the group that had learnt it by direct experience. In other words, the group who learnt the floor plans gained a better configurational understanding of the building than people who had been working in it for two years.

Although Moeser's (1988) study and similar research (e.g., Rossano et al., 1999) has demonstrated differences in the cognitive map as a result of learning from maps and direct experience, we know little about how these two types of information are combined in the cognitive map. The only research that has considered this topic has focused on the issue of orientation specificity. During direct experience the environment is viewed from many different perspectives, but a cartographic map shows the environment from one perspective, and for this reason Levine et al. (1982) argued that spatial information learnt from maps may be encoded in a cognitive map that is orientation-specific. They asked participants to learn a simple map showing four places, where, for example, place 1 was at the start of a path and place 2 was directly 'above' or ahead of place 1 on the map. Participants were blindfolded, asked to imagine standing at place 1, facing place 2 and then requested to make direction estimates to the location of other places they had learnt from the map. In other words they were making judgments in space that were 'aligned' with the map they had learnt. In a second condition, participants had to imagine standing at point 2, facing place 1 and make similar judgments. In this case the judgments were 'contraligned' with the map and accuracy was much poorer.

This has been called the 'alignment effect' and several researchers have found this to be a marked and consistent effect (e.g., Presson and Hazelrigg, 1984; Rossano and Warren, 1989), though Rossano et al. (1995) pointed out that the results related to this effect have been based on the mean scores of groups of participant in the different conditions. When Rossano et al. considered individual performance, they found a sub-group of participants in their experiments who did not demonstrate the alignment effect, though it is not clear why some individuals are better than others at manipulating a learned image, or whether these individuals would also be better at developing cognitive maps in more complex contexts.

Other researchers have also found that configurational knowledge gained from a map is orientation-specific (e.g., Peruch and Lapin, 1993; May et al., 1995) and also applies in practical wayfinding contexts. For example, Levine et al. (1984) asked participants to learn the layout of one floor of a building from a floor plan (placed on a wall) that was not aligned with the building. Despite the lack of alignment between the features on the map and the features they could see around them all the participants, incorrectly, assumed that 'up' on the map meant 'ahead' in the building.

Apart from the research into orientation specificity, there has been little research into how information derived from maps and from direct experience is integrated into the cognitive maps, or why there might be individual differences in this ability. Nonetheless, these are important issues, because few people learn large environments (like a city) only from direct experience, or only from a map, and therefore both sources of information have to be combined in the cognitive map. The specific contribution of other secondary sources of spatial information, such as tour guides or books, has not been investigated at all, though some research has been carried out into people's ability to learn spatial relationships from texts.

3.3.2 Written and verbal directions

Several researchers have investigated whether cognitive map knowledge can be generated from written texts (e.g., Franklin *et al.*, 1992; Denis and Zimmer, 1992; Ferguson and Hegarty, 1994; Tversky, 2000). For example, Ferguson and Hegarty (1994) found that cognitive map knowledge constructed from texts have properties similar to those constructed from traveling in real or simulated environments.

Taylor and Tversky (1992b) investigated the effect of texts that provided different perspectives on the same environments. They asked participants to learn about invented environments, like a small town, from texts that described the environments from either a route perspective (i.e., as if the reader was traveling through the environment) or a survey perspective (as if the reader was seeing the environment from above, with the location of places described relative to one another, in terms of cardinal directions). After participants had learnt the descriptions they were asked to say whether statements about the environments were true or false: some of the statements included route information and some included survey information. Participants from each learning condition were equally good at verifying either type of statement. In other words, they were good at inferring spatial information about a perspective different from the perspective that they had learnt. Taylor and Tversky, therefore, argued that participants formed cognitive maps of an environment that was independent of the perspective from which it had been learned. This is in contrast to some of the research with cartographic maps described above (e.g., Levine *et al.*, 1982), which has shown that encoding from secondary sources can sometimes be very specific to the perspective provided by that source.

3.3.3 Direction giving

The presence of an experienced guide may contribute to the development of another's cognitive map if they point out important places or relationships. There is a little evidence from studies of adults guiding children that the adults can structure environmental knowledge for the child and contribute to the development of the child's cognitive map. This has been reported anecdotally (Hart, 1981) and in some experiments (see Chapter 5).

People can give wayfinding directions effectively (e.g., Golding *et al.*, 1996) and researchers have investigated several aspects of how people describe routes, either in the environment or from maps. These have included studies of age differences in the ability to give directions (Blades and Medlicott, 1992), studies of gender differences in the way they are given (Ward *et al.*, 1986) and assessing how measures of spatial and verbal ability might be related to the ability to give directions (Vanetti and Allen, 1988). There have also been several studies of the structure and content of typical directions (e.g., Denis, 1997; Denis *et al.*, 1999; Wunderlich and Reinelt, 1982). As discussed above, there is much evidence that people can construct cognitive maps from written or verbal descriptions, including route descriptions of invented environments (Taylor and Tversky, 1992b; Tversky, 2000). However, there has not been any research into how people combine new information from other people into their existing cognitive maps of places.

3.4 Mediating Factors

There are many mediating factors which influence the use of both primary and secondary sources of information, and each is discussed in turn below. However, the effect of age on learning is discussed in Chapter 5, individual and gender differences are discussed in Chapter 6, and the effects that visual impairment might have on learning are considered in Chapter 7.

3.4.1 Familiarity and experience

How familiar a person is with a place will affect understanding of that place. Spatial familiarity is a poorly defined term and has received relatively little research attention. Intuitively, spatial familiarity can be interpreted as simply 'how well a place is known' (Chalmers and Knight, 1985). It is, however, more complex in nature, being difficult to identify and measure because it involves spatial and aspatial components. 'Familiarity' goes beyond just an awareness of a place, because it also involves affective components such as feelings of warmth, safety, and security, which complicate its meaning. Some people claim to be familiar with a place if they know its name, others if they recognize images of it, others if they have visited or passed through that place frequently, and others if they know about that place's geographic position or history. Spatial familiarity can therefore be described as being multidimensional (Gale *et al.*, 1990b).

Gale *et al.* (1990b) suggested that there are four dimensions of familiarity. The first of these is the ability to identify a place by recognizing its name, though this does not necessarily include having any spatial knowledge of the place. The second is the ability to recognize a place when shown a picture of it, although this does not require knowing where it is. The third dimension of familiarity is knowing the location of a place. This can be either egocentrically (in relation to one's self), topologically (relative to other places), or globally (in relation to coordinates or another abstract system). The fourth dimension is knowing about a place through frequent interaction. A fifth dimension that Gale *et al.* (1990b) ignored is the type of familiarity gained from having a knowledge of a place, such as its history or current affairs, which can be acquired from secondary sources like the media and education.

One factor in primary learning is the role of active experience in developing cognitive maps. Held and Rekosh (cited in Moore and Golledge, 1976) and Herman (1980) sought to explain why active interaction is so important. They noted that motor experience and sensor-motor interaction, necessary for movement, provide optimal opportunities for learning. That is, active exploration leads to more extensive cognitive maps than passive exploration. For example, Held and Rekosh found that participants with different opportunities to interact with an environment achieved different levels of knowledge about that environment. Similar results have been found in other studies, where participants actively using motor skills have produced more complete and accurate cognitive maps than passive travelers. For example, Feldman and Acredolo (1979) compared the cognitive maps of children who had learnt an unfamiliar office hall complex and the location of a hidden object, either through active exploration or through passive direction (they were led through the hall but were given no instruction of what to remember). Feldman and Acredolo found that the children who had explored the area for themselves were more likely to relocate the hidden object.

Foreman *et al.* (1990) compared how well children learnt a maze under four conditions of experience. The children either walked through the maze themselves, or their walking was guided by an adult, or they were taken through the maze in a pushchair while directing the person who was pushing, or they were taken through in the pushchair without any control over its direction. The children in the first three conditions learnt the maze successfully, but those in the last condition, who had experienced the maze passively and without any control over their movements, learnt least. This pattern of results suggests that when exploration is self-directed, or even if it is not self-directed but is still active (the guided walk condition in this experiment), a cognitive map can be formed effectively. However, in conditions when exploration is passive and outside the control of the person, a cognitive map may be less well formed. These findings may account for learning differences in other contexts (e.g., between car drivers' and passengers' route encoding), and they also have practical implications because they imply that people with disabilities (e.g., those who use wheelchairs) may need the opportunity to make navigation decisions while traveling if they are to learn new environments effectively.

Experience and length of residence in an environment are often treated as synonymous but this is not always the case. Length of residence does not necessarily mean more interaction with a particular area as an individual may be a passive explorer or never move far from their residence. Nonetheless, a number of researchers have found that the length of exposure does have an effect on cognitive maps. For example, Gärling *et al.* (1991a) found that length of residence in an area was a factor in estimating distance judgments between well-known landmarks. Montello (1991b) found that participants who claimed to know an area better responded faster when estimating directions, and those who had also lived for longer in the area were faster still and more accurate.

However, some researchers have argued that spatial knowledge develops rapidly within the first few weeks of residence, but then more slowly after the initial learning (Spencer *et al.*, 1989). Evans *et al.* (1982) found that as people learn about a setting, they learn the relative positions of items comparatively quickly, only fine-tuning exact locations with increasing experience. A similar conclusion was made by Devlin (1976), who investigated the cognitive maps of the wives of armed service personnel who had much travel experience and needed to learn new places frequently. Devlin found that their knowledge of important landmarks and their ability to find their way round new places developed quickly, but other aspects of their cognitive maps developed more slowly. However, more recent researchers have not always found a correlation between length of residence and spatial knowledge (e.g., Aitken and Prosser, 1990) or length of residence and the accuracy of distance estimation (Antes *et al.*, 1988).

3.4.2   Effort Effects

Muller (1982) described 'effort distances' as distances that can be measured in units, such as time, money, units of fuel, or psychological stress, that reflect the effort required to traverse a route. Muller argued that the greater the 'effort' to travel between two places the more likely that the cognitive distance between those places would be overestimated. Of the little research into effort effects, most has focused on the effects of travel time. A journey that takes a long time to travel 'feels' like a long distance and several researchers have found that distance estimations increase the longer it takes to travel a distance (e.g., MacEachren, 1980; Coshall, 1985; Saisa *et al.*, 1986).

Time taken to complete a journey will depend on the mode of transport, traffic congestion, and a person's ability to sense forward speed (Sadalla *et al.*, 1980; Golledge, 1992), nonetheless, as Saisa *et al.* (1986) have pointed out, time judgments have to be made every day. Zakay *et al.* (cited in Glicksohn, 1992) argued for the existence of an internal clock that processes and encodes temporal information, and suggested that as non-temporal information reduces or increases, more or less attention can be allocated to processing temporal data. Depending on the amount of attention available the internal clock will speed up or slow down with consequent effects on distance estimates.

3.4.3   Characteristics of the individual

Beck and Wood (1976a) and Wood and Beck (1990) suggested that the personality of the person exploring an environment might affect how well people form cognitive maps. Beck and Wood referred to 'rangers' who are happy to explore on their own; 'mixers' who like to explore but only as a member of a group; and 'fixers' who are hesitant about exploring except as passive members of a group. However, despite describing these three possible personalities they did little to establish the validity of these constructs, or to demonstrate empirical relationships between personality and spatial knowledge. In fact, if the results found by Foreman *et al.* (1990), described above, apply to large environments, whether people explore environments on their own or with others will be less important than whether they have active or passive experience of those environments. Aitken (1991) discussed environmental personalities with reference to Environmental Disposition Theory and Personal Construct Theory. The former theory suggests, like Beck and Wood (1976a), that people develop distinctive styles for dealing with environments, and that behavior within an environment may be explained through personality traits. In contrast, Personal Construct Theory places more emphasis on the personality being dynamic and assumes that the attitudes a person has toward the world can be continually changing.

Lundberg (1973) found that places with high emotional attachment were thought to be nearer than other places, citing the example of Vietnam, which was then in the news, and which was thought to be nearer to Europe than it actually was. Other researchers have also found that interest in a place and the importance attached to that place can influence estimates of distance (e.g., Bratfisch, 1969; Gilmartin and Lloyd, 1991), and Stea (1969) found that the perceived size of a country was correlated to its perceived economic and political importance. The perceived desirability of a place may also have an effect on cognitive maps. For example, Lowery (1973) found that people thought that desirable places were closer to their home than less desirable places, and Stea (1969) found that routes that were thought of as more beautiful and interesting were divided into more segments and were recalled better than other routes. Despite the early studies into the effects of personality on the cognitive map, and the effects of place attractiveness and importance, there has been much less recent research into these issues. This may be because this research has been restricted to making comparisons between types of personalities or places that have been defined by rather limited categories, and there has been little attempt to develop a theory of cognitive mapping that takes into account personality differences.

Metacognition may also play a role in learning environments. Metacognition refers to two different aspects of performance (Blades, 1991a). The first refers to a person's ability to judge his or her own cognitive abilities and limitations, and in cognitive mapping would include people's ability to judge when they have sufficient knowledge to support behavior and when they require additional information (e.g., to refer to a map or ask for directions when wayfinding). The second aspect of metacognition refers to the ability to carry out problem solving effectively, for example, by evaluating the problem, selecting the most relevant cognitive strategies to solve it, applying those strategies in an appropriate order and monitoring their outcome. In cognitive mapping this would include the strategies and combination of strategies that people use to learn spatial information.

Although metacognitive abilities are an important aspect of spatial learning, they have hardly been considered in cognitive mapping research, and there are only one or two studies. For example, Herman (1980) asked children to walk round a large model town for as long as they liked, until they thought they could reconstruct it from memory, but many of the children who said they had learnt the layout were unable to reconstruct it accurately. This suggests that the children were unable to monitor how well they had encoded the spatial information required to reconstruct the model town. In a study with adults, Kozlowski and Bryant (1977) asked participants to rate their own sense of direction, and then they were asked to estimate directions in a familiar area. There was a positive correlation between the estimates of sense of direction and the ability to estimate directions, and in a second experiment Kozlowski and Bryant found that self-assessment of sense of direction was also correlated with learning configurational information in novel environments. These results suggest that adults may have some awareness of their own cognitive map abilities, but how this self-awareness develops, and whether people with poor cognitive mapping abilities have different learning strategies than people with good abilities, are issues that have yet to be addressed.

3.4.4   Social and cultural factors

A few early researchers found that socio-economic class was related to the content of cognitive maps. For example, Orleans (1973) and Goodchild (1974) found that the working-class participants tended to draw sketch maps of smaller areas with fewer elements than their middle-class counterparts. In contrast, Golledge and Spector (1978) found that variables related to social status, such as education and income, did not have an effect on cognitive maps. It is not clear that socio-economic class itself will cause the differences in cognitive maps, because other, intervening, factors might be responsible for the differences. For instance, Van Vliet (1983) found children with higher socio-economic status had larger home ranges, and this greater experience may have had a positive effect on their cognitive maps. Lloyd and Heivly (1987) found that when socio-economic class, familiarity, and other variables are kept constant, residents of different neighborhoods developed different cognitive maps of the city, and as Lowenthal and Riel (1972) said, 'Where people are makes much more difference to the structure of the way they see the world than who they are.' Therefore any discussion of cognitive maps in terms of socio-economic status, without any consideration of related factors, has to be treated with caution.

Golledge (1991a) argued that culture provides the conceptual matrix that encompasses all experienced information, and therefore cognitive maps may vary in different cultures. This was demonstrated by Portugali and Haken (1992), who found that people from the same area, but from different cultures (Jews and Arabs) distorted their cognitive maps by omitting the areas that were predominantly populated by their rivals. Portugali and Haken suggested that nationalism, or 'culturalism', is one of the filters through which people build up their cognitive maps. Harris (1979) also suggested that cultural evolution will shape an individual's experience and knowledge, and pointed out that in different cultures there may be differences in home-range behavior, in experiences with spatial toys and activities, or in exposure to secondary sources of information. Such factors have been noted by Hazen (1983), who described how different cultures used a variety of techniques for wayfinding and navigation.

Spencer and Darvizeh (1983) found differences in the way that Iranian and English preschool children described familiar routes. The Iranian children provided more vivid and richer descriptions of the route, with more comments about personal experiences along the route and less information about landmarks and direction. Children's descriptions may have reflected differences in the type of information that they encoded about the routes, or they may have reflected cultural differences in verbal expression and assumptions about what is required when giving route directions.

3.4.5 Education

Self et al. (1992) argued that school curricula are a major factor in the development of spatial strategies and Saarinen et al. (1988) found that children with better school grades produced better sketch maps of an area. Such results might mean that people who receive a better education have more sophisticated cognitive map abilities, or they could mean that those with better education are better able to express their knowledge. Moore (1979) argued that overall educational level is not important in the construction of cognitive maps and what is more important is the development of the specific cognitive abilities needed for processing spatial information. These cognitive abilities might include understanding spatial relations, coordinating perspectives, and understanding rotation, abstraction, and scale reduction. However, as discussed in Chapter 6, little is known about the relationship between specific spatial abilities and cognitive map formation, or which abilities make the most important contribution to cognitive map learning.

Some authors have discussed how education and travel experience can contribute to children's cognitive maps of both local and distance environment. For example, Wiegand (1992) has described how children gain information from the formal curriculum, from maps and atlases, from educational and story books, and from travel experience. Wiegand stressed how all these sources of information can contribute to children's cognitive maps of the world. What is needed is a better understanding of which sources are the most important, and how learning information (i.e., cognitive map content) can best be combined with the most appropriate strategies (i.e., cognitive map processes) to provide the most effective cognitive map construction.

3.5 Conclusions

It is now generally accepted that cognitive maps are learnt through a process in which some aspects of the environment or secondary source take on more salience and are used to help structure and learn other data. The exact sequence of this learning and the factors which influence acquisition are, however, still contested and more analysis is needed to determine the specific processes of learning and how the environment itself and other mediating factors shape spatial knowledge. In particular, there is a need for studies that compare and contrast the same spatial information learnt through different sources to explore media effects. The model we outlined represents one possible conceptualization of the learning process and we explore its specific details and testing more fully in Chapter 9. The learning of spatial information is merely one aspect of cognitive mapping and other studies have concentrated on determining the constituent elements of cognitive maps and their structure and form. It is to this research we now turn.

CHAPTER 4

Structure and Form of Cognitive Maps

As spatial information is learnt it is processed and added to long term memory. A sizable body of research has investigated various aspects of the structure and form of cognitive maps as they develop, and how this relates to spatial behavior and other expressions of spatial knowledge (e.g., the drawing of maps). This research is centered on a number of themes, including the identification of the constituent elements of cognitive maps, the determination of different stages or levels of knowledge, how this knowledge compares in accuracy and content to real-world spatial relations, how spatial information is cognitively structured, what form cognitive maps take, and how this knowledge is processed for use. In this chapter we detail this research, outlining the main theories. In general, we consider these issues *per se*, as they apply to a whole population, concentrating on differences within and across populations in Chapters 6 and 7. The development of cognitive maps across the lifespan is addressed in Chapter 5.

4.1 Constituent Elements of Cognitive Maps

Golledge (1993b) suggested that all the elements of physical space have cognitive counterparts, and his model of cognitive map structure included six components of varying complexity. The first of these concerned the *individual occurrences* of elements. In physical space, elements such as buildings and landmarks may exist as unique occurrences, and have a specific identity, or label, or they can be identified by a generic label. Each element also has a location. In physical reality these locations remain fixed, but in cognitive maps they may become altered so that the locations are stored egocentrically, allocentrically, topologically, or even multidimensionally, rather than within strict coordinate systems (see next section). Each element also exists in time as well as space. Places are rarely isolated and are usually connected by routes, and these spatial *links*, in the form of linear elements such as paths and roads, are another component of cognitive maps. Linear elements can be distinguished by their gradient, width, surface, and other attributes, all of which aid encoding.

Places and routes form the basic building blocks of the cognitive map, but to organize this information other higher level information is required. The higher level information includes a knowledge of spatial *distribution*, which refers to the grouping of elements by common identity, by magnitude, or by temporal or functional characteristics to reveal a pattern. It also includes a recognition of *connectivity*, which refers to the distribution and linkage of paths into an overall understanding of a network. Networks may vary in complexity from a simple grid to complex patterns, and may also vary in terms of size and density.

A concept related to spatial distribution and connectivity is spatial *contiguity*, which refers to the order and separation of elements. For example, places encountered along a route can be thought of in the order they are experienced, or places in an area can be located relatively in terms of their proximity to one another. A further aspect of cognitive maps is *classification*, and Golledge (1993b) suggested that to make sense of spatial information it is often useful to stratify it in hierarchically ordered classes. For example, we can construct a city, town, village classification where cities are larger than towns which, in turn, are larger than villages. Golledge argued that stratification helps people to understand the geographic world by imposing an order on reality. The classification of information can be based on both physical facts and subjective judgments (Stevens and Coupe, 1978; Hart and Berzok, 1983).

All these components, in combination, provide the structure of cognitive maps. Individuals will differ in their knowledge of the same environments because few people will have a comprehensive knowledge of location, distribution, density, dispersion, pattern, connectivity, and hierarchy. Instead, the information known, and how it is organized, may vary greatly between individuals. Comprehensive spatial knowledge is not usually necessary when making spatial choices because much decision making and behavior in the environment can be based on three levels of knowledge.

4.2 Levels of Knowledge

Many of the theoretical descriptions of cognitive maps have emphasized three important levels of knowledge: declarative, procedural, and configurational. Liben (1981) described declarative knowledge as the database of specific spatial features, and although this is often used to mean information about landmarks, declarative knowledge also includes linear features like roads, or areal features such as parks.

Procedural knowledge consists of the rules used to synthesize declarative knowledge into information that can be used to facilitate an action. These rules are essentially wayfinding knowledge, which directs movement between places, an example of which would be the transformation of path elements into a navigable route. Thorndyke (1983) suggested that there are two types of procedural knowledge. The first is *unordered productions*. Here, behavior along a route is dependent on a series of independent pieces of spatial knowledge. Rather than information being combined into an understanding of the whole route, a person relies on taking actions at decision points along the route, and Thorndyke (1983) exemplified this by referring to a colleague who stated that she could take him to a place but not direct him to it. The second type of procedural knowledge is *ordered productions*. Here, order information is known and this allows whole routes to be remembered without having to traverse them.

Hart and Berzok (1983) suggested that ordered productions are divided into three stages. *Ordinal mapping* is when an individual is almost certain of the sequence of places, but is less sure of the relative distances that separate places. *Interval mapping* includes relative distances and times in the sequence, but not direction. Hart and Berzok (1983) suggested that this is the common strategy of encoding by people (e.g., commuter passengers) who do not need to know direction of travel to repeat the route. The third stage is *accurate mapping*, which contains information about direction to provide a complete set of procedural knowledge for a particular route.

Butler *et al.* (1993) suggested that people prefer to rely on ordinal or interval procedural knowledge when wayfinding because it is easier to do so. Butler *et al.* found that newcomers to a complex building preferred using ordered signs rather than interpreting you-are-here maps, because the latter involved encoding distance and direction. Similarly, Cornell *et al.* (1994) and Anooshian and Siebert (1996) suggested that wayfinding is based mainly on ordered productions, with people navigating by making choices based on recognizing familiar vistas and places along a route.

The highest level of knowledge is usually referred to as configurational knowledge. Configurational knowledge surpasses procedural knowledge by incorporating information about angles, orientation, and directions and distances between places (Golledge *et al.*, 1987). It forms a comprehensive spatial knowledge system that provides detailed information about the associations between places and their relative positions permits the connection of independent routes, and is the basis for making spatial inferences and propositions (Allen, 1985; Golledge, 1992).

Thorndyke (1983) argued that there are two types of configurational knowledge. One is the full configurational knowledge described above, but Thorndyke suggested that prior to such full knowledge a simpler, schematized knowledge was possible. This consists of simple, prototypical configurations of elements that form basic representations of an area, and Hart and Berzok (1983) termed these 'loose topological mappings' and suggested that locations are mapped on the basis of ordinal or categorical strategies, such as 'near to', 'parallel to', and 'in front of'.

A progression from declarative knowledge through procedural knowledge to configurational knowledge has been put forward by many researchers, and there has been much support for this description of cognitive map development (e.g., Golledge *et al.*, 1993). Nonetheless, there is also evidence that this progression does not occur in all cases. Some researchers have shown that it is not necessary to possess procedural knowledge of an area before possessing configurational knowledge. For example, Hanley and Levine (1983) and Holding and Holding (1989) both found that procedural and configurational knowledge can be learnt simultaneously, and Moar and Carlton (1982) found that networks of routes could be learnt without first learning the separate routes between them. Other studies have shown that configurational knowledge can be learnt very rapidly through travel, although accuracy and completeness may take a little longer to develop (Smyth and Kennedy, 1982; Gärling *et al.*, 1983; Magliano *et al.*, 1995). For example, Montello and Pick (1993) asked participants to learn routes through a hospital complex, and found that participants developed a configurational knowledge of the complex very rapidly. These studies suggest that the earlier (declarative and procedural) stages of cognitive mapping can be achieved very quickly.

Kitchin (1995) argued that configurational knowledge is merely an advanced form of declarative knowledge. According to this model, declarative knowledge includes both feature knowledge—the database of specific spatial features—and configurational knowledge—the database of spatial relationships and structures. Procedural knowledge consists of the rules and heuristics used to access and manipulate declarative knowledge for a specific spatial task. This removes procedural knowledge as a distinct stage of development and gives it a more general role as a set of rules and heuristics that apply to all types of declarative knowledge (Figure 4.1). Route knowledge, the information about specific routes, would be independent of its explicit link to procedural knowledge and be considered as one form of declarative knowledge. In this model, configurational knowledge can be learnt simultaneously with, or prior to, procedural knowledge and therefore it can account for both map-based and navigation-based learning.

Montello (1998) put forward a similar argument, suggesting that spatial knowledge develops quantitatively rather than qualitatively. Montello argued that people start to form a configurational understanding of an environment from their first encounters with it. This understanding is at first partial and does not include accurate information about distance, but with greater experience it begins to include metric information. In Montello's model there is no stage in which only landmark or only route knowledge exists, but some configurational knowledge begins to be acquired on first exposure, which becomes more complete and detailed with increasing experience in the environment. In other words, the same knowledge structures exist continuously, but include progressively more information at different times of development.

As discussed in the previous chapter, some forms of learning may lead to different forms of knowledge. Researchers who have compared map learning and navigation-based learning have found that maps lead to immediate configurational knowledge and navigation to procedural knowledge. Freundschuh (1991) suggested that although people learning an environment by direct experience might progress from route to configurational knowledge, people learning the same environment from a map can immediately gain metrically accurate configurational knowledge (see Chapter 3). Levels of knowledge may therefore be a function of learning medium and, in the case of direct experience, time (see Figure 4.2).

4.3 Frames of Reference

Directly related to levels of knowledge are frames of reference and the geometrical nature of cognitive maps. Frames (or systems) of reference are heuristics used to relate places to one another (Tversky, 1981; Moar and Bower, 1983) (see Figure 4.3). They help people to orientate themselves and provide a 'sense of direction' (Kuipers, 1978).

Old Model of Knowledge Structure

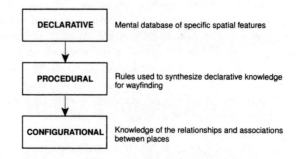

New Model of Knowledge Structure

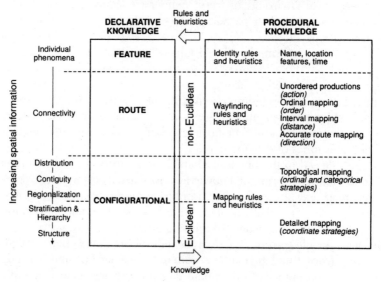

Figure 4.1. New and old models of cognitive map knowledge structures
Source: Kitchin (1995)

4.3.1 Development of frames of reference

Piaget and Inhelder (1956) and Piaget *et al.* (1960) suggested that there were three levels in the development of spatial knowledge, the topological, projective, and Euclidean. Piaget described these levels with reference to children's cognitive development, but he also saw them as underlying the development of children's cognitive map abilities (see Chapter 5). According to Piaget, in the topological level

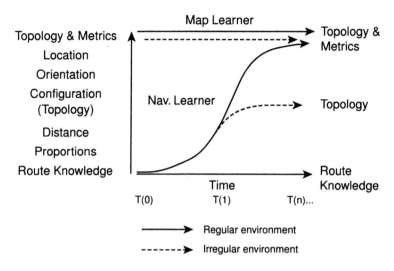

Figure 4.2. Levels of knowledge as a function of learning medium and time
Adapted from Freundschuh (1991)

of understanding, children are only able to appreciate a limited
range of spatial relationships and only consider the relationships
between a few objects or landmarks. With projective understanding,
children begin to appreciate that the relationship between objects or
places depends on the specific viewpoint of the observer. For
example, when objects X, Y, and Z are seen from one viewpoint
they are seen in that order, but from a different viewpoint they may
be seen as Z, Y, and X. Having recognized the importance of view-
points a child can then combine different views of the same area
into an overall framework for understanding that area. In the Euclidean stage of development the framework becomes more accurate
and includes information about distances between objects or landmarks. An Euclidean framework is an abstract frame of reference, so
that any object or place can be specified exactly (e.g., in terms of
coordinates), and spaces that are not occupied by objects can also be
specified by reference to the framework.

Although Piaget's description of spatial development has been
very influential and many of his terms and concepts are still retained
in the research into children's cognitive maps (see Chapter 5), there
are difficulties in interpreting it, because many aspects of his description and many of the distinctions he made (e.g., between projective
and Euclidean levels of understanding) were never fully clarified by
Piaget himself (see Blades and Spencer, 1994). Other researchers

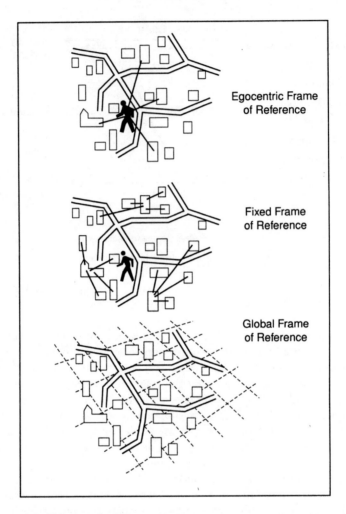

Figure 4.3. Frames of reference
Adapted from Hart (1981)

have put forward alternative descriptions that emphasize a more gradual and less stagelike progression in the development of spatial understanding. For example, Huttenlocher and Newcombe (1984) suggested that young children first encode objects or places relative to known salient landmarks, and may be able to estimate rough distances between objects and landmarks (Newcombe 1989). With increasing age children can relate objects to more than one landmark, and in doing so they can create local frameworks, which can eventually be integrated into ever larger frameworks. Newcombe, (1997) has summarized some of the evidence in support of this description. The main difference between Huttenlocher and New-combe's (1984) description and Piaget's description is that the latter explained children's development as a progression based on a series of cognitive stages characterized by distinct geometries (topological, projective, and Euclidean), but Huttenlocher and Newcombe descri-bed development as a gradual increase in the understanding of spatial relationships.

Adults may have fixed frames of reference that are based on landscape features or they may have more abstract or global frames (or Euclidean in Piaget's terminology). Tversky (1981) discussed three possible types of fixed frames of reference based on different landscape axes. These include *axes of symmetry*, which refers to natural features that bisect areas into two (e.g., a river); *main-line axes*, which refers to features such as roads or railways; or *landmark axes*, which link well-known salient features. When knowledge is rotated or translated to fit such natural coordinate systems the frame of refer-ence may contain distortions of alignment and rotation (Lloyd, 1989a) (Figure 4.4).

Tversky (1981) found that when participants were asked to describe spaces they demonstrated memory biases. These biases applied to frameworks for both small spaces (e.g., aligning intersect-ing roads to 90 degrees) or large spaces (e.g., rotating axes to cardi-nal directions). For instance, South America was thought to be due south of North America even though it is slightly to the Southeast, and Europe/North America and Africa/South America were given the same latitudes. Kitchin (1990, 1992) found a similar rotation error when participants recalled the vertical axis of Great Britain as north–south rather than southeast–to–northwest, and Glicksohn (1994) found that participants thought Israel was aligned north–south rather than fifteen degrees clockwise.

Global or abstract frames of reference (Figure 4.3) extend beyond fixed frames. These are frames of reference that individuals can use to orientate themselves in unknown environments, regardless of the direction faced (Gärling *et al.*, 1986b). With a global frame of refer-ence it is possible to locate all other known places within the same frame of reference. Examples of such systems include cardinal direc-tions, mapping coordinates, and latitude/longitude values.

Frames of reference can be thought of as one component of the rules and heuristics stored as procedural knowledge. They allow different parts of declarative knowledge (feature, route, and

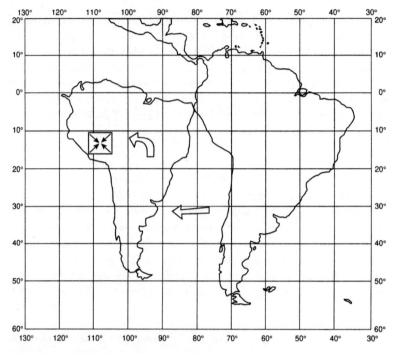

Figure 4.4. Rotation and alignment heuristics
Source: Adapted from Lloyd (1989a)

configurational information) to be accessed and used, and although there may be an underlying age-related progression, by adulthood, different frames of reference can be used in different contexts (Pick, 1976). For example, a fixed frame of reference will usually be of more use than an abstract coordinate system when trying to recall the location of an item within a room or wayfinding around a building, but an abstract system might be of more use when navigating in an area devoid of landmarks.

The frame of reference used will also be linked to the source of knowledge (e.g., whether from direct experiences, or from map-based information) and the position of the individual in relation to the environment. For example, Sholl (1987) asked students to point to landmarks (that were out of sight) on their college campus with which they were familiar from direct experience. The students were faster at pointing to campus landmarks that were ahead of them, and they showed this pattern of performance whichever way they were facing. This implies that the students applied a framework for local landmarks that was dependent on their own position, but that framework was not orientation-specific. Sholl also asked the same students to point to cities that they would know mainly from carto-graphic maps. The students pointed to all the cities equally well (i.e., irrespective of whether the cities were 'in front' or 'behind' them), but they were faster at this task when they themselves were facing north. This implies the students' framework for map-learnt informa-tion was independent of their own position, but that it was orienta-tion-specific. In other words there was a contrast between the type of encoding framework applied to environments learnt through direct experience and ones learnt from maps (see Chapter 3).

Franklin and Tversky (1990) also found that local space is con-ceptualized relative to a person's own position, but pointed out that the frameworks that are used for small spaces may be more varied than those described by Sholl (1987). Franklin and Tversky asked people to learn a description of a room that included different objects at various positions in front, behind, above, and below the partici-pants' assumed position (which could, for example, be standing or reclining). Participants' speed at identifying the objects around them was measured and Franklin and Tversky found that when a partici-pant was standing, reaction times were quickest for information along a vertical axis, followed by front–back and left–right axes. This changed when a participant was reclining, because in this condition reaction times were quickest for information along a front–back axis, followed by head–feet and left–right axes. From such results Franklin and Tversky argued that spatial processing takes place in spatial fra-meworks that are given more or less importance depending on the individual's body position. Maki and Marek (1997) also made the point that, when necessary (e.g., communicating spatial information), people can place their knowledge into the context of another's spatial framework (the listener's). In other words, the same spatial knowledge can be considered in several different frames of reference and can be used for different purposes (Tversky, 2000).

4.4 Geometrical Nature of Cognitive Maps

A number of researchers have considered the geometrical nature of cognitive map knowledge, to find out whether spatial relations are encoded as one-dimensional, two-dimensional or multidimensional metrics. If spatial memory perfectly matched a cartographic map then it would have a Euclidean metric (with uniform distances and directions across a plane). Richardson (1981a) examined which

Minkowskian metric best represented the two-dimensional config-uration produced through multidimensional scaling (MDS). Min-kowskian metrics are defined as:

$$d(x,y) = \left(\sum_{i=1}^{R} |x_i - y_i| \right)^{1/P}$$

where $d(x, y)$ refers to the distance from x to y, R is the number of dimensions, and P is the Minkowskian metric parameter. The city-block, Euclidean, and dominance metrics are defined respectively as $P=1$, $P=2$ and $P=\infty$ (Gatrell, 1983). Richardson (1981b) found that a city-block metric best represented the configurations used in his study, but noted that in some cases dominance and Euclidean metrics best represented the data. Wakabayashi (1990, 1994) also found that a city-block metric represented the cognitive maps of participants in a number of different cities.

Other constant uniform metrics exist, such as Rienmann metrics, which are used to measure celestial space, hyperbolic and spherical metrics, and these could also underlie the structure of cognitive maps (Cadwallader, 1979; Golledge and Hubert, 1982, Montello, 1991a). Pocock (1972) proposed that cognitive maps may be struc-tured using a time–distance metric, and there are other possibilities of non-uniform, non-constant metrics that vary across both time and space. At present, it is assumed that the spatial relationships encoded in cognitive maps are multidimensional in nature, supported by a non-Euclidean geometry (i.e., distance and direction standards vary across space), although this may be an incomplete, distorted, torn, or folded Euclidean metric (Montello, 1989). This latter suggestion is based on studies that have found multidimensional structures when using MDS, non-communicavity (when different distance estimates are given for the same route in forward and return directions), and intransivity in distance estimates (when the distances between three locations cannot be plotted, because participants have estimated that A > B, B > C, and A < C when A, B, and C are distances between points). Such studies have also found scale changes within two-dimensional spatial products like sketch maps, and found evidence for rotation and alignment heuristics and for hierarchical clustering.

According to the theoretical perspectives discussed above, cogni-tive maps will only become Euclidean in nature once they have been synthesized into an advanced spatial system that is dependent upon time and experience. With only partial experience the rips, tears, and inconsistencies within people's knowledge inevitably lead to an imperfect metric, or non-Euclidean framework, and many researchers have pointed out that an Euclidean metric may be an inappropriate standard for assessing spatial knowledge (e.g., Anooshian and Siegel, 1985; Downs, 1985). Euclidean, Ordnance Survey or Rand-McNally maps are only one standardized model of the world. They are sophisticated tools for aiding navigation, but may have little correspondence to how we actually view or understand the world, and therefore using them as standards to measure the accuracy of spatial knowledge may be inappropriate (Anooshian and Siegel, 1985). To understand more about the structure of cognitive maps it might be better to test spatial knowledge against several different metrics.

4.5 How Are Cognitive Maps Structured?

There are several theories as to how cognitive maps are structured and organized and some of the most influential can be considered under three headings: non-hierarchical, hierarchical, and schema theories, of which hierarchical are the most popular.

4.5.1 Non-hierarchical theories

Non-hierarchical theories contend that cognitive map knowledge is structured in a holistic fashion, does not contain nested levels of detail or separate codes for global or local properties, and therefore lacks any hierarchical structure. There are two principal ways of achieving such holistic structures: propositional networks and analog images (or a combination of propositional and analog data). Theories concerning images will be discussed in the next section.

Kaplan (1973) argued that cognitive maps require a network structure so that they can include generic information. He suggested that although hierarchical structures can occur as sub-sections of a network they are not sufficient storage mechanisms in themselves. This is because a non-planar network structure can encode distance and direction data within the structure itself, making it easier to retrieve information. Such a structure would allow the network to be coded as accurately as on a cartographic map, and would allow easy processing for tasks such as wayfinding and routefinding (Kuipers, 1978). Kaplan (1973) illustrated his argument by using the analogy of a city structure, and suggested that the mind, like a city, is not tree-like, and yet both contain complexity, richness, and the potential for diversity. As such, distortions and errors in people's spatial knowledge are the result of incorrect network coding.

Beck and Wood (1976b) speculated that cognitive map knowledge is organized in a net-like fashion, containing place-associative traces at space–time loci. The net is diffuse and topologically organized, with nodes acting to hold the net together and as recovery points for images. They were, however, unsure about how non-spatial attributive data were held and connected to the spatial network. Beck and Woods' theory corresponds closely to Lieblich and Arbib's (1982) view that cognitive map knowledge is coded as a world graph, where each node in the 'graph' represents a place, and these are connected by pathways. The world graph differs slightly in that each place can be represented many times, as different nodes.

4.5.2 Hierarchical theories

Hierarchical theories suggest that spatial knowledge is structured as nested levels of detail. Strong hierarchical theories represent an extreme position in the tradeoff between storage and computation and propose that all knowledge is encoded in a strict hierarchical fashion. In these theories, each item of information is stored once only within a tree-like structure and there are no links between branches except by moving up and down through the hierarchical structure. For this reason the spatial relations between all places are not explicitly encoded, but are inferred from other information such as processing time.

In contrast, partial hierarchical theories allow for spatial relations to be encoded between locations in different branches of the hierarchy. Such a structure increases the speed and accuracy with which spatial estimates can be made (McNamara, 1986). There is much evidence, from investigations of errors in cognitive maps, to support partial hierarchical theories. Cox and Zannaras (1973) suggested that superordinate structures would influence people's spatial and non-spatial cognitive estimates, and Stevens and Coupe (1978) found specific evidence of this. Stevens and Coupe asked participants to indicate, from memory, the direction from one North American city to another, and they noted particular patterns of error in this task. One of these concerned the direction from San Diego in California to Reno in Nevada. Most participants thought, incorrectly, that Reno was east of San Diego. Stevens and Coupe argued that this occurred because cognitive maps are structured using a partially hierarchical system of organization. In this structure, the relative location of the states is stored, and the location of cities is stored by reference to the states that contain them. When asked to make direction judgments between cities, people do not compute them directly, but infer them from the relative positions of the states they are in. Because California is generally west of Nevada, the inference is that all cities in California are west of cities in Nevada.

Just and Carpenter (1985) noted that it is difficult to imagine a whole map in detail, and the way we cope with this is to create a 'window' on the area in which we are interested. They suggested that the cognitive map contains embedded systems, and that processing involves moving up or down through this hierarchical system depending on situational demands. Distance estimation to locations separated by barriers is often higher than if the barrier was removed, and such evidence suggests that the barriers may act as boundaries between regions and therefore as branches in the cognitive hierarchy. Evidence for this effect can be found in studies using both metric distance and distance derived from ranking, which have found that barriers increased the distance estimates between places (e.g., McNamara, 1986; Newcombe and Liben, 1982; Newcombe, 1997).

Further evidence for a partially hierarchical system is provided by reaction times in making distance and direction comparisons. Wilton (1979) found that participants took longer to verify truth statements, such as 'Edinburgh is north of Sussex', when places were in the same spatial area (e.g., in England), than when they were in distinct spatial areas (e.g., England/Scotland). It seems that if places are in different spatial areas or categories, it is easier to infer the direction: Edinburgh is in Scotland, Sussex is in England, Scotland is north of England, therefore Edinburgh is north of Sussex. Places in the same category (or branch of the structure) take longer to process because there is no simple categorical way to divide them.

Additional evidence for hierarchical organization has been provided by studies that have found that environmental cues act as primers for other information. In other words, features in the environment are recalled because they are attached to more salient cues. Such grouping suggests that each cue acts as a focal point for a level in a hierarchical structure. As described in Chapter 3, Golledge et al. (1985) put forward an anchor-point theory, which described different levels of anchors or cues to which other data is attached. Their theory combines both network and hierarchical concepts to produce a model of cognitive maps in which places on the same hierarchical level form a network of spatial information.

Howard and Kerst (1981), Hirtle and Mascolo (1986), and McNamara et al. (1989) have all shown evidence of hierarchical structuring by identifying clustering in participants' recall of locations.

THE COGNITION OF GEOGRAPHIC SPACE

For example, Hirtle and Mascolo asked participants to learn a map that included ten places. The places on the map included two groups, one was a cluster of recreational sites (e.g., playground, golf course) and the other was an administrative cluster (e.g., post office, police station). After learning the map, participants were asked to estimate the distances between the places, and Hirtle and Mascolo found that participants estimated the distance between places in the same cluster as less than the distance of equally spaced places that were in different clusters. In other words, participants encoded the places with reference to the spatial groupings implied by similarity of function. Hirtle and Jonides (1985) also found that inter-cluster distances were overestimated and intra-cluster distances were underestimated, and Allen (1981) found evidence for the segmentation of route knowledge, because distances between places in different route segments were judged to be longer than the same distance between places within a segment. This implies that each segment contained independent information, but that this information existed within a framework or hierarchical structure.

In related experiments, McNamara *et al.* (1989) asked participants to learn a layout that included 28 objects that were randomly distributed in a large room, without any marked regions or boundaries. After learning the layout, participants performed a recall task in which they listed the objects, and a recognition task in which they had to say whether or not they recalled a target object as being present in the layout. For the recognition task, each target object that participants were asked about was preceded by a primer (e.g., the name of another object that had been present in the layout). The recall data revealed that participants grouped objects, subjectively, into different regions that could be described in a hierarchical framework. The recognition data showed that when a primer was from the same subjective region as the target object, participants' response time was quicker than when the primer was the same distance away from the target but in a different subjective region. This experiment demonstrated that even when there are no perceptual regions or barriers present, people still impose a hierarchy of regions on a space.

4.5.3 Schema

The term schema refers to both how knowledge is structured and how people think about the everyday geographic environment. Schemata provide a framework or outline of essential information about places or events that are derived from past experience and that can aid the recognition and learning of new environments (Medyckyj-Scott and Blades, 1992). For example, when visiting a city for the first time, a person can make assumptions about the layout of the city from past experience of visiting other cities (Williamson and McGuinness, 1990). An established schema might include general expectations about cities, including particular predictions about the location of places within the city (e.g., City Hall will be near the center, farms will be on the outskirts). Information about new cities can be 'fitted into' these expectations. In other words, a schema can influence what we expect to see, what we look for, and how we respond in new environments that we recognize as similar to ones that have been experienced before (Axia *et al.*, 1991).

Brewer and Treyens (1981) have suggested that there are a number of ways in which schema could influence recall, including the recall of places. The schema could determine which pieces of information are viewed and encoded. It may serve as a framework for the selective retention of material and can aid in the integration of new and old knowledge. Schemata may be used to guide the search for information in long term memory, and may influence the subset of information that is recalled. Although existing spatial schemata fulfil the important function of providing a framework that can be applied to new contexts and from which inferences can be drawn (e.g., where to find a hotel when visiting a new city), there may be occasions when a schema leads to incorrect inferences. For example, Blades and Banham (1990) asked young children to learn a model room that included several items of typical kitchen furniture but did not include a cooker. The children were later asked to reconstruct the model from memory, and were given a large variety of toy furniture (including a cooker) to do this. Children recalled the position of most of the items accurately in their reconstructions, but two-thirds of them incorrectly included a cooker. In other words, the children's reconstructions combined information that was specific to the layout they had learnt, and information from their schemata about kitchens that included the knowledge that kitchens include cookers. This is an example of how spatial schemata can be used to make assumptions (in this case incorrect ones) about environments.

As yet there is little research into how spatial schemata develop. One of the few studies to consider developmental differences in schemata was carried out by Dijkink and Elbers (1981) who asked children aged 7 to 13 years to make a model town. The children were given the components (old and new houses, factories, farms, and so on) and a road layout. Many of the younger children simply spread all the items across the layout without any geographical context at all. Some children placed buildings along roads, but made no attempt to distinguish the types of buildings. Only the oldest children produced a model that reflected the structure of a city (e.g., with public and older buildings near the center and newer buildings on the edge of the city). Dijink and Elbers's study suggests that learning the typical structure of a complex environment like a city may take some time to develop. But as yet there is no research into the number and type of experiences that would be needed to develop an effective spatial schema.

4.6   The Form of Cognitive Maps

There are several theories concerning the form of cognitive maps. Kosslyn and Pomerantz (1977) suggested that information can be in image-like units. Perceptual processes reduce perceived information to simpler and more organized units that are stored in a form that can be used to generate images (Farah, 1988). The generated images are not the same as visual experience, though they may appear to have some of the properties associated with visual images, but as they do not include all the details and qualities of an original perceived event they are best described as analog representations. There is some evidence that cognitive maps may include analog representations. For example, participants might be asked to learn a map that includes several features distributed across it. After learning the map participants are asked to imagine it, focusing on one of the features. A second feature is then named and participants are asked to imagine scanning between the two features (e.g., Kosslyn et al., 1978). Such studies have shown that participants take longer to scan between features that are further apart on the map and this implies that they are processing an image-like representation of the map.

In contrast to the view that spatial information is stored as images, Pylyshyn (1979, 1981) argued that both visual and verbal material is coded as conceptual propositions and that people do not use imagery when processing information. Pylyshyn suggested that participants can use imagery when asked to do so, because they will follow the task demands as closely as possible, and construct an image for the 'mind's eye' from propositional data, in which case imagery is a by-product of thought (West et al., 1985) and the results from scanning experiments can be accounted for by participants' tacit knowledge concerning physical laws of motion and their ability to draw on these to simulate the perceptual events that would occur if imagery was involved. If it is the case that people can generate mental images from propositions, or simulate scanning, in response to task demands, it is difficult to distinguish empirically between theories that emphasize imagery-based encoding and ones that emphasize propositional encoding (Lloyd, 1982).

Irrespective of the underlying coding, there is evidence that people may be flexible in encoding and recalling spatial information. Some researchers have suggested that differences in encoding may depend on the task demands (e.g., Eddy and Glass, 1981). Hintzman *et al.* (1981) suggested that direct learning through interaction, or sources which are learnt from multiple perspectives, may lead to propositional encoding but single-orientation learning, such as from a map, leads to analog memory. Other researchers have emphasized individual differences in processing information. For example, MacEachren (1992) suggested that there might be individual differences in processing information. He compared the ability of two sets of individuals to estimate distance and direction after learning a map and concluded that one group had encoded the information using imagery and the other had encoded the information propositionally. In a further study, when the individuals who used propositional encoding were given a strongly visual task they were slower in making estimates, but when presented with a less visual task the same group were faster in making estimates than those who had used imagery encoding.

Kitchin (1997) also found evidence for individual differences in encoding strategies in a study in which participants were asked to report how they had completed a task. In this study, respondents were divided into two groups of ten females and ten males, who each completed two of four tests designed to measure their configurational knowledge of the Swansea (South Wales, UK) area. The first group completed a sketch map and a cloze procedure test. The second group completed a projective convergence and an orientation specification test (see Chapter 8). In all cases, each individual undertook the tests whilst adopting a talk-aloud protocol describing what they did and how they were remembering information in order to complete the task.

Participants reported using eight different strategies, including both image-based and non image-based ones. One of the most frequently used strategies was the use of map imagery, which was used in two ways. First, some participants tried to recall a map that they had seen, usually an Ordnance Survey map, in its entirety. They had either stored this map as a complete image or as component images which they then reconstructed to perform the task. Second, some participants tried to construct maps with minimal structure, containing only those features that were necessary to complete the task. Participants implied or sometimes explicitly stated that these maps were constructed for the purpose of the task, and some claimed that they alternated between their minimal map or recalling an Ordnance Survey map depending on the difficulty of the question. In other cases the constructed map would be a combination of remembered and constructed maps intertwining elements from both: for example, one participant recalled the road network from his road atlas and into this he added locations that he had visited. Some participants reported that they had completed tasks solely in relation to a coastline, because their base maps were so minimal that this was the only feature they contained and therefore their responses were plotted in relation to it.

Other participants reported that they had imagined traveling along a route. This expression took two different forms. Most described a route strategy that was best described as 'replaying' a route traveled. Instead of imagining a journey between two locations, some participants constructed a minimal map which only contained the route between two places. Most of the latter route maps were created not by remembering a map but by constructing one, in other words by converting route knowledge into configurational knowledge. Participants would imagine traveling along a route and then simultaneously transpose this knowledge onto a 'mental' base map of the area which would then be used to answer the question. A few participants used their knowledge of travel times to work out the distances between places, and this was nearly always based on first-hand travel experience, where the amount of time taken to travel between two places was mentally converted into distances using an individual conversion standard.

Approximately one-third of all participants used the strategy of imagining being at a location and 'looking' in the direction of another location. For example, they would imagine standing at a location and looking across the space in front of them to judge distances, directions, or where two places were in relation to each other. This strategy is limited because it can only be applied in areas that can be viewed as a panorama, but it proved to be effective for judging spatial relationships between places along the coastline. Some participants constructed answers using abstract strategies that were based upon an amalgamation of real-life route knowledge and information learnt from a map, so that they tried to solve the task using a strategy never experienced. One of the ways they attempted this was by imagining looking down onto Swansea as if they had an aerial view of the city.

One participant worked out the positions of other locations solely in relation to where he was currently located, and some participants claimed to 'just know' the answer to a task. They did not need to employ any strategy of thought because they thought that they automatically knew where places were in relation to one another. Many implied some type of propositional coding, so that information was coded in the form 'along the seafront then in a bit', with participants knowing the directions and distances. Statements such as 'near to' or 'left of' were common, with no references made to any imagery. It is difficult to validate this strategy in that the participants could have been describing the answer resulting from another strategy. For example, a participant might know that a hospital is next to the university because they had just consulted a map image strategy.

4.6.1 Dual coding

According to Paivio (1979, 1986) the recall of verbal and visual information depends on different processing systems. Kulhavy et al. (1992) and Kulhavy and Stock (1996) applied a similar distinction, which they called 'conjoint retention', to learning texts with maps. They suggested that when a person is asked to learn a text that includes a spatial description (e.g., about a city) and the text is illustrated with an appropriate map, the verbal information from the text and the spatial information from the map are stored separately in memory and that there is separate access to each memory store at the time of recall. According to Kulhavy et al. such conjoint encoding has the advantage of improving recall.

In typical experiments, participants are given a description of an environment. Half of the participants are given the description with a map of the environment and the other half are given it with, for example, a list of all the placenames that are on the map. In other words, both groups experience the description with the same additional information, but for one group the information is spatially organized (in the map) and for the other group the information does not include any spatial relationships (in the list). When participants are later tested for their recall of the geographical description, the usual finding in these studies is that the group who have learnt the description with the map recall more information from the description (e.g., Kulhavy *et al.*, 1993, Stock *et al.*, 1995, Blades *et al.*, 1999).

4.7 The Expression of Spatial Knowledge

So far, the focus of the discussion has been the structure and form of cognitive maps, but there is also the question of how the information in the cognitive map is expressed in relation to different contexts and how it is retrieved. As pointed out in the previous chapter, people can use information from text or directions to generate configurational knowledge and several researchers have demonstrated the latter effect (Tversky, 2000). For example, Denis and Zimmer (1992) asked participants to learn an invented island either from viewing a map of the island or by reading a text that described the island with statements like 'In the extreme north-western part of the island there is a bridge. East of the bridge, there are skyscrapers...' Although participants' recall of locational information was better in the map condition, participants in the text condition had not only learnt the specific spatial relationships explicitly given in the text, but had also inferred, correctly, other spatial relationships that had not been given in the text. From the latter result Denis and Zimmer argued that people could generate configurational information from text. Other researchers have found similar results (e.g., Ferguson and Hegarty, 1994; Foos, 1980).

Several researchers have argued that cognitive maps derived from texts may have similar properties to ones gained through perceptual experience (e.g., Ferguson and Hegarty, 1994) and that similar processing mechanisms apply to cognitive maps learnt from text or from experience (e.g., Denis and Zimmer, 1992). A related point has been made by Tversky and Lee (1998), who asked participants to provide maps and written directions for a route they were familiar with. Tversky and Lee found that, despite differences due to the format (written or drawn) of the descriptions, both the map and the directions schematized the route in similar ways, and they argued that these reflected underlying similarities in the cognitive processes associated with spatial knowledge.

Landau and Jackendoff (1993) explored the spatial language associated with objects and places, and pointed out that spatial language used to describe places is usually fuzzy and contains only coarse geometrical properties. For example, language used to describe the location of an object or place usually relies on a limited number of prepositions (only 80–100 spatial locatives are used in the English

STRUCTURE AND FORM OF COGNITIVE MAPS

Table 4.1. Example spatial prepositions

near to	far from
on	off
in front of	behind
under	above
left	right
apart	near
there	here
east	west
north	south
backward	forward

Adapted from Golledge and Stimson (1997)

language) that are open to interpretation unless qualified with precise numerical information (Table 4.1).

Landau and Jackenoff (1993) argued that a language-based description of an object's location requires three elements: first, an object to be located (the figure); second, a reference object or background environment (the ground); and third, a relationship between figure and ground expressed as a spatial preposition. For example, the statement 'the car is on the road' describes the spatial relationship between the car (figure) and road (ground) using the preposition 'on'. Note that without a qualifier, *where* on the road is not expressed. It is usual for the larger or immobile objects to form the 'ground' (e.g., road) and confusion is often created when figure–ground relationships are mixed (e.g., the road is under the car) (Talmy, 1983). A number of figure–ground relationships can exist. For example, Tversky (2000) described a deictic relationship as one that relates to the speaker's point of view (e.g., 'the car is to the right of the house'), and an intrinsic relationship as one that relates a reference object (car) to the inherent sides of a reference object (house) (e.g., 'the car is in front of the house').

Several researchers have analyzed how people give directions (e.g., Denis, 1997; Couclelis, 1996; see below). For example, Wunderlich and Reinelt (1982) pointed out that when propositional statements are used to give directions they are divided into three phases: (a) directions within the visual or sensory field; (b) information about intermediate destinations and choice points; and (c) the approach to the final destination. Klein (1982) also suggested that because of their imprecision the direction giver and direction receiver must align their deictic, as well as perceptual, spaces. That is, they must

THE COGNITION OF GEOGRAPHIC SPACE

Table 4.2. Locating places with spatial language

Figure geometry	relationships
along	interior (in, inside)
across	contact (on)
around	proximal (near, around)
all over	distal (far, beyond)
throughout	negatives (out, off)
	vertical (over, above, below)
	horizontal (by, next to)
	front to back (ahead of, behind)
	axial (on top of, in front of)
	occlusion (beneath)
	earth orientated (up, east, north)
	object axis (forward, left, right)

Adapted from Landau and Jackendoff (1993).

share the same frames of reference with propositions determined to have the same spatial meanings. Consequently, although spatially imprecise, propositions can provide an effective means of spatial thought and communication by reducing complex information to simple, but rich, descriptive statements (Foos, 1980; Taylor and Tversky, 1992b). Indeed, Landau and Jackendoff (1993) noted that just a few different types of locational descriptor can convey elaborate combinations of spatial relationships relating to the figure itself and between the figure and the ground (Table 4.2).

4.8 Accessing and Using Spatial Knowledge

Clearly for cognitive maps to be useful they have to be applied to understanding the real world, to be put into practice. All recalled information has to be reconstructed in working memory from traces in long term memory. Smith *et al.* (1982) suggested that recall may depend on constructing information from several separate knowledge stores (whose data may be non-hierarchically or hierarchically structured and in imagery or propositional form). This is achieved through a system of frames. A frame is a knowledge template that is applicable in a given context and could be viewed as a knowledge structure with 'slots' in it, with each slot having access to different knowledge bases (Smith *et al.*, 1982). Depending on the task demands, the slots are left blank or filled so that the required information is made available. Consequently, knowledge is reconstructed within working memory to address a specific task (e.g., navigating a route).

Spatial mental models are constructed in working memory from available knowledge to address specific tasks. Both Foley and Cohen (1984) and Kitchin (1997) found evidence for the construction of a representation that draws selectively on information from the cognitive map depending on the nature of the task. Foley and Cohen found that participants who were familiar with an environment reported more abstract and less scenographic imagery than participants who were less familiar. Kitchin (1997), as described above, found eight generic strategies that were used to solve tasks, as well as a number of task-specific strategies. Anooshian and Siegel (1985) termed the cognitive map information in working memory 'procedural maps' because they are the product of procedural heuristics used to access and synthesize information from long term memory. These procedural maps are situational and context-dependent, reflecting their purpose and not necessarily their long term form. For our purpose, the term 'spatial mental models' is favored, rather than procedural maps, to avoid confusion with procedural knowledge.

Taylor and Tversky (1992a) speculated that spatial mental models might be thought of as analogous to an architect's three-dimensional model of a town, although applicable at different scales, which can be visualized from many perspectives, but not as a whole. McGuinness (1992) reported, however, that there exists a family of spatial mental models: high resolution, analogical, viewer-centered; hierarchically organized, simplified and schematized models which do not preserve metric distance; and models which can viewed from multiple perspectives. The type of model constructed will be dependent on existing knowledge, the scale of the environment, the specific task, and the level of detail required.

Couclelis (1996) outlined a schema for a spatial mental model with specific reference to direction giving. The model consisted of five stages (Figure 4.5). The first phase is initiation, consisting of the formulation of a deictic understanding (shared understanding) between the direction giver and the receiver concerning the nature of a request for directions. Once this is established, a direction giving schema is activated and the second phase of representation is entered. Because the direction receiver needs a verbal description a linguistic stance is adopted (if a map was required an imaginal stance would be adopted) and spatio-linguistic constructs are called up to aid direction giving. Initially a frame of reference is established to determine where the end point is in relation to the current position,

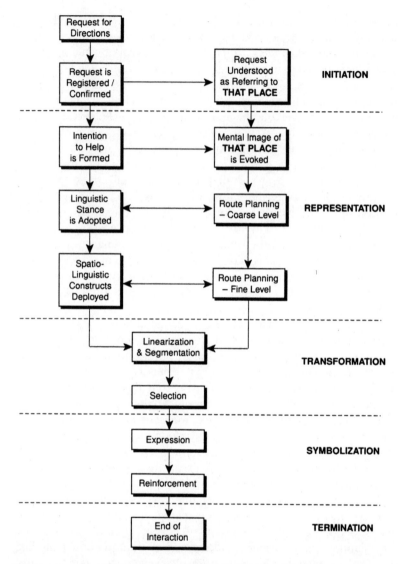

Figure 4.5. Using spatial mental models in direction-giving
Source: Couclelis (1996: p. 139)

and then a route is planned between these points at a course level.
This consists of establishing a deictic understanding of known places
along a route (e.g., the direction giver asks 'do you know where the
library is? Yes? Well you head to there and turn left...'). Then a

fine level planning stage is entered and specific direction details are formulated from detailed spatial mental models most probably composed of bird's-eye (aerial) and worm's-eye (vista) views. Once established, the third phase of transformation is entered. In this phase the spatial mental model that has been developed is transformed into a linguistic form. Because the route is traveled in sequence, the transformation often involves linearization (ordering) and segmentation (chunking), and a process of selection is needed to reduce complexity. The fourth phase is symbolization and concerns the actual process of communication, and in this phase the decisions about what is said (e.g., 'town hall' or 'large white building') are made. Descriptions are usually reinforced by qualifying statements such as 'okay?', and if the receiver is still unsure then the method of communication is rethought. The last phase is the termination, where the direction giver sends the direction receiver off along the route.

Mental models are persuasive because they help explain why people can find solutions to tasks relating to perceptions that have never been experienced—for example, imagining an oblique view of a town from an airplane. They also allow different sorts of data to be processed and integrated, for example route descriptions with information from maps; and for structure-effects (e.g., alignment heuristics, frames of reference, hierarchical coding or priming) to be applied to environments at different spatial scales.

4.9 Conclusions

At this time, most of the theories discussed lack concrete evidence, although opinions over some aspects—such as how spatial knowledge is structured—are gaining some continuity. Consequently, much more research is needed in order to determine the structure and form of spatial knowledge and how this knowledge is used in practice. In particular, there is a need to determine how information from different sources and collected at different times is integrated, and how cognitive maps are used in the real world in real contexts, for example, in navigating an environment. At present, most data generation takes place in the laboratory or at fixed locations.

In the next three chapters we consider differences within and between populations, highlighting the fact that, whilst there are general theories that seek to explain cognitive maps, there are often many exceptions to current models. Explaining these individual and group differences is essential for the building of more robust theories of cognitive mapping.

CHAPTER 5

Development of Cognitive Maps
over the Lifespan

Much cognitive mapping research has been devoted to studying the development of cognitive maps throughout childhood. Much less research has considered possible degenerative effects in old age. In this chapter we discuss research that has investigated the development of cognitive maps, concentrating on the larger body of work relating to childhood cognition.

The development of cognitive maps in children has, in the past, been studied in several different frameworks. These frameworks have been labeled nativism, empiricism, and constructivism. As these terms still occur in the literature on the development of cognitive maps they will be defined briefly, but in general the frameworks they describe have contributed little directly to the investigation of cognitive maps in children. Much more influential have been specific theories of cognitive map development put forward by Piaget and Inhelder (1956) and Siegel and White (1975). These theories have been the basis for many experimental studies, and therefore they will be discussed in some detail.

However, as we will point out, although these theories have stimulated much research they have not been very helpful in contributing to an understanding of how cognitive map abilities vary between different age groups, or what factors influence the development of cognitive maps. More recent research into children's abilities has been conducted within the information processing paradigm and has focused more specifically on the cognitive processes that are needed to form and develop a cognitive map.

We will discuss some of the evidence related to these theories. In doing this we will focus on studies of children's understanding of real or simulated large-scale environments. Such studies tend to be carried out with school age children, but this is not to suggest that younger children lack the abilities associated with cognitive maps, it is only that most studies with very young children have tested their recall of small spaces, like the layout of furniture in a room, or the pattern of toy buildings in a model layout. These environments can usually be seen from a single vantage point, and given their limited nature they do not offer the same richness of cues and information that form the basis for developing cognitive maps in the real environment. For summaries of the spatial research with very young children, see Bloch and Morange (1997) and Uttal and Tan (2000).

5.1 Traditional Theories

'Nativism' implies that children are born with predispositions and react to the world about them in predetermined ways, with set patterns of response that develop independently of learning context. The implication of this point of view is that knowledge is innate and simply opens up and unfolds with biological maturity (Matthews, 1992). Stea (1976) suggested that having a sense of place would be an evolutionary adaptation and followed Hewe's (1971) argument that 'geographical awareness' was part of the human nature. Although there is some evidence that the mind might be genetically equipped with very broad structures that organize spatial experience (e.g., O'Keefe, 1994), there is little support for any innate knowledge. Nonetheless some authors have argued that certain abilities may require little or no experience to develop. For example, Blaut (1991) and Stea et al. (1996) proposed a theory of 'natural mapping' and suggested that very young children have the ability to understand simple maps and aerial photographs without training. However, most of the studies that have investigated children's understanding of aerial photographs have only included children four years of age or older, and have been limited to asking the children to identify features on those photographs (e.g., Blades et al., 1998). As yet there is little evidence that children of this age can do anything more sophisticated with aerial photographs. Nor is there yet any evidence that children much younger than about three years of age can understand simple models or maps as representations of space (DeLoache et al., 1997) and therefore the theory of natural mapping remains open to debate (Blaut, 1997; Liben and Downs, 1997).

'Empiricism' is the opposing view to nativism. It implies that all behavior and knowledge is shaped and influenced by the environment (Langer, 1969). Cognitive maps are therefore developed through learning in the environment, and as experience increases a context-independent knowledge structure develops that supports behavior in a wide range of environments. Matthews (1992) summarized three empiricist theories. The first is the strongest form of stimulus–response theory where behavior and knowledge (responses) are solely determined by external reality (stimuli). The second is a variation of stimulus–response theory, in which there are expectancies mediating between the environment (stimulus) and the person. The third form of empiricist thought arises from cognitive behaviorism (e.g., Tolman, 1948). Here, the representation mediating between the environment and person is the cognitive map, which stores basic spatial relations learnt through previous events.

'Constructivism' is a synthesis of the positions of nativism and empiricism. Knowledge about the environment is not just accumulated (the position of empiricism) or slotted into a predetermined structure (the nativism position), rather it is organized and re-organized. According to Piaget and Inhelder (1956), this is accomplished by the processes of assimilation and accommodation. Assimilation is the incorporation of new information into existing frames of reference, and accommodation is the readjustment of those frames to cope with the assimilated information. In other words, there will be a gradual accumulation of information from experience and the processes of assimilation and accommodation will determine the organization and structure of this information.

These theoretical positions have generated some debate (see Spencer et al., 1989; Matthews 1992), but in themselves they are general statements of the possible alternative ways that environmental knowledge may be accumulated. As such they offer insights into the learning processes, but are not easily translated into unambiguous hypotheses that can be examined experimentally. More effective for stimulating studies was the theory put forward by Piaget, who described the development of children's environmental knowledge in terms of several stages (Piaget and Inhelder, 1956; Piaget et al., 1960).

5.2   Stage Theories of Cognitive Map Development

Piaget carried out the first research into children's cognitive maps. On the basis of this research he described the development of cognitive maps using terminology that remains current in the literature today, although there is rarely much acknowledgement that these terms and concepts stem from the analysis of a single (and rather small-scale) experiment by Piaget. In his experiment he asked children of different ages to make a model of their own home area. The children were given toys and materials to make the model. The children were also asked to draw a plan of a route from a familiar landmark to their school (on paper or in a sand tray). Piaget observed the children's performance and on the basis of their models and route maps, as well as what they said while making them, he put forward four stages of cognitive maps.

The first stage (stage I) does not really deserve to be called a stage because, according to Piaget, it was the period during which the child had little understanding of the environment beyond the ability to recognize individual and isolated places. In stage II, Piaget suggested that children developed an understanding of routes that was based primarily on their memory for movements through the environment. In other words, routes are encoded as a series of turns or movements. Only later (in stage IIIA) did children 'attach' landmarks to the encoded route information, but in this stage they encoded only some of the relationships between the landmarks. Piaget referred to this stage as the stage of partial coordination of landmarks and pointed out that although children could describe groups of landmarks with some accuracy, the groups were not necessarily coordinated. It was not until stage IIIB that children could recall a route accurately with all or most of the landmarks along it placed in correct relationship to one another, and Piaget called this the stage of full coordination of knowledge.

Piaget's theory of environmental cognition needs to be seen in the context of both his theory of spatial development and his more general theory of cognitive development, because the children's abilities and limitations in each stage summarized above are a reflection of the cognitive limitations in the related stages of their spatial and general development (see Blades, 1991b; Blades and Spencer, 1994). As such, Piaget put forward not only the first theory of cognitive map development but also, given its foundation in his spatial and cognitive theories, by far the most elaborate theory of cognitive maps. Unfortunately, with a few exceptions (e.g., Hart and Moore, 1973) most of the researchers who have referred to Piaget's theory of cognitive maps have focused mainly on the stages described above and have ignored their relationship to the wider theories, and this has led to a simplification of the concepts put forward by Piaget. Nonetheless, the important point is that Piaget's theory of cognitive maps led to other, related descriptions of cognitive mapping, and offered some specific hypotheses that were open to empirical testing.

One of the theories derived from Piaget's was put forward by Siegel and White (1975) and this was described in Chapter 3. As explained in that chapter, the focus of Siegel and White's theory was on how adults learnt novel environments, but the theory has frequently been applied to research with children. According to Siegel and White, the first stage of environmental learning was noting landmarks, followed by a second stage, in which behavioral decisions become associated with the landmarks ('turn left', move ahead', etc.). In this way a sequence of known landmarks can become a recognized route. In the third stage of learning, clusters of landmarks, called 'minimaps', are learnt—this is the equivalent to Piaget's stage of partial coordination. Then, in the fourth stage of learning, the relationships between all landmarks and places in the environment are understood. This was described as having a 'survey' representation—equivalent to Piaget's stage of full coordination.

Siegel and White's (1975) description of the later stages and the progression between them is derived directly from Piaget's description, but there are some differences in emphasis between the two theories. The most important is that Piaget believed that children passed through the stages of cognitive map development because their understanding and abilities in each stage were constrained by their more general level of cognitive ability. As the emphasis of Siegel and White's theory was on adult learning, the implication of their stages was that people progressed through each stage not because of maturing cognitive abilities, but because of the knowledge they gained from greater experience in the environment. There are also several differences in detail between the two theories. In particular, Piaget implied that young children learnt routes before they understood the relationships between landmarks along the route, and Siegel and White argued that learning landmarks preceded route learning. It can be noted that although both Piaget and Siegel and White gave several examples of 'landmarks' and 'routes', neither gave a clear definition of either of these terms (Blades, 1991b). This is a problem, because researchers who have investigated children's cognitive maps in the context of these two theories have often operationalized the concepts of landmarks and routes in very different ways, and this limits the comparisons that can be made between different studies.

To simplify the slightly different terminology that has been used by different developmental researchers we will refer to *landmark knowledge* (the understanding of individual features or places), *route knowledge* (the stage of partial coordination) and *configurational knowledge* (the stage of full coordination or survey knowledge). Configurational knowledge includes the understanding of the spatial relationships between several places in the environment (i.e., knowledge of directions and distances) and this has also been referred to as *Euclidean knowledge* or *vector knowledge* (e.g., Conning and Byrne, 1984).

In general, both Piaget's and Siegel and White's (1975) theories are correct. They both describe a sequence of improvement in cognitive map knowledge with age and experience, and it could hardly be otherwise. Children could not possibly have an understanding of the configuration of an environment before they had a partial coordination understanding, and to this extent both theories do no more than describe the increase and greater integration of knowledge over time. Several studies have shown that there is a progressive increase in children's knowledge. For example, Cousins *et al.* (1983) examined children's knowledge of their own school, using a number of tests. To assess the children's route knowledge they were asked to place photographs of landmarks along a line representing a route through the school, in the correct sequence and with the correct scaled distance between them. To assess configurational knowledge they were asked to point to unseen places off the route. Cousins *et al.* found that the children were only correct on the configurational tasks if they were already successful on the route tasks. The study by Cousins *et al.* was carried out in a very familiar environment, but other studies have tested the sequence in which knowledge is gained in unfamiliar environments. For example, Hazen *et al.* (1978) asked young children to learn a route through a sequence of four or six rooms, which each included different landmarks. The children learnt the route until they could walk it successfully: in other words, until the children had achieved route knowledge in the new environment. However, when the children who had learnt the route were asked to make a model of the rooms to show the relationship between all the rooms, few of them were able to do so, and this indicated that despite their good route knowledge they had not achieved a configurational understanding of the environment.

Studies such as Cousins *et al.* and Hazen *et al.* support the idea that configurational, or full, understanding is a later achievement than route, or partial, understanding. Nonetheless, Conning and Byrne (1984) showed that three to four year old children might have developed some configurational knowledge in both familiar and novel environments. In the familiar environments, the children walked round their home or the area immediately around their home, and in the novel environment, children walked paths through an unfamiliar garden. In all these environments the children were asked to point to out of sight places and they were able to do this with some success. Conning and Byrne argued that even young children, including ones with limited experience of a new environment, can develop an understanding of the spatial relationships between places that are not directly visible. Studies such as these imply that young children's abilities may have been underestimated by the theories described above. Given the implications of studies like Conning and Byrne, it would be useful to have further studies of very young children in real environments, but such studies are rare.

As pointed out above, Piaget's and Siegel and White's theories differ about the 'early' stages of cognitive map development. According to Piaget and Inhelder (1956) and Piaget et al. (1960), the second stage of cognitive map learning is encoding routes as a series of movements. However, there is little support for this suggestion. Children in the experiment by Hazen et al. (1978), summarized above, learnt the route through the rooms in one direction. After they had learnt the route in this way, they were taken to the end of the route and asked to find their way back to the beginning, and the children were able to do this. Other studies in real world environments (e.g., Cornell and Hay, 1984) have also found that children are good at walking a route in reverse. If children only learnt a route as a series of movements, they would be unable to retrace a route easily, because traveling a route in reverse requires movements that are different from the ones that were originally learnt.

One of the implications of Siegel and White's theory is that children will learn novel environments gradually, first by learning some landmarks and then connecting them into a route. This does not seem to be the case because some researchers have found that children can learn routes with little experience. Cornell and Hay (1984) found that many young children learnt a short route through a college campus, with seven choice points, after one experience of it. Gale et al. (1990a) and Torrell (1990) also found that some children could learn complex routes after brief exposure to them. These results imply that children can sometimes learn a route without first going through a distinct stage of landmark learning as suggested by Siegel and White.

Although they may not be correct in detail, Piaget's and Siegel and White's theories have stimulated much research into children's cognitive abilities. However, as both theories only suggest that children develop more complex and sophisticated cognitive maps with age or experience, the theories remain rather more descriptive than explanatory. Only comparatively recently have a few researchers investigated why children's ability to encode the environment might change and improve. These researchers have been influenced by the information processing paradigm and have considered what cognitive processes and strategies children use when learning new places.

5.3 Information Processing Approaches

One of the most detailed studies of cognitive map development was by Golledge *et al.* (1985). This was a case study of one 11 year old boy learning a new route through a suburban area. After being guided along the route once the boy was asked to retrace it five times and each time was asked to describe his wayfinding strategies, give a verbal description as if he was offering a set of directions to another child, draw a sketch map of the route, and, while watching a videotape of the route, point out what information and features he was using to encode the route. Golledge *et al.* found that the boy spent more effort encoding information at choice points on the route (i.e., changes of direction), and especially at choice points that involved more than one decision (e.g., crossing a road and changing direction). The sketch maps that the boy drew showed that he learnt the route in segments, and that these were combined as he gained greater experience of the route. Golledge *et al.* also analyzed the errors that the boy made, and found that more errors occurred at the more complex choice points, until enough information had been encoded about those points and they could be incorporated into the route without error.

It is difficult to generalize from a study like Golledge *et al.*'s (1985) experiment, because it only included one child learning a specific route. There is also the added complication in any such study that all the testing that took place between trials (e.g., giving directions, drawing sketch maps, watching videos of the route) may have contributed to the learning process, or at least made those processes different from the ones that would typically be used when learning a new environment from just direct experience. Nonetheless, the Golledge *et al.* study stands as one of the few that has attempted to analyze all aspects of the processes that may be involved in encoding a route, during repeated experience of the route.

Other researchers have considered specific strategies in route learning, but usually in the course of a single route experience. For example, Allen *et al.* (1979) showed seven year olds, ten year olds and adults a sequence of slides along a route, and after having seen the whole route the participants were asked to select nine slides that they thought would be most useful for helping them know where they were along the route. The adults selected scenes at choice points, but only one-half of the scenes chosen by the ten year olds and one-quarter of the scenes chosen by the seven year olds were at choice points. The results from the younger children in Allen *et al.* demonstrated that these children were less effective at selecting appropriate landmarks. In another study, Allen (1981) showed seven and ten year olds and adults another slide sequence of a route and asked them to divide the route into any number of segments. All three age groups were in general agreement that the route could be divided into six sections (e.g., three distinct residential areas, two different areas of a campus, and a park). The results from these two studies complement the findings from Golledge *et al.* (1985) in highlighting the importance of noting choice points, and the possibility of considering routes in terms of segments or sub-routes. These may be important aspects of cognitive map learning and as Allen and colleagues showed, there may be developmental differences in some of these aspects (e.g., identifying key points along the route), but not necessarily in others (e.g., segmenting a route). However, it is difficult to draw conclusions from the very small number of studies that have addressed these issues.

Future research will be needed to find out how general such findings might be, and most importantly, to establish the relative importance of different strategies in the formation of a cognitive map. We can presume that several strategies such as landmark learning and route segmenting (as well as others to be discussed below) all contribute to cognitive map development, but we do not know which ones are the most important, how each one develops with increasing age, or whether such strategies are combined in different ways at different ages. We speculate that some strategies, like route segmenting (on a short route) would place less cognitive demands on a child, than, say, encoding several landmarks along a route. If this was the case, those strategies that required less cognitive effort might be more developed in younger children. But these issues have hardly been considered or investigated in the research on children's cognitive mapping.

There has been a little research into specific wayfinding strategies in the real environment (Cornell *et al.*, 1989, 1992, 1999). For example, Cornell *et al.* (1989) took six and 12 year olds along a novel route through a college campus. Some of the children were told to think about the landmarks along the route they were walking, and some were told to consider more distant landmarks on the skyline. Paying attention to landmarks along the route helped both age groups to recall the route, but only the older children benefited from the advice to consider more distant landmarks. In another study, Heth *et al.* (1997) found that 12 year olds were better at noting permanent landmarks along a route, and reported using more distant ones than eight year olds. The eight year olds sometimes relied on temporary landmarks (for example, the position of a bicycle) and if the position of these landmarks had changed when they were retracing the route they were more likely than the older children to think they had traveled off the original route. These studies of real-world wayfinding confirm the earlier findings (e.g., Allen *et al.*, 1979) that there are developmental differences in noting and using landmarks.

Although all these studies have been important in considering the strategies that children use for learning a novel route, because of the nature of the environments that have been used they only address the earliest stages of cognitive map learning. Virtually nothing is known about the later stages, involving the combination of routes into full configurational understanding of the environment. One of the few studies to consider this was by Golledge *et al.* (1992) who asked children to learn two overlapping routes through a suburban area, and then draw a sketch map of both routes together. Although the children had learnt the separate routes successfully they were unable to draw a coherent representation of the whole area. How much additional experience the children would have needed about the individual routes, or what strategies they would have used to combine the information from the routes successfully, is not known. The development of configurational knowledge is important, but has received little attention. To some extent this is due to the difficulty of carrying out the types of studies that would be needed, because these would involve children learning several overlapping routes over a period of time, and then being tested for their understanding of the relationships between the routes. At the same time it would be necessary to assess the children's learning strategies, to find out which ones led to the most effective configurational knowledge. Given the time, safety, and practical constraints on research work with children (Blades, 1997), such studies would be difficult to organize, but they would be useful in extending our understanding of the later stages of cognitive map development. It is possible that, in the future, increases in the sophistication of simulations and virtual reality might provide the opportunity of testing children in realistic but safe environments. But as yet, nearly all the research into children's cognitive maps, especially in real-world environments, has concentrated on landmark and route learning.

5.4 Other Aspects of Children's Cognitive Maps

Other aspects of children's cognitive maps have also received little attention. Children may be particularly dependent on other people to help them learn about new places, but we do not know how adult guidance can structure children's environmental knowledge. Some studies have shown that if children learn a route or a room layout with the help of an adult they recall more spatial information (e.g., Darvizeh and Spencer, 1984; Golbeck et al., 1986), but others have found that the presence of an adult may result in the children learning less (e.g., Feldman and Acredolo, 1979). On the one hand the presence of an adult may help children focus on the most important aspects of an environment, but on the other hand, children may simply depend on the adult as a guide and pay little attention to the environment. These are issues that have not been resolved.

A related issue is the effect on children of the type of experience they receive in the environment. There is an assumption that children in Western societies may have less opportunity for independent exploration than they did in the past. This may be due to parental fears of traffic dangers and crime, as a result of which parents place more restrictions on children's own travel (Valentine, 1997), and Hillman et al. (1990) suggested that such limitations might be detrimental to the development of both spatial skills and cognitive maps. This was investigated by Joshi et al. (1999) who compared children between seven and 12 years of age who were driven to school, who walked to school with an adult, and who walked on their own or with other children. The children were given several spatial tests (e.g., locating north, understanding left and right, and a mental rotation task) and they were also asked to draw a sketch map of the area round their school. There were no differences between the groups on any of the spatial measures, or in the amount of detail and information included in the sketch maps. These findings suggest that if there are more limitations on children's independent travel now than in the past, those limitations may have little or no effect on the development of their cognitive maps. Further research will be needed to establish whether similar findings would also apply in other contexts, and for other age groups.

5.5 Learning from Secondary Sources

Given their more limited opportunity for mobility, children may be more dependent on secondary sources of information to learn about environments. How children interpret maps has been considered in several studies (Liben, 1997), and some researchers have also investigated whether children can relate maps to the environment (e.g., Blades and Spencer, 1994). Children have some appreciation of very simple maps of small layouts like rooms from about the age of three or four years (Loewenstein and Gentner, in press), and can use maps to find their way through mazes with several turns (Bremner and Andreasen, 1999). But there are only a few studies of older children's use of maps. For example, Ottosson (1987) asked children up to the age of 13 years to use a large-scale cartographic map to find their way round a suburban area. Nonetheless, none of this research has compared children's knowledge of an environment learnt from a map and their knowledge of the same environment learnt from direct experience. Studies with adults have shown that adults may learn different aspects of an environment depending on whether they learn about the environment from direct experience or from a secondary source like a map (e.g., Moeser, 1988). Whether the same effects apply to children, and the more general issue of how children incorporate information from secondary sources into their cognitive maps, are topics that have received little attention (Uttal, 2000).

Secondary sources are the only way that children can learn about environments that are too large to be explored directly, such as countries and continents. Compared to the research into children's cognitive maps of local areas, there has been little investigation of children's awareness of the wider world, though studies have shown that there are developmental differences in children's understanding of other countries and in their increasing appreciation of geographical and political concepts such as 'Europe' (e.g., Barrett and Short, 1992). There are also differences between children of the same age from different countries, with some demonstrating more complete cognitive maps of continents than others (e.g., Barrett and Farroni, 1996). Whether these differences in cognitive maps are due to education, general travel experience, or differential attitudes towards other countries, and whether children's knowledge can be influenced by specific teaching (e.g., Weigand, 1992) are all issues that require further research.

5.6 Cognitive Map Abilities in Old Age

Most of the developmental research into cognitive maps has concentrated on children's abilities and much less is known about developmental changes across the lifespan and in old age. There is evidence that spatial memory and abilities may be poorer in elderly people (Salthouse, 1991). However, almost all the research with elderly people has utilized spatial problem solving tasks and, as pointed out in the next chapter, we know little about the relationship between these problem solving tasks and the ability to form and retain a cognitive map. On tasks that might be thought to be most closely related to cognitive maps, there is a little evidence for decline in the performance of elderly people. For example, Ohta (1979) and Perlmutter *et al.* (1981) found that older adults performed poorly compared to young adults when asked to locate landmarks on maps they had learnt earlier, and Herman and Coyne (1980) found that older adults were poorer at imagining being at a location and pointing to other places. In routefinding studies, older adults made more errors when navigating through an environment they had experienced once before (Barrash, 1994) or when navigating with a map (Aubrey and Dobbs, 1990). Wilkniss *et al.* (1997) similarly found that route learning ability declined with increasing age. In this study, older adults had greater difficulty than younger adults in retracing a route and temporally ordering landmarks. This was still the case after studying a two-dimensional representation of the route to be learned.

There may also be differences in the way that older people and younger people encode the environment. Lipman (1991) found that older adults were more dependent on landmarks (rather than turns) when recalling routes, and Evans *et al.* (1982) found that older adults encoded different landmarks and places from younger adults. However, these variations in strategies may not be detrimental to the ability of older adults to form effective cognitive maps. For example, Kirasic (1991) found that older adults' route knowledge in familiar environments was no poorer than that of younger adults, and Ohta and Kirasic (1983) found that older adults were as successful at learning unfamiliar environments. They asked participants to find their way round a complex medical center, and found that the knowledge and efficiency of movement by the older adults did not differ from that of younger adults. Ohta and Kirasic suggested that, in practical contexts, there is no reason to expect older adults to perform any less well than young adults. Making a similar point, Hunt (1992) argued that even if older people had some slight decrement in their spatial skills, they could compensate for this by their greater general knowledge and reliance on other cognitive abilities. Given the limited research with older adults, this is an aspect of cognitive maps that requires further investigation.

5.7 Conclusions

The investigation of children's cognitive maps has, to date, been rather limited. Although the theories put forward by Piaget (1956), and by Siegel and White (1975) provided a suitable framework for the early studies, much of the research has not progressed beyond descriptions of children's performance at different ages. One problem is that very young children have been shown to have achieved the later stages of cognitive map knowledge in very limited environments (e.g., Conning and Byrne, 1984), but have not demonstrated such abilities in more complex environments (e.g., Cousins *et al.*, 1983), and therefore it is difficult to identify stages of cognitive map development that are independent of the environment in which children are tested. A more useful approach has been the information processing approach which considers the strategies that children use to generate a cognitive map but, as yet, this work is also limited because there has been no overall program of investigation, and the little we know about children's processes and strategies has come from rather diverse experiments with different age groups. Nonetheless, understanding the processes underlying cognitive map development and the relationship between these processes and other cognitive abilities offers one of the best ways forward. Similarly, there is a need for a much more focused research program that considers cognitive maps over the whole lifespan, and in particular in relation to old age. If cognitive maps do degenerate in old age this has a number of consequences in relation to independent travel for older persons, where a fear of getting lost may limit spatial behavior.

CHAPTER 6

Individual and Gender Differences in Cognitive Mapping

In this chapter we turn our attention away from understanding the generic processes that underlie cognitive mapping to examine differences between cognitive maps, both between individuals within a group and across groups, in this case defined by gender. As we detail, such examinations are important because they reveal commonalities and differences which help determine the nature of cognitive maps and how they develop. We discuss other cross-group differences in the next chapter, when we consider differences between the cognitive maps of disabled and non-disabled people, focusing in particular upon comparisons of the cognitive maps of sighted and non-sighted people.

6.1   Individual Differences in Cognitive Maps

Many researchers have reported differences in cognitive map abilities. Such reports are usually in the context of experiments that have made comparisons between two or more groups of participants, e.g., between different age groups, between males and females, between young and elderly, or between people with disabilities and others. There is also evidence for differences depending on training or experience (e.g., between people with greater or lesser travel experience). As most researchers concentrate on group differences there has been less emphasis on individual differences in cognitive mapping ability, though of course, in any experiment some participants within a group are likely to perform better than others in the same group. Sometimes such differences are reported, for example in studies of special populations where the number of participants might be quite small and there are often large differences in individual performance (e.g., with participants who are visually impaired—see Chapter 7). But in most studies little attention is paid to variations within a group. This is a pity, because many cognitive map tasks are complex and involve a combination of strategies and processes, and differential performance between participants might indicate differences in the way that they approach the same task. There is clear evidence for individual differences in spatial reasoning and problem solving, and as some of those processes may be related to cognitive map abilities it is likely that there will also be individual differences in the formation of cognitive maps.

As Allen (1999) pointed out, many spatial abilities are likely to be important components of cognitive maps. The degree to which there are individual differences in any spatial process will depend on the nature of the process itself and probably on its complexity, because the more complex the process, the more likely it is that alternative strategies are possible.

Some researchers have suggested that specific spatial processes are automatic, and if this is the case, individual differences would not be expected. Hasher and Zacks (1979) argued that spatial location is encoded automatically, for example, when looking for a previously read article in a newspaper it is often easy to recall the position of the article on the page, even though this information would not have been deliberately encoded. Similarly, most people can recall the layout of furniture in a room without having intentionally learnt the relationships between all the items of furniture. Hasher and Zacks defined automatic encoding in terms of several criteria including the following: participants should be able to recall spatial location as well in incidental conditions (i.e., when they have not deliberately learnt the location of items) as under intentional conditions (i.e., when they have explicitly learnt them); that recall of spatial location will be equally effective with or without training; and that there will be no developmental differences in the recall of location (in other words, children and adults will perform similarly in location tasks). These are strict criteria and have not been fully supported by researchers testing the automaticity hypothesis. Naveh-Benjamin (1987, 1988), for example, found little support for each of the criteria and some researchers have found that people perform poorly in some location tasks (e.g., Patel et al., 1999). Nonetheless, even though a strict interpretation of Hasher and Zacks' theory has not been supported, there is little doubt that participants do perform well above chance in many tasks involving incidental spatial location (Naveh-Benjamin, 1987). Put another way, encoding spatial location may not be as automatic as Hasher and Zacks suggested, but if all encoding is considered on a automatic–intentional continuum, then location encoding falls towards the automatic end of this continuum.

As such, it is unlikely that there will be marked individual differences in the ability to encode information about location.

Other spatial processes, such as perspective taking or mental rotation, are complex and effortful. A task that requires imagining an array from alternative perspectives (Newcombe and Hutten-locher, 1992), or visualizing a shape that has been rotated in space (Just and Carpenter, 1985), can be performed in more than one way. As these spatial tasks can be attempted using different strate-gies, individual differences in performance are to be expected, and such differences have been found (e.g., Just and Carpenter, 1985). All these spatial processes are dependent on other processing abilities like working memory capacity or speed of processing, and these differ between individuals (Allen, 1999).

However, most studies of spatial processes have investigated participants' performance in small-scale tasks that involve table-top arrays or pictures of objects. These tasks are somewhat removed from exploring and encoding large-scale environments like buildings, neighborhoods, and cities, and there is little research into the rela-tionship between the spatial processes involved in small-scale tasks and the spatial processes required for cognitive maps.

In one of the few investigations into these relationships, Allen *et al.* (1996) tested participants with six spatial tasks (e.g., recognizing incomplete pictures, searching for hidden shapes in a complex pattern, or imagining how an unfolded object will look when it is folded into a three-dimensional shape); with perspective-taking tasks (in a model town); and with paper and pencil maze and map tasks. Participants were also tested on six environmental learning tasks (which included learning a route through a city and then being measured on both route and configurational knowledge). Allen *et al.* found that participants' ability in the spatial tasks did not directly influence the environmental learning tasks, but abilities on the spatial tasks influenced the perspective and maze tasks, and in turn perfor-mance on these influenced the environmental learning. In other words, there were links between performance on spatial tasks and cognitive map tasks, but there were not direct effects of one on the other. Nonetheless, if there is a relationship between spatial abilities and cognitive mapping (even an indirect one) it would be a useful research initiative to discover more about these relationships, and how individual differences in basic information processing might have implications for individual differences in cognitive mapping abilities.

A related issue that requires investigation is whether people who have deficits in information processing capacity have deficits in their cognitive maps, and if so, how those deficits might be overcome. In other words, it is not only important to identify individual differences, but where necessary discover at what level remedial intervention would be appropriate. As yet we know little about the spatial and information processing abilities that are involved in cognitive mapping, or the relative importance of these abilities. It is one of the limitations of cognitive map research that so little attention has been directed at the basic processes and strategies that are involved in environmental learning (Allen, 1999).

Irrespective of individual differences in cognitive processes, many other factors may influence individuals' cognitive maps. Within the same environment there will be differences in cognitive maps depending on individuals' knowledge and experience of that environment, and there may also be differences depending on an individual's experience of different places (e.g., Devlin, 1976). Individuals who have had greater experience of learning new environments may be able to form more complex cognitive maps. Murray and Spencer (1979) compared sketch maps drawn by a group of participants who had lived in many places, a group who had lived in two places, and a group who had only lived in one place. The group with more experience drew more complex, better organized maps that included more detail. Although the comparisons in this experiment were made between groups of participants, the results imply that individuals' cognitive maps may vary depending on how much previous cognitive mapping experience they have had.

There will also be differences in the way that people use external aids to learn about new environments. There has been some research into the different effects of learning a new environment from secondary information such as maps (e.g., Levine et al., 1982; Moeser, 1988). There has also has been a little research into how people encode information from maps and this research has found individual differences in the way that people learn maps (e.g., Rossano and Morrison, 1996). For example, Thorndyke and Stasz (1980) gave participants several trials to learn invented maps of a town and a country. Thorndyke and Stasz included novice and expert map readers and found that the experts were better at encoding map information. They analyzed the learning strategies used by participants and found that the experts were better at assessing how much they had encoded and then focusing on those aspects of the maps that they had not yet learnt. There were individual differences in how well participants learnt the maps, and these differences were apparent even within the expert group. Gilhooley et al. (1988)

also found differences in the map learning strategies of novice and expert map readers, and Ungar *et al.* (1997) found marked differences in the way that novice map readers learnt tactile maps.

It might be assumed that people who are more effective at encoding information from a map will be able to form a better cognitive map of the area represented by the map. But the experiments described above only used invented maps and so there has been no research into whether individual differences in the use of secondary sources will lead to individual differences in the formation of cognitive maps. However, one group of researchers have noted individual differences in the application of map-learnt information to a route following task. Rossano *et al.* (1995) asked participants to learn a layout of places from a map and then estimate, from memory, the direction between pairs of those places (see Chapter 3). Earlier research had shown that estimates were more accurate if the direction being judged was one that corresponded to the orientation of the learnt map and it was labeled the *alignment effect* (Levine *et al.*, 1982). Rossano *et al.* found that although most of their participants demonstrated the alignment effect, a sub-group of participants did not, and this implies that there might be differences in individuals' ability to apply map-learnt information to the environment.

6.2   Gender Differences in Cognitive Maps

Many researchers have reported gender differences on tasks related to cognitive maps, with males often performing better than females. There is a large literature on gender differences in spatial ability and much debate about how significant these differences are (e.g., Kitchin, 1996c; Self and Golledge, 2000). We will begin by giving, briefly, some examples of the research that has found gender differences, and then consider the implications of such differences.

It has been suggested that gender-related differences in spatial knowledge and ability are present across the lifespan (e.g., Kirasic *et al.*, 1992) with differences starting to appear from the early school-age years, and this has been found in several studies investigating children's knowledge of familiar areas. For example, Siegel and Schadler (1977) found that four to six year old boys were better than girls at constructing a three-dimensional model of their own classroom, and Hart (1979) found that boys' models of their neighborhood were better organized in terms of both configurational relations and distances. Matthews (1986) tested six to 11 year old children's cognitive maps of their local environment. The children were asked to draw a sketch map of the area, and interpret a map and an aerial photograph of the area. By the age of 11 years the boys performed the tasks better than girls and their sketch maps were more accurate and more detailed.

In a study of larger spaces, Bettis (1974) tested the geographic knowledge of 1700 11 year old children about their state. The children were asked to interpret graphs and maps, name places and identify features, and of 45 questions, boys performed better than girls on 42 and were equal on three questions. In another study, Beatty and Troster (1987), examined 1800 undergraduates, and found that males consistently performed better than women on tests of geographical knowledge.

Gender differences have also been reported when children or adults learn new spaces. For example, Herman and Siegel (1978) asked children to learn a novel environment (a model town) and then reconstruct the layout. They did not find gender differences in five year old children, but the seven and 11 year old boys were better than girls of the same ages. Herman *et al.* (1979) tested students who had been at college for three weeks and found that males recognized more campus buildings. In another study Devlin and Bernstein (1995) examined how well first-time visitors to a college campus learnt about the campus from a computer simulation of a campus tour. After learning from the simulation, participants were given a wayfinding test (via the screen) and males made fewer wayfinding errors than females. Studies of elderly people have also found gender differences in environmental learning. Elderly males have been shown to be better at learning new environments from a slide presentation (Kirasic *et al.*, 1992) and that they are also been found to be better at navigating with a map (Aubrey and Dobbs, 1990).

It is difficult to know how to assess the gender differences reported in the cognitive map literature. Although many studies have found evidence of better performance by males, there are a large number of cognitive map studies that have either not found any differences, or not reported differences. Some authors have argued that although males might perform better than females on some spatial tasks the reverse might be true on other spatial tasks (Self *et al.*, 1992). Other authors have argued that even if gender differences in cognitive abilities have been found in the past they may be diminishing or disappearing (Feingold, 1988). Whether the differences reported by some cognitive map researchers represent a significant pattern or not would require a meta-analysis of a large number of cognitive map studies.

Meta-analyses have been carried out on studies of spatial abilities (rather than cognitive maps) and these have been important for focusing attention on where there might be significant differences between males and females. Linn and Petersen (1985) carried out a meta-analysis of nearly 200 reports of gender differences in spatial abilities. They divided spatial abilities into three categories. First, spatial perception, in which participants have to determine spatial relationships in respect of a frame of reference. Second, mental rotation, in which participants have to imagine how objects will appear if they are rotated. Third, spatial visualization, in which, for example, participants have to find hidden shapes in complex designs, or imagine how a folded piece of paper will appear if it is unfolded. Linn and Petersen found that although there were no differences on tasks involving spatial visualization, males were better than females on tasks involving mental rotation and spatial perception.

Only a few researchers have compared participants' performance on small-scale tasks and cognitive map tasks. For example, O'Laughlin and Brubaker (1988) gave participants a mental rotation test, and they also showed participants a film of the interior of a house and then asked them to draw a sketch map of its floor plan. O'Laughlin and Brubaker found that males were better in the mental rotation task, but there were no gender differences in the mapping task. This might imply that there is no relationship between mental rotation and cognitive mapping, but other researchers have found different results. Montello et al. (2000) gave participants a mental rotation task and also asked them to learn a college campus. The males performed better on the rotation task, and they were also better than the females on some, but not all, of the measures used to assess their knowledge of the campus. In contrast to O'Laughlin and Brubaker, the latter result could mean that males were better at both small-scale and cognitive mapping tasks. However, we cannot draw clear conclusions from a small number of studies with divergent results, and what is needed in this area is a much better understanding of the spatial abilities that contribute most to the development of cognitive maps. On the one hand, the frequent finding that, for some spatial abilities, males are better than females (Linn and Petersen, 1985) would lead to the hypothesis that, if these abilities are important in the development of cognitive maps, we might also expect gender differences in cognitive map skills. On the other hand, if these abilities are not relevant to cognitive mapping, the fact that males have better small-scale spatial abilities may not imply anything about gender differences in cognitive mapping.

Various theories have been put forward to explain gender differences on small-scale tasks. These explanations include ones that emphasize biological variables, such as hormonal differences, and explanations that focus on social effects, such as differences in gender expectations and experience.

Male and female hormones have also been linked to differences in spatial abilities (McGee, 1983). For example, Shute *et al.* (1983) measured male hormones (androgens) in male and female students who were given a series of spatial tasks, and they found different relationships between androgens in male and females. Spatial performance was better in males with lower levels of androgen, and better in females with higher levels of androgen (though other researchers have not confirmed these findings, see McKeever *et al.* (1987). Evidence from people with disabilities also suggests the role of hormones in spatial ability. People with Turner's syndrome, who have low levels of androgen, show poorer levels of spatial performance (Witelson and Swallow, 1988), as do males with hypogonado-tropic hypogonadism who have lower levels of testosterone (Hampson, 1995). Females with congenital adrenal hyperplasia, who have higher levels of androgen, have better spatial skills (Resnick *et al.*, 1986). Chiarello *et al.* (1989) also found that spatial abilities in females varied in relation to hormonal differences during the menstrual cycle. It should be emphasized that the studies that have found relationships between levels of hormones and spatial ability have nearly always measured ability in terms of small-scale tasks, and little is known about the relationship between hormonal levels and performance in tasks like wayfinding and cognitive mapping. In these latter tasks, the complexity of the task and the effects of experience and social factors may be as important as, or more important than, any small differences in basic spatial abilities. Though, of course, people who have slightly poorer initial spatial abilities may have less confidence in exploring and gaining the experience that might contribute to more effective cognitive mapping.

Gender differences have also been explained in terms of the different strategies that males and females may use in spatial tasks. Blough and Slavin (1987) argued that early verbal precocity in girls means that they are more likely to apply verbal strategies to visual–spatial problems, but boys are more likely to apply spatial strategies. Blough and Slavin suggested that women were slower at spatial tasks, with slower mental rotation and mental comparisons, but had a bias towards accuracy, and that social–cultural stereotyping might reinforce these differences in strategy. Some researchers have noted gender differences in cognitive mapping strategies. For example, Lawton (1994) found that males and females used different strategies in a wayfinding task. Lawton assessed self reports of the strategies that males and females used, and found that males claimed greater reliance on orientation (making more references to cardinal directions and metric distances), but females relied more on landmarks and relations between landmarks. In other words, the males considered configurational or Euclidean information more often than the females. Lawton also asked participants to assess their anxiety about traveling in new environments and found that the use of configurational information was correlated with lower anxiety scores. Other researchers have also suggested that females place more emphasis on landmarks (McGuiness and Sparks, 1982) and that males make more use of configurational information such as cardinal directions and metric information in route instructions (Dabbs *et al.*, 1998; Matthews, 1986; Miller and Santoni, 1986; Ward *et al.*, 1986).

In a related study, Lawton (1996) gave male and female students experience of finding a route through a building and then asked them to complete a questionnaire about their wayfinding strategies in the building ('indoors'), a questionnaire about how they planned routes between cities ('outdoors'), and another questionnaire about the anxiety they felt in various wayfinding contexts. Males were more likely to report an orientation (or configurational) strategy, and females relied more on information about the route (both indoors and outdoors). Females also reported higher levels of anxiety when wayfinding. In another study, Schmitz (1997) gave boys and girls (ten to 17 years of age) five trials to find their way through a complex maze of paths and tunnels. There were no gender differences in the amount of information they had learnt about the maze by the end of the last trial, but girls mentioned more landmarks and boys made more references to directions. The girls reported more anxiety about the task on the first trial, and for both boys and girls there was a correlation between anxiety and information recalled, because children who expressed higher anxiety recalled less about the maze.

Liben (1981) suggested that both strategy and anxiety differences in learning new environments might be influenced by social assumptions, so that when males are faced with a problem they are encouraged to master the task, but females are conditioned to seek assistance, and Liben linked this to females' lack of confidence in carrying out tasks. This may be related to the higher levels of anxiety reported by females in studies like the experiment by Schmitz (1997) described above. However, the measures of anxiety and cognitive mapping abilities in that study are correlations, and therefore it is not possible to draw a causal relationship between these two factors. It may be the case that people with greater anxiety are poorer at learning new environments, or that people who are poorer at learning environments have past experience of being disorientated and have therefore become anxious as a result. Nonetheless, the present evidence indicates relationships between anxiety and poorer performance, and females report greater anxiety.

Irrespective of the actual performance of females, several surveys have shown that females believe they have poorer spatial abilities and a poorer sense of direction than males (Lunneborg and Lunneborg, 1984; Thompson et al., 1981), and Harris (1981) found that both males and females believed that females had greater difficulty with tasks that involved spatial reasoning. These assumptions may reflect reality, or they may, in part, reflect differences in the way that males and females assess their own performance, because when Lunneborg and Lunneborg (1984) compared self-rated abilities and actual abilities, they found that males overestimated their own competence and females underestimated their own abilities.

Several researchers have suggested that one of the factors in gender differences is the different social and spatial experiences of males and females. Children's toys that are linked to gender include, for example, dolls and doll houses for girls, but model kits, construction toys, and sports equipment for boys (Hughes, 1999). The toys associated with boys might be ones that involve more spatial reasoning than the ones associated with girls, though this is an issue which needs investigation. Males are assumed to have have more involvement in games and activities that involve spatial abilities, such as ball games, model making, and computer games, and these might influence the development of related abilities (Self and Golledge, 2000; Tracey, 1987). More importantly, males may have more direct experience of the environment. Goodchild (1974) and Moore (1979) suggested that women have a more detailed image of their immediate surroundings, but men have more composite images of a larger area, and Matthews (1986) argued that this is the direct result of socialization and upbringing. Indeed, Gilmartin and Patton (1984) suggested that males and females are 'programmed' by society to conform to accepted, traditional gender roles, leading to differing patterns of spatial behavior. As a result, women experience less interaction with the environment and receive stereotypical social and media pressure to move away from activities that build spatial and cognitive mapping abilities. There is evidence that females have more strictly defined ranges than males (Brown and Broadway, 1981), and that women's patterns of movement may be limited by factors such as the fear of personal crime (Pain, 1991; Valentine, 1990). The limitations on females' experience may be particularly pronounced at younger ages, for example, Hart (1979) found that boys had greater freedom to explore, but girls were encouraged to stay at home and participate in the routines of family life. Liben (1981) argued that if girls are given less encouragement to explore and have less opportunity to acquire spatial knowledge this may have an effect on their later cognitive map abilities.

In contrast to the view that females have less experience, Self *et al.* (1992) argued that in contemporary Western societies females may now have as much active environmental interaction as men. Self *et al.* also pointed out that gender differences in spatial ability tend to be greater in societies in which gender roles are clearly differentiated and in which these roles are emphasized from the early years. The reverse may also be true, and in societies in which gender roles are less distinct there may be less evidence for gender differences in spatial performance. Self and Golledge (1994) also pointed out that specific training in spatial skills can lead to improvements in those skills in both males and female, often with slightly greater improvements in females. If performance can be improved by training it would support the view that poorer spatial abilities are due to lack of practice and experience rather than some underlying and more fundamental cognitive deficit. As Golledge and Stimson (1997) have pointed out, if spatial abilities can be improved by increased experience, there is no reason to expect that the slightly poorer spatial abilities of females would be of any real hindrance to the development of their geographical abilities.

6.3 Conclusions

In summary, there has been very little research into individual differences in cognitive mapping ability. Most experiments report group performance or differences between groups (see Chapter 7) and this may mask individual variations in performance. Indeed, it can often be the case that in-group variation is larger than between-group variation and this raises questions of the validity of cross-group comparisons (Kitchin 1996a; see Chapter 8). Such variations between individuals, however, may be important in providing insights into the different ways that people encode or use information that is relevant to cognitive maps, and this would be a useful area for future research. In particular, there is a need to investigate the specific reasons why the cognitive maps of individuals differ and how interventions might be used to help improve those with poor cognitive mapping skills (e.g., for use in the classroom).

There is some evidence for gender differences in spatial abilities, and where these differences have been found it has usually been shown that males perform better than females, especially on small-scale tasks involving mental rotation and spatial perception. However, it is not yet known how important these abilities are in the development of cognitive maps (Allen, 1999). There is evidence for gender differences in a few cognitive mapping studies, but it is important to be cautious in interpreting these findings, in case undue weight is given to what might only be a small proportion of studies. Until there are appropriate meta-analyses of cognitive map studies, it is difficult to know whether the gender differences found in some studies are the reflection of a real difference or a matter of chance, and if they are real differences, how significant they are. Given the findings from training studies, it appears that a small amount of additional experience is enough to reduce or erase any gender differences in ability.

CHAPTER 7

Cognitive Mapping and Disability

In this chapter we continue our discussion of the differences in cognitive maps between groups through an examination of the effects of disability. It is often assumed that the cognitive maps of people with disabilties will be less well developed in comparison to the cognitive maps of people without disabilities. In general, the difference between people with and without disabilities is often thought to exist regardless of the disability, because people with disabilities may have had more restricted spatial behavior. Given the centrality of sight to spatial perception, it is perhaps no surprise that most research concerning the cognitive maps of disabled people has concentrated on those with visual impairments. As a consequence, we focus our discussion on people with visual impairments, and the differences between their cognitive map abilities and those of people with sight.

7.1 Cognitive Maps of People with Visual Impairments

Vision is often quoted as the spatial sense *par excellence* (Foulke, 1983). This is because, as Brambring (1982) noted, sight is vital to locomotion as it allows the immediate perception of objects and the opportunity to easily orientate oneself. In particular, vision allows a person to perceptually differentiate perspective, to recognize the invariant structure of an environment (Sholl, 1996), and makes available information about the location of objects not just in relation to the viewer, but also relative to one another (Morrongiello *et al.*, 1995). In addition, vision permits the use of distant landmarks that would not be available through other senses. As such, vision provides an external frame of reference for coding spatial information. People with no vision or limited vision have to rely on sequential learning using tactile, proprioceptive, and auditory senses to construct spatial relationships (Bigelow, 1996).

Many researchers have suggested that people with visual impairments experience a world different from those who are sighted (see Spencer *et al.*, 1989). This has led researchers such as Golledge

(1993a) to argue that, after communicating by reading and writing, the inability to travel independently and to interact with the wider world is the most significant problem produced by visual impairment. Indeed, Clark-Carter *et al.* (1986) reported that at least one-third of people with visual impairment or blindness make no independent journeys outside their homes, and most of those who do venture outside their home independently adhere to known routes, because exploration is stressful and can lead to disorientation (Golledge, 1993a; Hill *et al.*, 1993).

7.1.1 Theories of spatial development

Three theories have been put forward to explain the possible deficits in the cognitive maps of people with visual impairments (Fletcher, 1980) and these will be summarized in turn.

The *deficiency theory* suggests that the cognitive map abilities of people with visual impairments are lacking compared to those of people with sight. The assumption behind this theory is that vision is essential to the formation of a cognitive map and that the information received from senses other than vision cannot provide an adequate base for the development of a cognitive map. The deficiency theory was proposed by von Senden (1932), who said that people with visual impairments would not be able to build up an overall impression of space from their fragmentary experiences of it: 'Imaginative retention of a completed whole is not possible with tactile impressions... the blind man can grasp only succession and relation, but cannot later produce the completed whole as the sighted do' (1932: p. 288). However, both the experimental evidence (discussed below) and the clear ability of many people with visual impairments to learn and navigate new environments have demonstrated that such a negative view of the abilities of people with visual impairments is not tenable.

The *inefficiency theory* proposes that although people with visual impairments have the potential to achieve the same levels of spatial knowledge as people with sight, their abilities are underdeveloped because they have less effective ways of encoding and applying spatial information. The implication is that people with visual impairments have access to processes and strategies that are similar to those used by people with sight, but these processes are best applied to perceptual information gained from vision, and when they can only be applied to haptic or auditory information a person with a visual impairment is at a disadvantage. In other words, people with visual impairments are inefficient users of the same cognitive processes used by people with sight. Therefore, they may be able to develop a cognitive map of an environment, but their cognitive map is likely to be less elaborate than one developed by a person with sight. For example, people with visual impairments may have an effective cognitive map that can be the basis for successful navigation, but they may have greater difficulty estimating directions and distances. People with visual impairments may have greater difficulty identifying small changes of direction, for example when traveling a route that includes a shallow curve they may encode it as a straight path. Such effects have been found in studies which have shown that participants with visual impairments have greater difficulty updating their position as they navigate through a novel space (e.g., Rieser *et al.*, 1986; Rieser *et al.*, 1992). In other words, they were less efficient at processing distance and direction changes and therefore less able to develop an accurate configurational knowledge of the space.

The *difference theory* suggests that the cognitive maps of people with visual impairments may be equivalent to those of people with sight, but they might develop in different ways or consist of different structures. There may be a developmental delay in achieving the same level of knowledge as a person with sight, and this will be confounded by other factors, like reduced environmental experience, less access to secondary sources of spatial information such as maps, and the likelihood that navigating large novel spaces is a stressful experience that detracts from effective learning. In other words, lack of vision does not necessarily prohibit the development of a cognitive map, but may reduce how quickly such a map can be generated. The difference theory is based on research by Worchel (1951), who asked participants to walk short routes (e.g., round the four sides of a square or along the three sides of a triangle), and found that people with visual impairments were poorer at these tasks than people with sight. Juurmaa (1973) suggested that in tasks like these people with visual impairments were at a disadvantage because they would have had less experience at recognizing or imagining 'optically familiar' shapes like squares and triangles. Juurmaa and Lehtinen-Railo (1994) suggested that differences occur between people with visual impairments and people with sight because of the former's 'lack of experience in bringing their representations into effective use and operation' (1994: p. 170). The implication of the difference theory is that if people with visual impairments are given sufficient experience and training they should be able to acquire a cognitive map that is as effective as one developed by a person with sight.

These theories are summarized above because they are still frequently cited, usually with the acknowledgment that there is no support for the deficiency hypothesis. The inefficiency theory leads to the conclusion that people with visual impairments will usually show a deficit on tasks related to cognitive maps, but the difference theory offers a more optimistic assessment of their spatial abilities, indicating that, with enough practice, people with visual impairments will achieve the same level of expertise as people with sight. These two latter 'theories' are perhaps better thought of as the two possible positions that might be true of the cognitive map abilities of people with visual impairments. Either they will always have a deficit compared to people with sight irrespective of how much experience they have, or, if they have enough experience, they will be able to perform cognitive map tasks as well as people with sight.

There are difficulties in assessing these alternative positions experimentally, because for any results that show that people with visual impairments perform less well than people with sight (i.e., support the inefficiency hypothesis) it can be argued that the deficit in ability is due to lack of experience—either specific lack of experience of the environment in which they are being tested, or general lack of experience over the life span because of their more limited mobility (i.e., support for the difference hypothesis). The only way to distinguish these two positions is to find evidence that people with visual impairments can perform as well as people with sight in cognitive map tasks (this would provide evidence for the difference hypothesis, and only for that hypothesis).

This leads to the second difficulty, because studies of participants developing cognitive maps in *unfamiliar* environments have usually given all participants equal and controlled experience of those environments. If people with visual impairments perform less well in unfamiliar environments, this may be accounted for by the fact that they would need more experience than people with sight to learn the same environment. In a study of a *familiar* environment it is difficult to know that participants with visual impairments and participants with sight have had the equivalent spatial experience in that environment, and the lack of equivalent experience could be given for any deficits exhibited by the former group. The types of studies that would address these issues are ones in which the participants with visual impairments were given continuing experience or specific training to find out if they can reach the same level of ability as a sighted control group. However, there are practical difficulties in carrying out such studies in real environments, because of the time and practice that might be required.

There are many limitations to interpreting and comparing the research with people with visual impairments, because different studies may include groups with quite different levels of visual impairment or different levels of mobility training and environmental experience (see Kitchin and Jacobson, 1997). In addition, several researchers have found marked individual differences in the performance of people with visual impairments. For example, Loomis et al. (1993) asked participants to learn the position of several items in a room. They learnt the items from a single position and were then asked to move to a new position and point to the items from this new position, or were asked to imagine being at the new position (without moving to it) and asked to do the same pointing task. There were large individual differences in the ability to do this accurately, with some of the participants who were congenitally blind performing poorly, and others being successful. Other researchers have also found significant individual differences in cognitive map tasks (Ungar et al., 1996), and these differences could be the result of variations in previous experience and/or the selection of more appropriate strategies by some participants.

7.1.2 Empirical studies in unfamiliar environments

Many of the cognitive map studies with people with visual impairments have tested people in 'laboratory' environments, ranging from table-top layouts to simple mazes built in a room, and it may be difficult to extrapolate from these studies to how people develop cognitive maps in the real world. On the one hand, real environments might be much harder to learn because of their greater complexity, but on the other hand, the real environment offers far more information (e.g., auditory and tactile feedback) that may be particularly beneficial for the learning strategies used by people with visual impairments. It is, of course, not possible to use slides, films, or virtual reality to simulate new environments for people with visual impairments and therefore, in the past, studies of their cognitive maps have tended to rely on two predominant methodological approaches: testing people in familiar, well learnt environments (usually the person's neighborhood or in a frequently used building), or testing people in novel environments in the laboratory (usually small environments with limited cues). This means that there has been little research into the development of cognitive maps in real-world spaces, and so little is known about the processes that contribute to real-world learning. It is only recently that researchers have started to investigate the formation of cognitive maps in the real-world, and compared the way that people with visual impairments and people with sight develop cognitive maps of new areas. The following discussion of cognitive maps will necessarily be selective, but we will place greater emphasis on the results from studies of real-world learning, because we will argue that these probably provide the most realistic assessments of people with visual impairments.

Several researchers have demonstrated that people with visual impairments can learn routes successfully. Passini and Proulx (1988) gave congenitally blind and sighted participants two guided tours along a 250 meter route through a building, and then asked them to describe how they would retrace the route. Finally they walked the route on their own, giving a verbal protocol as they did so. After completing the route they made a map of the route (using magnetic pieces on a board). One-third of the participants with visual impairments and two-thirds of the participants with sight were able to retrace the route without making errors, and participants who did not complete the route accurately only made one or two errors each. In other words, people who were congenitally blind were able to encode sufficient information about a novel route to walk it on their own after limited experience of it. The two groups were equally good at making a map of the route, with one-third of each group making maps without errors, and there was no difference between the groups in the number of configurational errors they made in the map task. These findings suggest that the participants who were congenitally blind were good at generating a cognitive map of the route from their experience of walking it.

In Passini and Proulx's (1988) study there were differences in the way that the participants with visual impairments planned the route and described it during the journey. The former made more planning decisions and had to make more decisions along the route; they also used a greater variety of cues and information to find their way and, not surprisingly, those cues included more references to immediate landmarks that were accessible to touch. The verbal protocols given by the participants with visual impairments reflected the different wayfinding strategies that they had to use to retrace the route. As such, the results from this study support the difference theory, because Passini and Proulx found little difference between the visually impaired and sighted groups' performance, but it is clear from the verbal protocol that their performance was based on different route information and learning processes.

Several researchers have pointed out that the environmental information that will be important for visually impaired people will be different from the information used by people with sight. Golledge (1991b) assessed the cues used by people navigating through a college campus and found that the features used by people with visual impairments (who depended, for example, on local landmarks, sounds, smells, and the texture of the paths) did not overlap at all with the features used by people with sight (who considered, for example, more distant landmarks, the shape and heights of buildings, as well as visually distinctive features and colors). Other researchers have also noted the very different cues used by people with visual impairments, and the difficulty of navigating in environments where such cues are unavailable or are masked by other information (Kitchin et al., 1998; Passini et al., 1986). The issue is whether these alternative cues, and the processes that are needed to encode them, can result in cognitive maps that are as complete and as effective as the cognitive maps of people with sight. The results of Passini and Proulx's (1988) study, described above, suggest that people with visual impairments could generate a cognitive map of a building, because they were able to make maps of the building that were as accurate as maps made by people with sight. However, given the typical design of a building, several assumptions could be made about its layout (for example, that junctions were at right angles) and these assumptions could have contributed to all the participants' success in mapping the route.

Passini and Proulx (1988) investigated wayfinding performance and only considered configurational knowledge incidentally by asking their participants to draw a map. Other researchers have examined the development of configurational understanding more directly by asking participants to learn the relationships between places. Some of these experiments have been in table-top or small spaces. For example, Klatzky et al. (1994) gave participants a range of different tasks including manipulative ones (e.g., assembling shapes) and locomotive ones (e.g., being guided along two sides of a triangular route and then being asked to walk back to the start point on their own). In general there were few differences between blindfolded, sighted participants and participants who were visually impaired. These results imply that people with visual impairments can perform some spatial tasks, including ones like path completion, which requires configurational understanding, as well as people with sight.

Passini et al. (1990) also tested several groups of participants in a small space, but assessed participants' ability to do more than encode the layout of objects, or complete simple paths. Passini et al.

built a small maze and tested participants in several tasks that included learning a route through the maze, retracing a route in reverse,
finding short-cuts back to the start point, combining two routes that
had been learnt separately, and learning a route through the maze
from prior experience of using a model of the maze. The sighted
group in this experiment had the highest overall performance, then
the visually impaired group, and then the congenitally blind group.
Nonetheless, levels of performance were comparatively high, and all
the tasks were performed without error by at least some participants
in each group. Passini *et al.* concluded that both congenitally blind
and visually impaired people had all the necessary abilities for developing cognitive maps. Passini *et al.* did not speculate about why the
participants with visual impairments in their experiment performed
less well than the sighted group, but it may have been the case that
an artificial maze built in a room would put the visually impaired
groups at a greater disadvantage than the sighted group, because of
the very much reduced number of available orientation cues.

Other researchers have investigated routefinding in the real
world and included tests of configurational knowledge, for example,
making a novel short-cut or pointing between unseen places (e.g.,
Dodds *et al.*, 1982; Hollyfield and Foulke, 1983). Dodds *et al.* asked
11 year olds to learn two different but overlapping routes round two
blocks. Half the children were congenitally blind and half were late
blind. The children were given several trials to learn each route and
made pointing estimates between places along the routes on each
trial, and, at the end of the experiment, they also made pointing
estimates between places on the two routes. All the children were
able to learn the routes after just a single experience of each one.
The late blind children were generally successful in the pointing task
and significantly better than the congenitally blind children, though
one of the congenitally blind children performed at the same level as
the late blind group. The children also made maps of each route,
but only one of the congenitally blind children was able to construct
a recognizable map of the environment. These findings showed that
all the children with visual impairment could learn the route without
difficulty, but the congenitally blind children only gained a limited
understanding of the configuration of the routes. One interpretation
of these findings would be that congenitally blind children will have
difficulty generating cognitive maps of new areas (as proposed by the
inefficiency theory), but alternatively, the point made earlier may
apply and the poorer performance of the congenitally blind group
may have been due to the fact that they would have needed more

practice and experience to achieve the same level of performance as the other, more successful children (as proposed by the difference theory).

In another route learning study Jacobson *et al.* (1998) examined the abilities of 30 participants in Belfast (UK). One-third were totally blind, one-third were visually impaired and one-third were sighted. The route was 1.5 kilometers long and included 16 choice points. Participants were first guided along the route, and then had three trials when they retraced the route on their own. During these trials they were asked to give a verbal description of the route and were given tests of configurational knowledge, including pointing between landmarks on the route, making distance judgments, and constructing maps of the route. Route learning was measured by assessing the number of errors made by the participants as they retraced the route. The sighted group learned the route faster, and made fewer errors on the second and third trials, and could complete the route almost without error by the third trial. The visually impaired and blind groups learned slightly more slowly, making more errors on the first and second trials, but by the third trial they had also learned the route almost without error. There was no difference between the groups in their pointing estimates, which were generally accurate. Nor was there any difference between the groups' distance estimates. The maps were coded for the accuracy of the choice points represented in them, and for their 'completeness', 'shape', and 'orientation'. There were no differences between the groups for these measures. Taken together, these measures indicate that the people with visual impairments were able to learn a long and complex route comparatively quickly, and in doing so they were able to use configurational information to build up a cognitive map of the environment that was equivalent to the cognitive maps of the sighted group. Such results indicate that in some real-world contexts people with visual impairments may be able to develop cognitive maps very effectively.

In the experiment by Jacobson *et al.* (1998) there was little evidence that people with visual impairments were much slower than people with sight at generating a cognitive map of a new area, and this finding does not lend support to either the inefficient or difference theories, and raises the question of why the participants with visual impairments performed so well. One possibility, which requires further investigation, is that the process of data collection (e.g., pointing and making maps) focused the learning of the visually impaired groups. Previous studies (e.g., Dodds *et al.*, 1982) that have found less accurate performance by participants with visual impairments have used similar assessment measures, but in the Jacobson *et al.* experiment participants were asked for a much greater range of information (verbal protocols, distance and direction judgments, and map making) than in previous studies and this may have benefited their route encoding. The importance of such learning strategies will be discussed later in this section.

7.1.3 *Empirical studies in familiar environments*

The studies discussed above have involved participants without sight learning new environments. Other researchers have considered how well people with visual impairments have encoded very familiar environments. Casey (1978) asked student participants who were visually impaired to make a model of their campus, and they were able to do this with some accuracy, but their models were not as complete and well organized as the models produced by participants with sight. Byrne and Salter (1983) compared the ability of participants who were totally blind and participants with sight to point to familiar places in their own neighborhood. The blind group were poorer at pointing to places, especially if they had to point from an imagined place in the environment (rather than their actual position). Bigelow (1991), in one of the few longitudinal studies, carried out a 15 month study with five to seven year olds who were totally blind, visually impaired, or sighted. The children were tested in their own homes and asked to point to places in their houses, or in their neighborhood, and these tests were repeated every two months. The eight children who were sighted and the two children who were visually impaired were all able to do all the pointing tasks by the end of the 15 month period, and most had completed the tasks successfully during the first trial. In contrast, the two totally blind children were unable to complete most of the pointing tasks, even by the end of the study. Rather than point directly to the requested place, the children who were totally blind often pointed to the route they would take to get to the place, and Bigelow suggested that these children's cognitive maps were based on the functional aspects of the environment (i.e., on routes) rather than a configurational (i.e., Euclidean) understanding of the environment.

Other researchers have found similar results with both adults and children (e.g., Rieser *et al.*, 1980; Ungar *et al.*, 1997), but these researchers used measures of distance estimation. For example, Rieser *et al.* asked totally blind, late blind, and sighted adults to estimate distances in a familiar building. Three places in the building were named and the participants were asked to say which two were closest together and which two were furthest apart. This was repeated for 140 groups of three locations, and under several conditions, including making comparisons based on the travel distance between the places (functional distance) and making comparisons based on the straight line distances between places (Euclidean distance). Rieser *et al.* found that all three groups performed similarly when asked to base their estimates on functional distances, but when asked for estimates based on Euclidean distances, the sighted group performed best and the congenitally blind group worst, with the late blind group in between. The congenitally blind group exaggerated the Euclidean distance between places that were separated by corners and turns (i.e., ones that had greater travel, or functional, distance between them). The bias in considering places in terms of functional distance meant that the cognitive maps of the congenitally blind group were different from those of the sighted group (and less accurate compared to a cartographic map of the building). In other words, despite their familiarity with the space, the people who were totally blind had not developed the same cognitive maps as people with sight. Ungar *et al.* (1996) tested children's knowledge of a familiar area (their own school environment) using the same procedure as Rieser *et al.* The children were blind or visually impaired and nearly all the children in both groups made distance estimates that were more closely correlated to travel, or functional distance, than to Euclidean distance.

7.1.4 Summary

In the experiments discussed in this section there are several contrasting results. In general, participants who are totally blind show poorer cognitive map abilities than participants who are visually impaired or participants with sight (e.g., Bigelow, 1991; Byrne and Salter, 1983; Dodds *et al.*, 1982; Rieser *et al.*, 1980). This implies that lack of any visual experience (usually from birth, because the majority of totally blind participants in these experiments were congenitally blind) is detrimental to the development of cognitive maps. However, Jacobson *et al.* (1998) demonstrated that participants who were totally blind could learn the configuration of a route as well as other sight groups.

It is important to find out what accounts for these variations in results, and what accounts for the individual differences reported in some studies. At present, most researchers have compared groups who differ in sight, or differ for onset of blindness, and, less often, have included analyses of age, education and gender (e.g., Passini *et al.*, 1990). However, analysis of such group variables does not contribute to an understanding of why some people with visual impairments are more successful at developing cognitive maps than others. A possible explanation is that some individuals have developed better learning strategies than others, but with one or two exceptions (e.g., Hill *et al.*, 1993; Passini and Proulx, 1988) researchers have not usually considered the cognitive strategies that people with visual impairments adopt when learning a new environment.

What is needed in future research is a move away from global comparisons between groups, and more detailed analyses of individual learning strategies. Hill *et al.* (1993) examined participants' ability to learn the layout of objects in a large room and suggested that success on this task depended on the ability of participants to establish orientation and a frame of reference, and found that several strategies were related to successful performance. These strategies included: systematic exploration; establishment of a clearly defined anchor-point as an origin; establishing patterns in the structure of the environment; and establishing landmark cues. Hill *et al.* found that the best performance was nearly always based on an anchor-point (object to object) strategy similar to that identified in the cognitive mapping and environmental learning processes by Golledge (1978) and Couclelis *et al.* (1987).

However, in most discussions of the strategies used by people with visual impairments the emphasis has been on the strategies that directly incorporate aspects of the environment (like noticing regular street plans, or salient landmarks). These are, without doubt, important components of environmental learning, but much less emphasis has been placed on other cognitive strategies (e.g., mentally rehearsing a route, dividing a route into distinct and memorable sections, imagining the configuration of landmarks, comparing distances between places, and so on) and, as yet, we know little about how important such learning strategies might be, or whether the ability to use them differs between people with visual impairments and people with sight. Although there has recently been a greater emphasis on the analysis of the spatial strategies used by children and adults in small spaces (e.g., Millar, 1994; Thinus-Blanc and Gaunet, 1997), and in tasks like learning tactile maps (Ungar *et al.*, 1997), there has been far less research into the learning strategies that might be used in the real world.

As well as such learning strategies there are external aids that can contribute to the development of cognitive maps. For example, Espinosa *et al.* (1998) investigated how people with visual impairments learnt a two kilometer route under three different conditions. In one condition participants were guided along the route, in a second condition they were guided along the route and given a verbal description of it, and in a third condition they were guided along the route and given a tactile map of it. After the introduction to the route, participants were asked to retrace it on their own, and while retracing it they were asked to point between places along the route and to work out short-cuts between places. The participants who were shown the tactile map learnt the route more accurately, made more accurate pointing estimates, and located better short-cuts. Espinosa *et al.* therefore argued that tactile maps can make a significant contribution to the development of a person's cognitive map. Other researchers have also stressed the advantages of tactile maps, especially ones that can be presented in conjunction with auditory information (e.g., Jacobson, 1998).

Research into the cognitive maps of people with visual impairments has important implications. Like a sighted individual, a person who is visually impaired or blind must be able to traverse space at a reasonable pace (Golledge, 1993a) and undertake such mobility with grace, comfort, and safety (Foulke, 1983), and better insights into the cognitive maps of people with visual impairments may contribute to the training of effective spatial strategies and mobility skills (Ungar, 2000).

7.2 Other Disabilities and Cognitive Maps

Cognitive map research could also contribute to a understanding of the spatial abilities of other groups with disabilities, but as yet there is very little research into their cognitive maps, and therefore only a few examples of this research can be given in this section. Vujakovic and Matthews (1994) asked a group of geography students and a group of wheelchair users in Coventry (UK) to draw sketch maps of the city center. The maps produced by the wheelchair users were more detailed and included more references to barriers and other mobility constraints, and their cognitive maps of the center were limited to the areas that were accessible.

Other researchers have considered the effects of neuropsychological impairment on cognitive map abilities. Some of these investigations have been single case studies. For example, Sellal *et al.* (1996) described an elderly woman (LB) who suffered from delusion of place, and while in hospital recovering from a viral encephalitis believed that she was in her own home. Sellal *et al.* tested her ability to learn the layout of a small room by asking her to explore the room and then identify a model representation of the room (from several alternative models). LB was unable to do this and explored the room only briefly and then based her choice of model on part of the features in the room. As LB had good recall of familiar, well learnt places and demonstrated good recall of novel verbal memory, her failure to encode the room suggested specific deficits in learning unfamiliar spaces. Sellal *et al.* suggested that LB's particular problem was that she only identified individual parts or features in new spaces and did not encode the configuration of the space as a whole, and if so it would not be possible to generate a cognitive map of a new area.

Golledge and Stimson (1997) summarized studies carried out with people with learning difficulties. They concluded that, in familiar environments, the participants with learning difficulties had a good understanding of local landmarks and travel routes, and the distances between places. However, compared to a group of control participants, the ones with learning difficulties were less competent in tasks that required an understanding of Euclidean relationships. In other words, they had a less developed configurational understanding of the environment. In contrast to the research in familiar settings, Passini *et al.* (1995) investigated how a group of people with dementia of the Alzheimer type learnt their way round an unfamiliar environment. They were asked to find a route through a building, and then retrace it. The majority of a control group were able to do these tasks, but none of the Alzheimer group could complete the routes without help. Although the latter were able to retain the overall goal of the task (to reach a room in the building) they were poorer at planning a series of sub-goals to complete the route, in particular being inflexible in the wayfinding strategies they attempted and not adapting them to the new environment. Although Passini *et al.* were concerned with routefinding rather than the development of cognitive maps, it is clear that the Alzheimer group would have had had difficulty developing a cognitive map of the building or any other new environment.

7.3 Conclusions

As yet there have been few studies of the cognitive maps of people with disabilities other than visual impairment, and most of these have included participants with different types of disability (whether physical or neuropsychological) and with different degrees of impairment, and the participants have been tested in different ways in different environments. Some of the research has focused on identifying the differences between groups and rather fewer have attempted to identify the specific spatial difficulties of people with disabilities (e.g., Passini *et al.*, 1995). As a consequence, much of the research is descriptive rather than motivated by specific theories and hypotheses. Nonetheless, this research is important in highlighting the difficulties that people with disabilities might have both in traveling through an environment (Vujakovic and Matthews, 1994) and in learning new environments (Passini *et al.*, 1995). To a limited extent, some of these difficulties might be overcome by improving the design of an environment to make it more accessible or more memorable (Golledge and Stimson, 1997), but the most important way to help people with disabilities will be to identify their cognitive difficulties in developing configurational awareness, and provide training or support in the use of cognitive strategies that help to overcome those limitations. More research is needed therefore that focuses on this latter need.

CHAPTER 8

Methods and Methodological Issues

To examine the theories relating to how we acquire, learn, and store spatial information cognitive mapping researchers use a number of techniques to generate and analyze data. In general, participants are required to perform tasks within a controlled environment. In this chapter, some of the data collection tasks that have been used to generate data are summarized, along with methods to analyze these data, and issues arising from their use are discussed.

8.1 Unidimensional Data Generation

Unidimensional techniques are used to determine a participant's knowledge of the spatial relationship between two locations, and these can be divided into two main categories: distance tasks and direction tasks.

8.1.1 Distance tasks

Montello (1991a) classified tests designed to measure cognitive distance estimates into five categories. These were: psychophysical ratio scaling; psychophysical interval and ordinal scaling; mapping; reproduction; and route choice.

The first two of these methods use traditional psychophysical scaling techniques which differ in their level of measurement. Montello (1991a) described four *ratio scaling* techniques, two of which are applicable for testing the cognition of large-scale distances:

(a) *Magnitude estimation* requires a participant to assign a number to a distance, scaled in relation to a given known scale value. For example, the distance between London and Paris could be assigned a scale value of 100 and a participant would then be required to estimate the distances between other locations in comparison to this value, with places thought to be closer together being given a lower value and places further apart receiving a higher value. Allen *et al.* (1978) and Cadwallader (1979) have both used this technique to obtain distance estimates.

(b) *Ratio estimation* requires a participant to mark on a line the distance to a location with the length of the line representing a known distance. For example, a participant could be told that the length of a line represents the distance from New York to Los Angeles. They would then be asked to mark the distance from Chicago to Denver, where Chicago is at the start of the line. Ratio estimation has been used by many researchers to collect distance estimates, for example, Lowery (1973), Briggs (1976), Day (1976), Phipps (1979), MacEachren (1980), Coshall (1985), Okabe *et al.* (1986), and Lloyd and Heivly (1987).

Both ratio scaling and ratio estimation are techniques that require an understanding of scale, and therefore participants' responses may be influenced by their ability to make scaled comparisons as well as by their estimates of distance, and such techniques would be inappropriate for participants (such as children) who are unable to make scale comparisons.

Montello (1991a) classed *psychophysical interval and ordinal scaling* techniques into four classes:

(a) *Paired comparison* requires a participant to decide which one of a pair of distances is longer (e.g., Biel, 1982). For example, a respondent would be asked which is the longer distance, 'Shop A to Shop B or Shop C to Shop D'. In a similar triad methodology, participants might be presented with the names of three locations and asked to judge which of the three is furthest from the other two (or which two are nearer together) (e.g., Allen, 1981; Ungar *et al.*, 1996).

(b) *Ranking* requires participants to rank distance in an order along the dimension of length. For example, participants might be asked to say, for a number of places in the same environment, which one is closest to a given reference point, then which is next closest to the reference point, and so on (e.g., Allen *et al.*, 1978; Newcombe, 1997).

(c) *Rating* requires participants to assign the distance between places to a set of predetermined classes that represent relative length (e.g., Baird *et al.*, 1979). For example, participants might be presented with a series of three categories, long, medium, and short, and asked to assign their distance estimates between locations to one of the three classes.

(4) *Partition scales* require participants to assign distances to classes of equal-appearing intervals of length (e.g., Cadwallader, 1979). This is usually an adapted form of ratio scaling, with respondents marking off distance estimates at set intervals along a line.

The interval and ordinal techniques are often used to collect data for non-metric multidimensional scaling, where the data is converted into two-dimensional data for analysis.

A third category of distance estimates is *mapping*, and this requires several places to be represented simultaneously at a scale smaller than the estimated environment, with the distances being measured from this representation for comparison with the actual distances (Montello, 1991a). To avoid the necessity of making scale transformations, participants can be asked to provide distance estimates at the same scale of the estimated distance. This is referred to as *reproduction*, for example, respondents could be asked to pace out the distance that is equivalent between place A and place B (e.g., Herman and Klein, 1985). Although this technique has the advantage that a participant does not have to make a scale transformation of the distance, it is only appropriate for comparatively short distances.

The last category of distance estimation is *route choice*. This means inferring judgments of cognitive distance from the choice of route an individual makes when he or she is asked to take the shortest route between two locations. Here, the length of the route chosen can be compared to the lengths of alternative routes.

In some studies, participants have been asked to estimate straight-line, or Euclidean, distances between places (e.g., Antes *et al.*, 1988; Baird, 1979; Buttenfield, 1986) and in others functional, or route, distances between places (e.g., Cohen *et al.*, 1978; McNamara, 1986). For some groups, accuracy in estimating straight-line and functional distances might vary. For example, people with visual impairments are often better at estimating the functional distance than the straight-line distances between places (Rieser *et al.*, 1980).

In some experiments, participants have been asked to estimate distances in standard units (e.g., Cadwallader, 1976; Saisa *et al.*, 1986). For example, Matthews (1981) asked children to estimate distances, in yards and miles, between places in their home town, and Day (1976) asked participants to mark a dash along a line with miles marked along its length. Other researchers have asked for estimates of the time it took to travel between places (e.g., MacEachren, 1980; Matthews, 1981). Time estimates can be made directly in units (e.g., minutes) or by asking participants to imagine traveling a distance and measuring how long this takes (e.g., Hanyu and Itsukushima, 1995). However, there are limitations in asking people to estimate either distance or time units, because people may not be very proficient at making such estimates.

As the above discussion indicates, there is a variety of methods for obtaining distance estimates. Some may be more or less appropriate for specific environments (e.g., reproduction techniques can only be used for short distances), or for particular populations (e.g., Newcombe, 1997, has pointed out that young children find it difficult to rank distances), but most techniques could be used for most investigations of cognitive maps. However, the choice of technique is not always justified by experimenters. In most studies only one technique is used, and therefore there is little evidence about the validity of these distance measures. In experiments which have used more than one method of estimating the same distance, the results suggest that there can be marked differences in estimates obtained in different ways. For example, Hanyu and Itsukushima (1995) asked participants to estimate the time it took to walk a stairway (in seconds), and they also measured how long the same participants took to imagine walking the stairway. The time estimates were nearly twice as long as the measures of imagined walking. It may not be surprising that such estimates differ, because they probably depend on different cognitive processes, but it is then difficult to decide which estimate, if either, reflects 'distance' in the cognitive map.

Just as there has been little research into the validity of distance measures, there has been no research into the reliability of these measures, and we have little evidence about how the same person would carry out the same estimation task at different times. Underlying the use of most of these measures is the assumption that if an individual estimates the distance from A to B on one occasion he or she would give the same estimate from A to B if asked to do so a second time. It may well be the case that all the measures summarized in this section are reliable, and would always elicit the same response from the same individual, but this needs to be addressed with a systematic program of experimentation to establish test–retest reliability measures for all these techniques. As there are a large number of methods for eliciting distance judgments, and it might be suspected that some have greater validity and reliability than others, if it could be determined which measures are the most valid (and the conditions under which they remain valid), then the less valid measures could be avoided. As it is, researchers investigating cognitive distance have to make comparisons between a large number of studies that have used quite different measures to obtain distance estimates, but without knowing how the validity of those measures compares.

These comments about the validity and reliability of measures can be applied to many of the other techniques used to elicit information about cognitive maps (e.g., direction estimates, sketch mapping and so on). We will only repeat the point briefly in reference to other measures, but we emphasize here that the failure to assess the measures that are used in cognitive mapping studies has probably been to the detriment of this research field. As we discuss later in the chapter, one of the difficulties in comparing studies is the fact that different researchers have usually tested people's knowledge of different environments. This is especially true for large environments, because participants in different studies inevitably live in different environments, and this is an unavoidable aspect of cognitive map research. But the problem of making comparisons is compounded when different researchers have also used different measuring techniques. If all techniques could be demonstrated to be equally valid and reliable (in all environments) then at least one potentially confounding aspect of generalizing between studies could be ignored. If techniques are not equally valid and reliable, then studies that have used the less valid methods could be treated with greater caution.

8.1.2 Analyzing distance tasks

In this section we give examples of how distance estimates can be analyzed. There are several ways that distance estimates can be considered in relation to actual distances in the environment (Guth, 1990):

- *Absolute error* scores refer to the calculation of unsigned error for each distance estimate. This calculation is the difference between the estimate and the actual distance without taking into account whether the participant underestimated or overestimated the distance. This measure provides a general indication of accuracy, but is limited because overestimations and underestimations may, sometimes, cancel each other out.
- *Constant error* is a way to find out if there is a systematic tendency to underestimate or overestimate distances. This is determined by calculating the signed error, so that a positive score indicates a tendency to overestimate distances and a negative score indicates a tendency to underestimate distances.
- *Variable error* can also be calculated for a number of scores (e.g., all

the estimates by a participant in a study) to give an indication of the range of estimates. For example, a person who always underestimates distances by ten percent will have a lower variable error than a person who is sometimes correct, sometimes underestimates by ten percent and sometimes underestimates by 20 percent.

The use of these different measures can be informative in contrasting how different individuals or different groups of participants make distance judgments (e.g., Ungar *et al.*, 1997).

Psychophysical ratio scaling, mapping and reproduction distance data are often analyzed using *linear/non-linear regression*. Here, the cognitive distance estimates are regressed onto the objective distance values and the relationship between the two assessed. The r-squared value indicates the degree to which the cognitive distance estimates vary from the objective distance values. There is a debate about whether the relationship between cognitive and objective distance is linear (see Cadwallader, 1973) or non-linear (see Briggs, 1973b; MacEachren, 1980; Baird *et al.*, 1982; Gärling *et al.*, 1991a) and therefore data can be analyzed in two ways. *Linear regression* posits a straight-line relationship between cognitive and objective distance ($Y=a+bX$, where Y is the cognitive distance, a is the intercept, b is the slope, and X is the objective distance). In contrast, *non-linear regression* posits a curved-line relationship ($Y=aX^b$) (see Figure 8.1).

Ratio scaling and metric distance estimates and interval or ordinal distance data can be analyzed using *multidimensional scaling techniques* (MDS). Although the estimates are obtained by asking

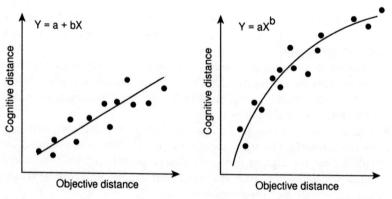

Figure 8.1. Linear and non-linear regression

people to judge the distances between two places, the use of MDS permits the construction of a 'map' showing the relationship between a number of places and in this way the spatial relationships between all places (i.e., configurational information) can be generated from the data collected from the original unidimensional data (Aitken *et al.*, 1989). The distances can be either all metric (metric MDS) or all interval/ordinal (non-metric MDS). The purpose of the technique is to discover a pattern or structure from the collection of individual distance estimates, and present that pattern visually (Golledge, 1977).

MDS algorithms work to minimize the difference, or stress, between the patterns of proximities in a matrix of distances and the space created (Montello, 1991a). The stress value is a residual sum of squares values, a positive dimensionless number that can be expressed as a percentage (Gentry and Wakefield, 1991) and it indicates how well the configured coordinates fit within the optimal dimension solution (Buttenfield, 1986). It is not a measure of accuracy, but rather an indication of how adequately the configuration demonstrates the original matrix data. The resultant coordinates may exist in one of a number of dimensions, but usually the results are constrained to two dimensions so that the locations in cognitive space can be compared to the original environment (Buttenfield, 1986). This comparison is usually performed using bidimensional regression (see Golledge and Spector, 1978), after the configuration has been rotated to make it maximally congruent with the real-world configuration (see later). A minimum number of distance comparisons between all places in an environment is necessary to construct a MDS configuration.

MDS is open to a number of criticisms. First, the validity of inferring a latent two-dimensional configuration from unidimensional data is questionable. For example, people may be able to estimate the distances between locations without possessing a knowledge of where those places are in relation to each other, and consequently the technique may suggest an underlying structure to an individual's knowledge that does not exist. Second, unless the optimum stress value is two-dimensional, the results have to be constrained to two dimensions for comparison to Euclidean metrics (Harman and Betak, 1976), and consequently the MDS configuration will not be a true representation of the knowledge possessed by the individual. Third, the coordinates in the center of the configuration may possess more accuracy of representation than those on the edge and therefore the method may also introduce geometric bias into the configuration (Montello, 1991a). Fourth, the technique is non-associational because the configuration that is generated does not necessarily show the associations and relations that are understood by participants (Buttenfield, 1986). When participants use techniques such as sketch mapping and model construction, they can update and alter the relationships between objects and places in their products, but this is not possible with MDS because in this latter technique relational data is inferred. For these reasons it is possible for MDS techniques to misrepresent participants' cognitive maps (Curtis *et al.*, 1981). But despite these problems, MDS remains a common method of analyzing cognitive map knowledge because it gives the opportunity to convert one-dimensional distance estimates to a two-dimensional configuration, and this makes it possible to examine distortions in cognitive maps (Gärling *et al.*, 1997).

8.1.3 Direction tasks

A second type of unidimensional test concerns direction estimation. Participants are asked to estimate the direction between two places in the environment, usually by pointing from a given place to a target place. Pointing tasks have been used in a number of studies and can be used appropriately with both sighted people (e.g., Anooshian and Young, 1981; Kirasic *et al.*, 1984; Herman *et al.*, 1985) and people with visual impairments (e.g., Bigelow, 1991; Espinosa *et al.*, 1998). In general, this technique involves standing at, or imagining being at, one location and pointing to another location. Pointing can be used in environments of different sizes, for example to locate out-of-sight places in rooms (e.g., Hardwick *et al.*, 1976), in buildings (e.g., Evans *et al.*, 1980) or in cities (e.g., Espinosa *et al.*, 1998). One version of the pointing technique involves participants drawing a line, on paper, across a compass representation to indicate the direction to a place (Tversky 1981, Kitchin 1996a), and MacEachren (1992) used an on-screen version where participants were presented with a junction and were asked to align a line, using the mouse, so that it pointed in the direction of another location.

The issues of validity and reliability that were raised with reference to distance tasks (above) also apply to direction estimates. For example, there has been no systematic investigation of the reliability of direction estimates, but it would be important to establish that every time a person made a direction estimate between the same two points (under the same conditions), that he or she gave a similar estimate. This type of study would not be difficult to carry out, and, assuming that the same direction estimates are similar under the same conditions, it would strengthen any assumptions drawn from studies depending on direction estimates. The only study of the validity of direction-giving tasks found that participants' performance differed depending on whether they were asked to make direction estimates by turning their body, or by pointing with a dial (Montello *et al.*, 1999). The fact that different ways of obtaining direction estimates produced different patterns of results has serious implications for any interpretation of performance based on a single method of collecting direction estimates. As such, the validity of direction estimates requires much more investigation.

8.1.4 Analyzing direction tasks

Like distance estimates, direction estimates can be assessed in terms of absolute, constant and variable error (see above). Direction estimates can be analyzed in two main ways. First, the direction estimates are compared to their objective counterparts. Like distance estimates, this can be achieved through linear/non-linear regression (Kitchin, 1992). For this, direction estimates are regressed onto objective direction values with the r-squared value indicating the level of variance between the data sets. However, there are problems associated with such use, because (a) direction estimates are constrained to a 360 degree range, and (b) due to the circularity of this range the cognitive direction estimates can be no more than 180 degrees from the objective direction value. Estimates that fall between 270 and 359 produce large residuals when regressed onto objective values between zero and 89, and care must therefore be taken to alter values so that the difference between them falls below 180. Once the data has been transformed, effective regression can take place. As an alternative to regression, accuracy scores reflecting the absolute and relative accuracy of direction estimates can be calculated (Jacobson *et al.*, 1998). The absolute accuracy score (AAS) represents the average percentage difference between the objective direction values (ODV) and the cognitive direction estimates (CDE) (Figure 8.2).

$$AAS = \left(\frac{\sum_{i=1}^{n} \left(\frac{ODV^i - CDE^i}{180} \right) * 100}{n} \right)$$

where n = number of direction estimates.

The relative accuracy score (RAS) represents the average percentage difference between objective angle segments (OASs) and cognitive angle segments (CASs) (Figure 8.3). Once again, care must be

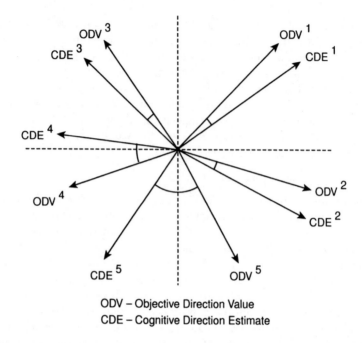

ODV – Objective Direction Value
CDE – Cognitive Direction Estimate

Figure 8.2. Calculating an absolute direction error score
Source: Jacobson *et al.* (1998)

taken in both cases to convert difference over 180 degrees to lesser values.

$$RAS = \left(\frac{\sum_{i=1}^{n} \left(\frac{OAS^i - CAS^i}{180} \right) * 100}{n} \right)$$

where n = number of angle segments.

In the second instance, using a series of pointing estimations it is possible to construct a two-dimensional map of place locations using a technique known as *projective convergence*. For this technique, vectors are drawn on a base map to represent a participant's pointing estimates. The point at which the vectors to a place, from two pointing locations, intersect the intersection is taken as the cognitive position of that place. If two or more vectors intersect then the cognitive position is taken as the average position of the intersections (see Figure 8.4, panel a). If there are no intersections then a cognitive position cannot be calculated. If distance and direction data has been collected then

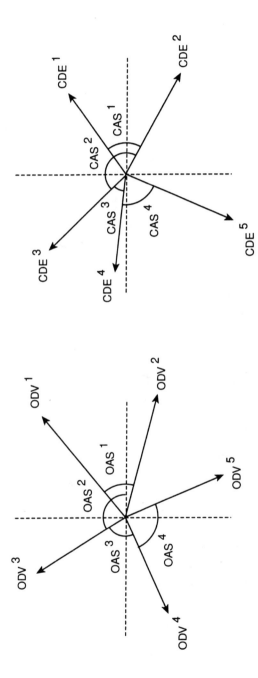

Figure 8.3. Calculating a relative direction error score

Source: Jacobson *et al.* (1998)

137

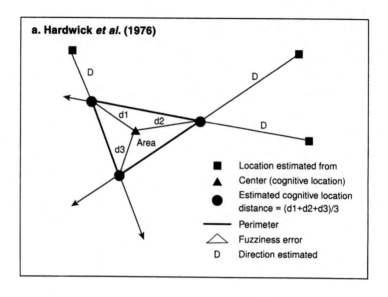

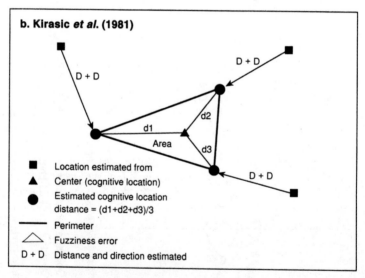

Figure 8.4. Methods of projective convergence

the vectors are only extended for a scaled distance, and the cognitive location is taken as the average position of the end places (see Figure 8.4, panel b). If there are more than two vectors then the area of the shape created can be used to indicate the level of place cognition.

Although projective convergence techniques are useful, they are open to several criticisms. First, like MDS, they assume that a knowledge of the relative locations of a number of places can be assessed through unidimensional data generation, and second, estimates over long distances often produce very large errors.

8.2 Two-dimensional Data Generation

Two-dimensional techniques of data collection are used to elicit a participant's knowledge of configurational spatial relationships, in other words the relationships between a number of locations. Techniques used to measure this type of knowledge can be divided into three categories: graphic tasks, completion tasks, and recognition tasks.

8.2.1 Graphic and modeling tasks

Sketch mapping has been a frequently used technique for gathering information about configurational knowledge, even though it has many limitations (see below). Graphic tasks include several variants of sketch mapping.

- The *basic* sketch map technique depends on eliciting a freely drawn sketch map that has been minimally defined by the researcher. A participant is given a blank piece of paper and asked to draw a map of a given environment, with a general instruction such as 'Draw a map of London', but without any instructions about what should be included.
- The *normal* sketch map technique imposes more constraints than the basic approach. The researcher is often interested in more specific features and will word the instructions appropriately to obtain the required data, for example, 'Draw a map of London. Include and label any districts you think you know the location of.' This method gives the researcher some control over the type of sketch maps produced.
- For a *cued* sketch mapping task, a participant is provided with a portion of the map and asked to complete specific features. Pocock (1973) used this method to compare the route maps of particular roads in Durham (UK), and Pearce (1981) used cued sketch mapping to collect the route knowledge of a trip between Townsville and Cairns in North Queensland. In Pearce's study, participants were given a sheet of paper that included three locations and a scale bar, and they were asked to draw a map of the

route including as many features as they could recall, with a suggested list of possible attributes. This use of cued sketch mapping introduces a common scale to the results, but may also influence the results because some of the information is inevitably provided by the researcher.

- The *longitudinal* sketch map technique allows the researcher to study how the sketch map evolves, because a participant is asked to sketch the map on layers of tracing paper that can be turned over as the participant continues to draw (e.g., Humphreys, 1990). Alternatively, the sketch mapping can be recorded on video for later analysis. The advantage of the longitudinal technique is that a researcher can study the evolution of the map and this may provide information about participants' retrieval strategies when drawing the map.

- Wood and Beck (1976a, 1989) suggested that more could be gained from the sketch map technique if participants were taught a *sketch map language.* The graphical map language that Wood and Beck invented was called Environmental A, and it included a vocabulary and a set of rules or grammar. The vocabulary consisted of signs, marks, and the labels for points, lines, and areas, and the grammar suggested ways in which the point, line, and area symbols could be assembled into structures. The data were collected using a series of overlays similar to a longitudinal study, but these were not constrained by time; rather each layer was used for particular features. For example, there might be one layer for landmarks, one for roads, one for attitudes, and so on. The advantage of Environmental A was that the information collected was much more comprehensive than just the layout of places and roads, because the technique also elicited personal meanings and values. However, with a few exceptions (e.g., Spencer and Dixon, 1983) the technique developed by Beck and Wood has rarely been used to collect data. Nor has it inspired the development of similar techniques.

The fundamental assumption behind the use of the sketch map technique (as with all other methods of data collection) is that the technique is reliable in the sense that if a person draws a sketch map twice they will produce a similar product each time (assuming that no additional environmental learning has taken place between the times of drawing). If people failed to produce similar maps each time the technique would only have limited use. Blades (1990) investigated whether the sketch map technique was reliable by asking participants to draw a familiar route on one occasion, and then to draw the same route again a week later. The sketch maps were scored for the type and number of elements included, and there was a high correlation between what participants drew on the first occasion and what they drew the second time. Blades also found that judges who were given a number of the sketch maps from both occasions were able to pair the ones that had been drawn by the same participant. In other words, what participants drew on one occasion was very similar to what they drew on another occasion, and this indicates that sketch mapping is a reliable technique.

There are several advantages in using the sketch map technique to gather cognitive map data, because the technique requires participants to express environmental features in relation to one another (Gärling *et al.*, 1997). It is also a simple and comparatively quick method to employ, and one that has some ecological validity, because most adults are familiar with the idea of drawing sketch maps as a way to provide directions for other people.

Nonetheless the use of sketch maps has several limitations, most importantly because it depends on graphic skill, and many people may not have the ability to express their cognitive map as a sketch map. This limitation to the technique applies particularly to certain populations such as children, who certainly have cognitive maps well before they can express themselves by drawing a sketch map (Blades, 1997), and to people who are visually impaired, who may not be able to express their knowledge by drawing. It is possible to overcome the limitations of graphic skill to some extent. For example, people with visual impairments have been asked to make 'sketch maps' by drawing on pads that give a raised line image (Jacobson, 1998) or by using magnetic pieces that can be attached to a metal board (Ungar *et al.*, 1997), and children have been given toy items (roads, houses, and other features) to use in making models of familiar environments (e.g., Piaget *et al.*, 1960; Hart, 1981). A limitation of these aids is that participants are given just some of the elements for the sketch map or modeling process and this may influence the way that that map or model is constructed. One way round this is to provide participants with all the possible elements that may be needed to make a model—for example, Siegel and Schadler (1977) gave children models of all the items in their classroom and asked the children to reconstruct the configuration of the room—but this is only possible for cognitive maps of very small environments.

The type of sketch map that is produced will also be affected by several factors that may confound the way that a person draws the sketch map. Many people will, without prompting, consider the task as one in which they are expected to produce a representation that resembles a cartographic map, with expected symbols and labels for the features that are included. The first features that are drawn, the size of the paper, and people's unwillingness to adjust details after they have been drawn may all affect the outcome of the sketch mapping process (Beck and Wood, 1976b). In a similar way, making models will be constrained by the elements that are provided, the size of the surface available for the model, and participants' willingness to make changes to elements that have already been positioned (Hart, 1981). Apart from limitations associated with the production of sketch maps, there are also difficulties in scoring and analyzing them (see below).

Irrespective of the limitations of the sketch map technique, there are contexts in which sketch mapping is the only way to obtain information about participants' cognitive maps. When the environment that is being examined is too large for other data collection techniques, sketch mapping may be one of the few appropriate methods. For instance, researchers have asked participants to draw sketch maps of Europe (Axia *et al.*, 1998) or the world (e.g., Pinheiro, 1998; Saarinen *et al.*, 1996), or have given participants the shapes of countries and asked them to construct maps of continents (e.g., Barrett and Farroni, 1996).

8.2.2 *Analyzing graphic and modeling tasks*

Graphic tasks have been analyzed in several ways. One way that researchers have analyzed sketch maps is by subjective classifications using a set of predetermined criteria. Lynch (1960) was the first to produce such a classification for evaluating sketch maps of urban environments (Table 8.1). He divided the elements of the city into five main categories: paths, edges, districts, nodes, and landmarks. He then used his classification to assess people's maps of three cities (Los Angeles, New Jersey, and Boston), noting the number of times each element occurred.

Lynch's classification is essentially a content classification. Content classifications divide the environment in a sketch map into categories of features, and these are measured by counting the number of features that can be included in each category.

Other researchers have used similar classifications. For example, Pearce (1981) used three elements of Lynch's classification (landmarks, districts, and paths) with two more socially based criteria, namely textural and social classes. The texture class related to items

Table 8.1. Lynch's original classification

Category	Verbal description
Paths	Paths are the channels along which the sketch mapper moves. They may include streets, walkways, railways.
Edges	Edges are the linear elements not considered as paths by the sketch mapper. They are the boundaries between two phases, linear breaks in continuity such as shores or walls.
Districts	Districts are the medium-to-large scale sections to the city, conceived as having a two-dimensional extent, which the observer mentally enters, and which have some common identifiable character.
Nodes	Nodes are points, the strategic spots in the city into which an observer can enter, and which are the intensive foci to and from which he is traveling. They may be primarily junctions, places of a break in transportation, a crossing or convergence of paths.
Landmarks	Landmarks are another type of point-reference, but in this case the observer does not enter them as they are external. They are usually a rather simply defined physical object: building, sign, store, or mountain.

on the sketch map which formed a general reference to the landscape without having any specific locational significance, and the social class referred to any items which related to social activity.

Appleyard (1970) extended Lynch's classification, so that not only were sketch map contents evaluated but also the map's style, structure, and accuracy. Appleyard suggested that maps were either predominantly sequential in nature (linear features) or spatial (place features such as landmarks and districts) and that they could range from being topological (non-metric) to being positional (Euclidean). Appleyard hypothesized that spatial maps develop from sequential maps, as route knowledge develops into configurational knowledge. Other researchers have also suggested similar classificatory schemes for analyzing sketch maps (e.g., Pocock, 1976; Aginsky et al., 1997) or model constructions (e.g., Hart, 1981).

Some researchers have also suggested classification of drawing styles, to reflect developmental differences in map drawing ability. For example, Matthews (1984) described three categories of children's drawing that he labeled 'pictorial' (maps that were just pictures of environmental features, like houses and trees, drawn in 'side' view), 'pictorial-plan' (a combination of the other two categories), and 'plan' views (using a plan format and drawn from an aerial perspective). This sort of classification has less to do with the content or structure of a cognitive map and more to do with preferred drawing style, but the fact that children may be limited to different styles at different ages, and that some of these styles (e.g., pictorial) are not suitable for expressing configurational information, highlights the fact that sketch mapping may not be an appropriate technique for participants who have not achieved a certain level of drawing ability.

Even the rather basic classificatory scheme put forward by Matthews (1984) was unsuccessful in categorizing children's drawings. For example, in one study more than two-thirds of sketch maps were classified as pictorial-plan maps, i.e., they were hybrid maps that did not fall into any clear category (Matthews, 1984). This is a difficulty associated with any classificatory system, as there will often be sketch maps that overlap categories because the maps include elements associated with two or more categories. Few category schemes have been used in more than a few studies, and the failure of any one category scheme to be frequently and effectively used in a range of different studies indicates the limitation of any one of these subjective schemes. When researchers have tried to apply schemes developed by previous researchers it has often been with difficulty, for example, Murray and Spencer (1979) found it difficult to apply Pocock's (1976) scheme to their sketch map data. Other researchers have suggested that some classifications lack reliability, for instance, Kitchin (1995) also used Pocock's scheme, but found that it had low levels of inter-rater reliability.

8.2.3   Completion tasks

A second technique for generating two-dimensional data is the completion task. In this technique, a participant is provided with some data and asked to complete the task. The cued sketch map, described in the previous section, is an example of a completion task. Completion tasks can be divided into three classes: *spatial cued response tasks*, *reconstruction tasks* and *cloze procedures*.

Spatial cued response tasks differ from sketch mapping because the tasks provide a framework for participants who are only required to place points in the given framework, and this reduces the drawing component of the task to a minimum. There are various cued response techniques, but the basic method is that of Thorndyke and Hayes–Roth (1982), who asked participants to place a single location in relation to two given points along a route. The information that was given included a scale and orientation information for the participant. Kitchin (1990) altered the methodology so that participants were asked to place several locations in relation to a given pair of locations. McGuiness and Sparks (1982) used a similar method, in which participants were given the location of three places and were then asked to draw in all the roads, paths, bridges, and steps between those places. Other researchers have added more information for participants to use. For example, Buttenfield (1986) provided participants with a map outline, and Beatty and Troster (1987) asked participants to place locations on a map of the USA. At other scales, participants have been asked to place landmarks on a street plan (Ohta, 1979) and complete floor plans of buildings (Evans *et al.*, 1980).

Alternatively, a minimum of information can be provided. For example, Lloyd (1989a) used a minimal spatial cue by providing participants with just a reference point and a scale. The reference point was centrally located and surrounded by a circle and participants were told that the circle represented the distance to the furthest point away from the reference point. Participants were then asked to locate all other places in comparison to these sources of information. Other researchers have used a similar method by presenting participants with a series of circles with center points (e.g., Kirasic *et al.*, 1984; Kitchin, 1996a). Participants were told that the center point represented a particular place and that the distance to the outer circle was equal to a known place, then they were asked to draw a line from the center point which represented the distance and direction of a target location.

As another alternative, participants can be asked to carry out similar spatial cued response tasks that vary the amount of information that is provided. Kitchin (1996a) varied the amount of spatial cueing (two locations, or two locations and a coastline) and varied the amount of location cueing (free choice of places to locate, or 25 named places to locate) (see Figure 8.5). Spatial cued response tasks remove the graphic aspects involved in sketch mapping, but the fact that information is provided can have an influence on measures of accuracy. For example, Kitchin (1997) found that four groups of participants who each completed one of the tasks in Figure 8.5 produced different results. Spatial cueing accounted for approximately 5–10 percent of the variance between groups,

THE COGNITION OF GEOGRAPHIC SPACE

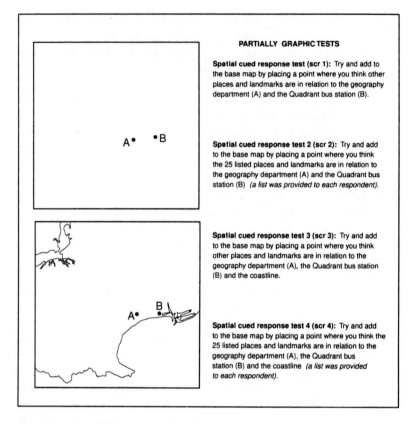

PARTIALLY GRAPHIC TESTS

Spatial cued response test (scr 1): Try and add to the base map by placing a point where you think other places and landmarks are in relation to the geography department (A) and the Quadrant bus station (B).

Spatial cued response test 2 (scr 2): Try and add to the base map by placing a point where you think the 25 listed places and landmarks are in relation to the geography department (A) and the Quadrant bus station (B) *(a list was provided to each respondent).*

Spatial cued response test 3 (scr 3): Try and add to the base map by placing a point where you think other places and landmarks are in relation to the geography department (A), the Quadrant bus station (B) and the coastline.

Spatial cued response test 4 (scr 4): Try and add to the base map by placing a point where you think the 25 listed places and landmarks are in relation to the geography department (A), the Quadrant bus station (B) and the coastline *(a list was provided to each respondent).*

Figure 8.5. Examples of spatial cued response tasks
Source: Kitchin (1995)

and locational cueing accounted for 20–30 percent of the variance between groups. In effect, spatial cueing provided a significant anchor on which participants could 'hang' their answers, but location cueing introduced bias by requiring participants to locate places when they did not know the location of those places.

Cloze procedure tasks are highly cued, spatial completion tests. These tasks require the respondent to 'fill in' a missing space: a non-spatial example would be a sentence like 'a dog barks but a cat _____?' Robinson (1974) and Boyle and Robinson (1979) extended this procedure to spatial tasks. A base map is covered in a grid, and the information contained in some of the squares is deleted. Participants are then asked to identify particular elements in the blank squares with the aid of the contextual information retained in the

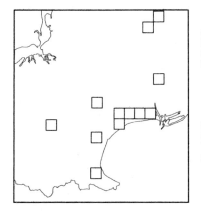

Cloze procedure test 1 (cz1): Write in the blanked out boxes the number of a place or landmark that has been removed. Write the place that number represents in the spaces below.

Cloze procedure test 2 (cz2): Write in the blanked out boxes the number of a place or landmark, from the 15 listed below, that has been removed *(a list was provided to each respondent).*

Figure 8.6. An example of a cloze procedure test
Source: Kitchin (1995)

remaining squares. For example, Kitchin (1996a) used the cloze procedure to test the cognitive map knowledge of the Swansea (UK) area by undergraduate students (Figure 8.6).

Other examples of the method include research by Beatty and Troster (1987) who asked participants to identify individual states on regional maps of the USA containing the outlines of the states. In a second experiment, participants were shown an outline map of the USA with the state boundaries missing and 48 points located across it. Thirty of the points represented cities, while the remaining 16 points were distracters, and participants were asked to match a list of the cities to the points and also to add ten features, such as the Atlantic and Pacific Oceans, Texas, Florida, and Canada. Lastly, participants were given a map of three states marked with their boundaries and 30 points and were asked to match 18 cities to the points. Burroughs and Sadalla (1979) used another technique called sentence frames. Participants were asked to complete a set of sentence frames that took the form of: '_____ is close to _____' and '_____ is essentially next to _____'. These were then used to identify main reference points in a person's cognitive map.

The cloze procedure tasks have the advantage that they can be altered to suit any scale, be analyzed easily, and they eliminate individual differences caused by drawing skills. There are, however, a number of limitations to the technique, because it imposes a structure on the data because participants are, in effect, forced to locate places in the spaces provided. The results of the exercise can also be influenced by the technique's parameters: the size of the grid used, the frequency of deletions, the sampling of the deletions, and the level of contextual information that is retained in the open squares.

8.2.4   Analyzing completion tasks

Spatial cued response tasks are best analyzed using bidimensional regression (see Tobler 1965, 1976, 1978; Kitchin, 1993, 1996a, 1996b; Wakabayashi, 1994). Bidimensional regression measures the degree and direction of any association between configurations (see Figure 8.7a) and gives a regression-like relationship, that is an extension of a product moment correlation and ordinary least-squares regression procedures, between two sets of coordinates (Tobler, 1965). The calculation is sensitive to rotations, translations, and changes of scale, and calculates how large these are (Tobler, 1976). Although reflection may be required to make the cognized coordinates best correspond with the objective coordinates, it cannot be accomplished using current bidimensional regression techniques, which are not sophisticated enough to perform such a task (Murphy, 1978; Gatrell, 1983). In bidimensional regression the parameters **a** and **b** of the standard regression equation become:

$$a = \begin{pmatrix} a_1 \\ a_2 \end{pmatrix} \quad b = \begin{pmatrix} b_{11} & b_{12} \\ b_{21} & b_{22} \end{pmatrix}$$

This translates into a bidimensional regression of the form:

$$\begin{pmatrix} u_j \\ v_j \end{pmatrix} = \begin{pmatrix} a_1 \\ a_2 \end{pmatrix} = \begin{pmatrix} b_{11} & b_{12} \\ b_{21} & b_{22} \end{pmatrix} \begin{pmatrix} x_j \\ y_j \end{pmatrix} + \begin{pmatrix} e_j \\ f_j \end{pmatrix}$$

where $\{u_j, v_j\}$ are the cognized coordinates, $\{x_j, y_j\}$ are the actual coordinates, and e_j and f_j are the residual errors. The parameters a_1 and a_2 are analogous to the intercept term of OLS regression and perform the translation, and the scaling and the rotation are accomplished by the matrix of b_{ij} values (analogous to the slope coefficient in OLS regression) (Figure 8.7b). A rigid Euclidean rotation is maintained by constraining b_{12} to equal $-b_{21}$, while constraining $b_{22} = b_{11}$ ensures the scale on both the axes is adjusted by the same amount and thus the regression grid remains equilateral (Murphy 1978).

A number of result variables are produced which indicate different facets of the goodness-of-fit between the real world and cognitive data sets (see Figure 8.8). The $\mathbf{r}^2$ value represents the degree of variance in the cognitive coordinates that can be explained by objective coordinates and is thus a measure of association between the two configurations. It is calculated as:

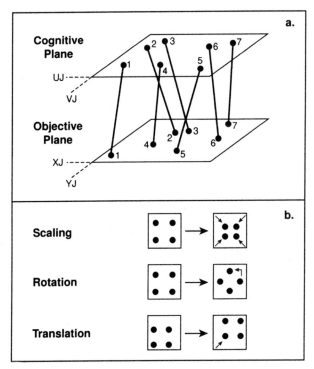

Figure 8.7. Bidimensional regression
Source: Kitchin (1995)

$$R = \sqrt{1 - \frac{\sum_{i=1}^{n}(x_j - u_i)\sum_{i=1}^{n}(y_i - v_i)}{\sum_{i=1}^{n}(x_j - u)\sum_{i=1}^{n}(y_i - v_i)}}$$

where (x_i, y_i) are the real world coordinates, (u_i, v_i) are the cognitive coordinates, (x, y) is the mean center of real world coordinates, and n is the number of points (Wakabayashi, 1994).

R^2 varies between zero and 100, with 100 representing a perfect fit. The scale is an index that measures the scale change needed to produce the best fit between the cognitive space and the real-world space. A scale value less than one indicates that the cognitive space needs to be contracted (reduced) to fit the real-world space; a scale value greater than one indicates that the cognitive space needs to be expanded.

The angle value is the angle to which the coordinate axes must be rotated to produce the best fit with the real-world space. An angle value with a positive value indicates the counter-clockwise rotation needed to produce a best fit; a negative value the clockwise

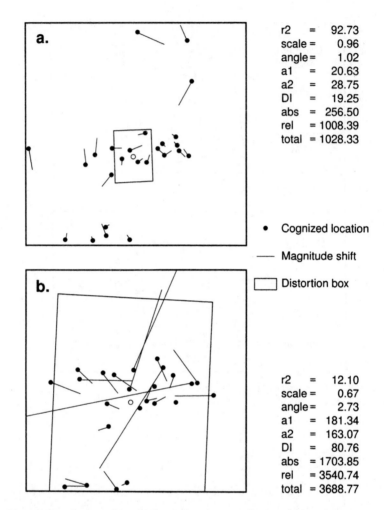

Figure 8.8. Output from bidimensional regression analysis
Source: Kitchin (1995)

rotation. The a_1 value is the horizontal translation, with a positive value indicating a west-to-east shift and a negative value indicating an east-to-west shift; a_2 is the vertical translation, with a positive value indicating a south-to-north shift and a negative value indicating a north-to-south shift (Lloyd, 1989b).

Each of these bidimensional regression variables reveals a different facet about the association between the cognitive space and real-world space and allows the reason for any differences between spaces to be determined. For example, r^2 values for two different individual data sets might be very similar but the two data sets might differ in terms of the scaling (scale), rotation (angle), and translation (a_1 and a_2) needed to produce the best fit. It is therefore important to examine all these variables to fully understand individual cognitive maps and their relationship to real-world spaces.

Waterman and Gordan (1984) have extended bidimensional regression analysis using the results to calculate the amount and nature of distortion in spatial products. The distance between the $\{u_j, v_j\}$ and $\{x_j, y_j\}$ coordinates is the quantity that is minimized by the bidimensional regression transformations. They argued that this distance is the most suitable basis of comparison between different spatial products. The distortion distance (D) is calculated as:

$$D = \sqrt{\sum (x_i - u_i{}')^2 + (y_i - v_i{}')^2}$$

where x_i and y_i are the observed x and y coordinates and $u_i{}'$ and $v_i{}'$ are the predicted u_i and v_i coordinates of a point.

Using D a distortion index (DI) can be calculated:

$$DI = 100D / D_{max}$$

where D_{max} is calculated as:

$$D_{max} = \sqrt{z - (x^2 + y^2)/n}$$

where:

$$x = \sum x_i; \quad y = \sum y_i; \quad z = \sum (x_i^2 + y_i^2), \quad n = \text{number of points}$$

The distortion index is, in effect, a standardized measure of relative error (Lloyd, 1989a) and can be displayed graphically using a distortion box, which indicates the orientation of maximum and minimum distortion for each point (see Figure 8.8). The distortion box's diagonal is the distortion distance, D. At a glance the box reveals the amount of distortion and its primary orientation and the length of its sides (D_1 and D_2) are calculated as:

$$D_i = \sqrt{E}, \quad D_2 = \sqrt{F - E}$$

where:

$$E = Q\sin(2S) + (P + R + (P - R)\cos(2S)/2$$
$$F = \sum ((x_i - u_i)^2 = (y_i = v_i)^2)$$

where:

$$P = \sum(u_i - x_i)^2, \quad Q = \sum(u_i - x_i)(v_i - y_i), \quad R = (v_i - y_i)^2$$

$$S = \arctan(22Q/(P - R)/2 \quad (if \ P = R \text{ take } S = \Pi/4)$$

As well as the distortion index, Waterman and Gordan's (1984) calculations provide measures of absolute and relative distortion. *Absolute distortion* refers to the distance between the real and cognitive locations. *Relative distortion* indicates the degree to which locations in the cognitive configuration are correctly positioned in relation to one another. The *total distortion* combines both of these elements. However, this technique can only be used to compare different cognitive maps of the same environment and the value does not indicate whether the distortion is large or small.

Cognitive and objective line-based data can be compared in two different ways. First, the *sinuosity* of a line, its 'wiggliness' or 'curviness', can be compared. The sinuosity ratio is calculated as:

$$\text{Sinuosity Ratio} = \frac{T}{D}$$

where T is the total path length, and D is the straight-line distance from the origin to the end node.

Figure 8.9 displays three lines representing the coastline of Swansea Bay. Diagram a shows the real outline marked with the position of the Geography department and Mumbles Pier. Diagrams b and c show Swansea Bay as drawn by two participants. To compare the spatial properties of the three lines the sinuosity ratio has been calculated. The coastline has an objective sinuosity ratio value of 1.53. Both the cognized bay drawings have values which are less than this (1.38 and 1.21), which indicates that the drawings lacked the natural sinuosity of the coastline.

However, the sinuosity ratio only gives an indication of how 'curvy' the line is. It does not describe the line's other properties, and two lines that look very different can have the same sinuosity value. An alternate method of comparing two lines is to convert them into a series of matching points for comparison using bidimensional regression. Each line must have the same start and end nodes and be divided into exactly the same number of equidistant segments. In this way two lines which represent the same feature can be compared regardless of scale, rotation, and number of segments. This method was used by Kitchin (1995) to analyze line data representing the coastline.

It is also possible to assess and compare the shape of cognitive and objective polygons (e.g., an island). Shape is a difficult concept

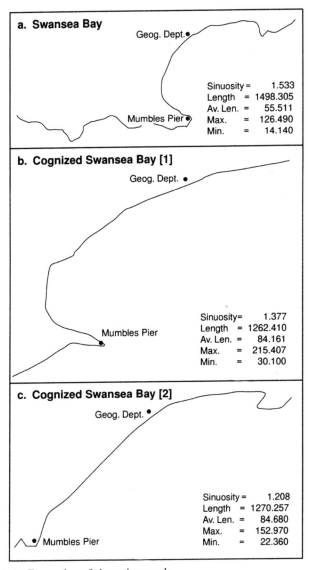

Figure 8.9. Examples of sinuosity results
Source: Kitchin (1995)

to quantify but several *shape indexes* have been devised. Most indexes compare the shape of an area to simple shapes such as circles, squares, and triangles. The most popular shape to compare a polygon to is the circle. In these indexes, the polygon's compactness is being assessed. The circle is the most compact shape because it has the smallest possible perimeter relative to the area contained within. A simple example consists of calculating the ratio between the perimeter length and its area:

$$\text{Shape Index } 1 = \frac{P}{A}$$

where P is the perimeter and A is the area of the shape.

The difficulty with this index is that index value will alter with size despite the shape remaining the same. It will also differ if the units are changed. Other indexes are more sophisticated using complex algorithms that control for differences in scale and shape. For example, one of the easiest to calculate is:

$$\text{Shape Index } 2 = \frac{4^*A}{\pi^*(L)^2}$$

where A is the area and L is the longest axis across the polygon.

These more complex indexes use simple measures such as the longest axis across the shape and the diameters of circles that can enclose the shape. Figure 8.10 shows the shape indexes of three out-lines of mainland Britain. Shape a is the real digitized outline and b and c are its cognitive counterpart as drawn by two participants. The first shape index shows that participant c's drawing was not as irre-gular as the others because the index is smaller. This means that

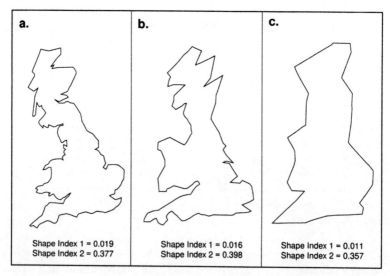

Figure 8.10. Examples of shape indexes applied to cognitive map data
Source: Kitchin (1995)

although its area was equivalent to the others the perimeter was much shorter. The second index is a measure of compactness. If the shape was a circle it would achieve an index value of 1; a hexagon has a value of 0.83; a square a value of 0.64; and an equilateral triangle a value of 0.55 (Ebdon, 1985). The results from the three examples show that participant B's drawing is more triangular than the 'real' drawing and participant C's drawing was not triangular enough. These indexes give a useful quantitative comparison between the outlines drawn by a participant and the 'true' outline allowing the investigation of polygon data. Sanders and Porter (1974) used such measures to compare the outlines of the African continent.

Cloze procedure data is best analyzed by calculating an *individual accuracy score*. This score is simply a percentage of how well an individual performed when assigning answers to questions ((100/total number of questions) * total correct answers). A score of 100 would indicate that all the boxes had correct locations assigned to them, and a value of zero would show that all the boxes had an incorrect place assigned to them.

8.3 Recognition Tasks

In recognition tasks, participants are usually asked to identify a learnt or familiar configuration. For example, a participant might be shown various building plans and asked to say which plan represents a particular building with which they are familiar. There are three types of recognition tasks. The first type are *iconic tasks*, which require the respondent to correctly identify features on a map or aerial photograph of a familiar area. For example, Matthews (1984, 1985) asked children to draw the route they took from home to school on a piece of tracing paper laid over an aerial photograph of their local area.

The second type are *configuration tasks*, which require a participant to identify which of several configurations displays the correct spatial relations. In Evans *et al.* (1980), participants walked routes through buildings and were then showed several floor plans and asked to identify those that they had walked through. In another study, Evans and Pedzek (1980) showed participants triad configurations, half of which were correct configurations of the places and half incorrect. They were either non-rotated or rotated by 60, 120, or 180 degrees. Participants were shown the configurations one at a time and asked to say which configuration had the places correctly located relative to one another, despite the rotation, and the reaction times were noted. Kitchin (1996a) used a similar method, but presented eight triads simultaneously. These were depicted in either the correct

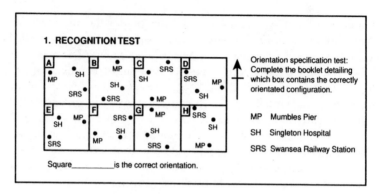

Figure 8.11. An example of a recognition test
Source: Kitchin (1995)

orientation or with orientations that were rotated, reversed, or both, and participants had to indicate the correct one (see Figure 8.11).

The third type of recognition task is one that requires the verification of statements. Here, participants are presented with text descriptions of a spatial relationship, each of which they have to declare true or false. For example, a participant might be presented with a statement such as 'The church is to the south of the museum, true or false?' Both Wilton (1979) and Ferguson and Hegarty (1994) have used this recognition method to investigate the hierarchical nature of spatial relationships.

Recognition tasks have the advantage of being easily scored, usually as the percentage of correct responses. As these tasks involve participants selecting from a limited range of choices, it is important to compare each participant's score with chance expectations, because some correct responses might be due to participants guessing one of the presented alternatives. Recognition tasks can be useful for populations who might not be able to describe or express spatial information in a recall task. For example, children might identify a familiar route on an aerial photograph more effectively than they would be able to draw that route (Matthews, 1992). Recognition tasks are also useful for investigating specific aspects of the structure of cognitive maps (e.g., Ferguson and Hegarty, 1994).

8.4 Qualitative Approaches to Studying Cognitive Maps

The methods so far described have been quantitative in nature. In other words, participants have been asked to express their knowledge either through precise judgments (e.g., estimating distances, or pointing directions) or in ways that are usually analyzed using quantitative methods (e.g., the scoring of sketch maps in terms of the number of landmarks or place labels). Tasks that generate qualitative data can also be used to assess individuals' cognitive map knowledge and abilities. Qualitative tasks usually require participants to verbally describe a route or layout.

Researchers have long been cautious about the use of qualitative methods to investigate cognitive processes (e.g., Nesbitt and Wilson, 1977). Such methods are limited because people have only a limited ability to comment on their own cognitive processes, and the usefulness of qualitative methods will depend on the investigation being undertaken. Nonetheless, 'think aloud' protocols have proved to be useful for some aspects of spatial research. For instance, they have been used to elicit how people make spatial choices (Gärling *et al.*, 1997), or how people learn spatial information from maps (e.g., Ungar *et al.*, 1997).

Qualitative methods have also been used specifically to investigate cognitive maps. For example, Taylor and Tversky (1992a) asked participants to give a verbal description to investigate the hierarchical structure of cognitive maps. They used the order in which places were mentioned to determine the clustering of landmark data. They did this by calculating the recall distance between every paired combination of landmarks in the environment. The recall distance was operationalized as the number of places mentioned between two locations during a description. For example, the recall distance between A and D in the alphabet would be two, as two other places would be mentioned between them (B and C). Accordingly a half-matrix of recall distances between all pairs of landmarks could be constructed and processed using a program called ADDTREE. This produced a tree-like diagram where a horizontal path length represented the recall distances between places and the branches represented the degree of clustering (see Figure 8.12). Using this method, Taylor and Tversky (1992a) found that text-based descriptions led to chain-like recall whereas map-based learning led to cluster-like recall.

In another example of the use of qualitative data, Kitchin (1997) explored the environmental knowledge and strategies of students in Swansea by interpreting the information they provided in semi-talk aloud protocols and debriefing interviews. These were analyzed by imposing an order on the data to reveal patterns within it. In this example, a series of structural frames were used to analyze the

Town: Map Drawing Order

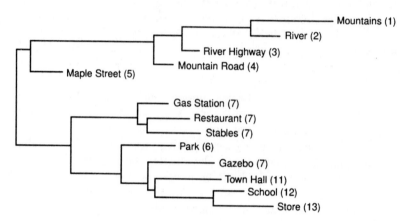

Figure 8.12. Hierarchical orderings revealed in text data

protocols. Structural frames are categories defined by the information provided by the participants. Every strategy of spatial thought identified was recorded into a frame (see Table 8.2). In this study, it was found that participants used a range of spatial thought strategies that were not consistent across individuals or across tests.

The above methods of analysis focus on categorizing qualitative data in terms of categories or patterns. An alternative approach is the use of *interpretative analysis*, which means that, rather than just identifying patterns, the researcher attempts to interpret the data to gain greater insights into it (Kitchin and Tate, 1999). The core of interpretative qualitative analysis consists of describing data, classifying data, and finding out how concepts interconnect. Kitchin *et al.* (1998) used this approach to explore the cognitive maps of 30 individuals, ten of whom were totally blind, ten partially sighted, and ten sighted. They were asked about their experiences of traveling in macro environments and their strategies of wayfinding. The interviews were analyzed using an interpretative approach to gain insights into wayfinding strategies and spatial problem solving, and provided rich descriptions of how people behave in space and how they think about spatial problems.

Collecting qualitative data can be useful, but such verbal protocols need to be treated with caution, mainly because people have only a limited insight into their own cognitive processes. Verbal protocols also have other limitations, because participants may only give

Table 8.2. Text analyzed using structural frames

	C1	C2	C3	C4	C5	C6	C7	C8
F1	pr	p	p					r
F2	pr	p	p			pr	p	
F3	p	r	p					
F4	pr	r						
F5	pr					p		r
F6	pr							
F7	pr	r	p		p	pr		
F8	pr	r	p		p			p
F9			pr		r			
F10	pr	r	p	p				
M1	pr	r				r		
M2	p	r	p		p			
M3	p	r	p					
M4	pr		p					r
M5	r		p		p			
M6	pr	p		p				pr
M7							pr	
M8	pr	p	p					
M9	p	r			r	r		
M10	pr	pr	p	p	p			

Key:

F1–10	female respondents
M1–10	male respondents
C1–C8	different strategies of spatial thought:

C1	imagining or constructing various types of maps
C2	referring to the coastline
C3	imagining the route or traveling between two locations
C4	using travel time to work out the separation between locations
C5	imagining standing at a location and 'looking' in the direction of another location
C6	imagining looking down vertically or obliquely
C7	working out where places are in relation to the current location
C8	just know—propositional coding

p	strategy used on a projective convergence test
r	strategy used on a recognition test

Adapted from Kitchin (1997)

partial reports of what they are thinking, or may simply describe what they are doing rather than the strategies they are using. In general, the complexity of reasoning in any cognitive map or spatial task is likely to mean that verbal protocols only provide partial insights into the reasoning behind the task. There is a further limitation in the analysis of such data, because the patterns imposed on it are inevitably the ones imposed by the researcher, and the analysis of verbal information always requires subjective judgments about the division of that information as the researcher must make decisions about the unit of analysis. The unit can be a sentence, a phrase, or specific factual references, and the choice of unit will have implications for the later analysis of the data.

One problem with qualitative data which is common to other forms of data collection, and has been discussed previously, is the issue of reliability. This may be a particularly serious problem with regard to qualitative data, because it might be the case that people do not provide consistent verbal protocols. Just like other methods of cognitive map collection, there is a need to check the reliability of qualitative methods. For example, to find out whether participants who are asked to give think aloud protocols provide similar protocols each time they are asked to carry out the same task.

Nonetheless, qualitative methods can provide a good starting point in areas of research that have received little previous attention. For example, the study by Kitchin *et al.* (1998) provided information about the real-life wayfinding of a group of people (those with visual impairments) whose actual wayfinding had hardly been investigated before, and the information gained from such studies can then be used to generate hypotheses for further investigation.

8.5 Aggregating Individual Cognition Data

So far we have discussed the analysis of individual sets of cognitive mapping data. However, researchers may want to compare the cognitive map abilities of groups of individuals, for example, men and women (see Chapter 6). Often this has been achieved using a strategy of *collective aggregation* (e.g., Magana *et al.*, 1981; Golledge *et al.*, 1985; Lloyd, 1989a). Collective aggregation entails aggregating each group's raw data sets together and creating a new 'average' data set (see Figure 8.13), which is then compared across groups. An alternative method is to use a strategy of *individual aggregation*: analyzing all of a group's individual data sets separately and then aggregating together all of the results and creating an 'average' group result (see

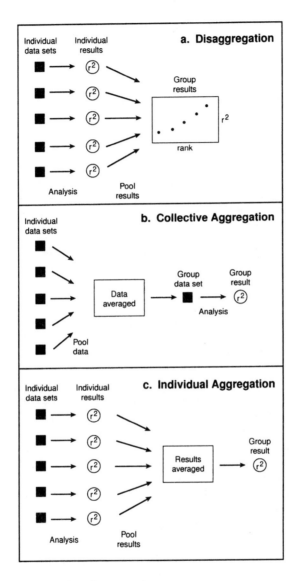

Figure 8.13. Strategies of aggregation
Source: Kitchin and Fotheringham (1997)

Figure 8.13). The group results can then be compared across groups. These procedures can be applied to all forms of unidimensional and two-dimensional data.

Kitchin and Fotheringham (1997) have suggested an alternative

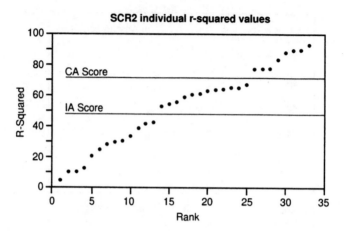

Figure 8.14. Comparing the results of different aggregation strategies
Source: Kitchin and Fotheringham (1997)

way to combine data, using a strategy of disaggregate comparison. For this, all of a group's individual data sets are analyzed separately and the results are pooled only for comparison (see Figure 8.14). They warn that the strategy of collective aggregation can lead to erroneous comparison of individual cognition (note: not place cognition, see next section). This is because the strategy of aggregating raw data together and then producing an average for each common data entry removes variation from the data sets. This can lead to an inflated set of results when the group data set is analyzed. Similarly, individual aggregation removes the variation in the pattern of individual results. Disaggregation avoids this pitfall, as all individual cases are still identified and the differences between individuals can be noted. For example, Figure 8.14 shows the collective (CA), individual (IA), and disaggregate bidimensional regression r-squared results from a spatial cued response test. The members of this group had a diversity in knowledge which the collective aggregate method clearly inflates (CA: $r^2 = .72$; IA: $r^2 = .48$). The most effective way, therefore, to compare groups' cognitive maps is to use a strategy of disaggregation using statistical tests such as a two-sample t-test to find out if there are significant differences in the groups' individual performances.

8.6 Generating and Analyzing Place Cognition Data

Place cognition refers to an individual's or group's overall cognition of specific locations. It is often investigated by researchers who want to find out which places hold more salience for individuals. Place cognition is also investigated by researchers who want to explain commonalities and divergences between participants in the same environment. For example, a researcher might conclude that Shop A is consistently located in the same location by all participants, but Shop B is much less consistently placed, or that all the distance estimates that include Shop C, as either the start or destination, are less accurate than other estimates. All forms of unidimensional and two-dimensional cognitive mapping data can be converted from 'individual' data to 'place' data through collective aggregation (see previous section).

For distance data, place cognition can be assessed by examining the variability of answers to the same questions across participants. Those questions with answers that have a higher standard deviation have a greater variability in response and reflect less consistent place cognition. The same procedure cannot be used on direction data, because direction data has a fixed circular scale. Instead, absolute and relative accuracy scores can be computed for each question for each individual and these can then be grouped into question responses before their standard deviations are calculated. Again, the questions with the larger standard deviations have more variability and this indicates less consensus of opinion amongst group members.

Place cognition can also be assessed for two-dimensional data. For example, Gould (1975) used an aggregate of contents analysis of sketch maps to create an information surface map that represented how many times a place was mentioned (e.g., how well it was known). He used the number of times each place was mentioned to create a contour map. This type of analysis gives an indication of the places that are well known, providing an indication of the general geographical knowledge of a group. Alternatively, a similar map can be constructed by asking participants to rank the saliency of a number of places. These places can then be assigned weights, and contours drawn to fit these weights (e.g., Gould and White, 1974). However, Thill and Sui (1993) suggested that this method is flawed because participants may have difficulty ranking large numbers of places, and they suggested that the rankings should be treated with fuzzy estimation, acknowledging the difficulty in assigning places to discrete categories, before the isolines are calculated.

Place cognition data from spatial cued response tests can be assessed by calculating the magnitude shift and standard deviation ellipse of each location. The magnitude shift is the distance and direction from the average cognitive location of a place to its

equivalent real-world location. The average cognitive location is calculated by summing all the cognitive estimates (u, v coordinates) and
dividing by the number of estimates. A standard deviation ellipse
represents the dispersion or variability of a group's cognitive estimates of a location and describes the scatter and shape of the estimates (Gale, 1982). The ellipse is centered on the average cognitive
location, with its size representing the degree of variability and its
shape representing the main axes of dispersion (Golledge and
Spector, 1978). To calculate the ellipse, the length of the shortest
axis, the length of the longest axis, and the orientation of the ellipses
need to be known. These can be calculated by: (a) producing a set of
transposed coordinates (x' and y') by subtracting the average cognitive coordinates (u, v) from the real-world (x and y) coordinates; and
(b) calculating the ellipse rotation (clockwise from vertical):

$$\text{rotation (R)} = \tan \frac{(\sum{}^2 - \sum y^2)^2 + 4(\sum x'y')^2)}{2 \sum x'y'}$$

then (c) calculating the standard deviations along the horizontal (x)
and vertical (y) axes of the ellipse.

$$\text{Standard deviation X axis} = \sqrt{\frac{\sum (x' \cos R - y' \sin R)^2}{n}}$$

$$\text{Standard deviation Y axis} = \sqrt{\frac{\sum (x' \sin R + y' \cos R)^2}{n}}$$

where n is the number of points.

By plotting the magnitude shift and standard deviation ellipses it
is possible to observe the place cognition of an area (Figure 8.15).

Place cognition can also be calculated from cloze procedure data,
in which a place accuracy score is calculated that is simply a percentage of how many of the group's individuals successfully matched a
feature to the question. A value of 100 would indicate that all participants correctly assigned a feature to a question, and a value of zero
would indicate that no participants had correctly matched feature
and question. Table 8.3 presents the place accuracy scores for 25
participants completing a cloze procedure test (see Figure 8.6). The
residual errors from this analysis can be displayed graphically to
illustrate the cognitive errors of participants across geographic space
(Figure 8.16).

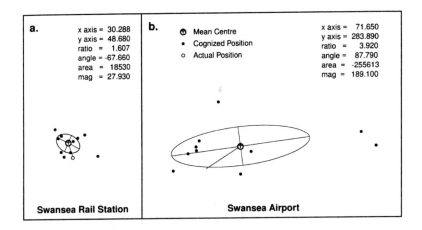

Figure 8.15. Standard deviation ellipses

Table 8.3. Place cognition from cloze procedure data

↓	place	1	2	3	4	5	6	7	8	9	10	11	12	13	14	15	box score	place accuracy ↓
1	Mumbles Pier	**24**	1	0	0	0	0	0	0	0	0	0	0	0	0	0		96.00
2	Railway Station	0	0	0	0	0	0	0	0	0	0	0	**14**	*12*	0	0		53.85
3	Athletics Stadium	0	1	1	1	0	0	0	1	0	0	0	*4*	**8**	6	*3*		32.00
4	The Vetch	0	0	0	0	*3*	0	0	*11*	**7**	2	1	2	0	0	0		26.92
5	Morriston Hospital	0	0	0	0	0	0	1	0	0	1	0	0	2	*10*	**9**		39.13
6	Sketty Park	0	0	0	0	1	2	**15**	2	0	0	*5*	0	0	0	0		60.00
7	Ferry Terminal	0	0	0	0	0	**19**	1	2	0	*3*	0	0	0	0	0		76.00
8	Oystermouth Castle	0	**21**	1	2	0	0	0	0	1	0	0	0	0	0	0		84.00
9	Hendrefoilan	0	0	0	2	0	0	2	1	0	0	**19**	0	0	1	0		76.00
10	Singleton Hospital	0	0	1	0	**16**	0	7	1	0	1	0	0	0	0	0		61.54
11	Leisure Centre	0	0	0	0	0	1	0	0	7	**17**	0	1	0	0	0		65.38
12	Swansea Airport	0	2	0	**18**	0	0	0	0	0	0	1	0	0	1	3		72.00
13	Clyne Halls	0	2	**22**	1	1	0	0	0	0	0	0	0	0	0	0		84.62
14	Guildhall	0	0	1	0	2	0	0	**8**	*12*	0	0	0	1	0	0		33.33
15	DVLA	0	0	0	0	1	1	0	0	0	1	0	*3*	3	**8**	*9*		30.77
		2	0	0	2	1	3	0	0	0	1	0	2	0	0	2		← missing data (26)

(the correct box number for each location is in bold; italics are large residuals).

Source: Kitchin (1996)

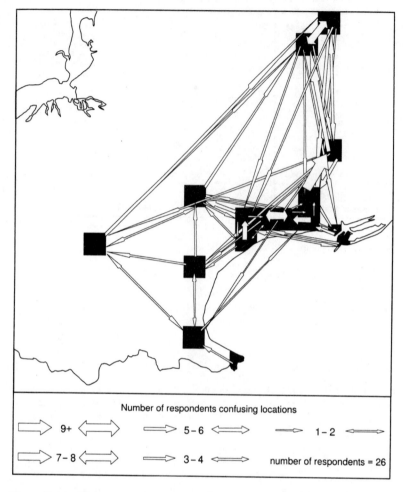

Figure 8.16. Displaying residual errors for cloze procedure data
Source: Kitchin (1995)

A similar place accuracy score can be calculated for recognition data with a value of zero indicating that none of the participants identified the correct feature/relationship, and a value of one hundred indicating that all respondents correctly identified the feature/relationship. Table 8.4 presents the place accuracy scores for 109 respondents completing a recognition test (see Figure 8.11).

Table 8.4. Place cognition from recognition data

	c	c1	c2	c3	c4	c5	c6	c7	n	accuracy score
1	56	**18**	1	1	1	**31**	0	1	0	51.38
2	83	**17**	1	1	0	0	3	4	0	76.15
3	73	**24**	1	2	1	7	1	0	0	66.97
4	64	5	1	4	2	**24**	**8**	1	0	58.72
5	33	**49**	0	4	**17**	1	0	2	3	30.28
6	83	6	3	4	1	0	**8**	2	2	76.15
7	17	**32**	2	0	**49**	1	1	5	2	15.60
8	33	**46**	2	0	**14**	**8**	2	2	2	30.28
9	79	**14**	2	1	1	0	1	**9**	2	72.48
10	27	4	0	2	**8**	**65**	1	0	2	24.77
11	68	**23**	3	0	0	10	2	0	3	62.39
12	75	**14**	0	4	2	1	0	**9**	4	68.81
13	59	1	1	2	2	7	**33**	2	1	54.13
14	59	**38**	0	3	1	1	1	1	5	54.13
15	79	4	1	**9**	1	1	2	5	7	72.48
16	73	**19**	1	3	2	1	2	3	5	66.97
17	88	7	1	4	1	2	3	1	1	80.73
18	55	**21**	0	3	2	**17**	1	1	**8**	50.46
19	86	**9**	1	3	1	4	0	1	4	78.90
20	80	7	2	**8**	0	6	2	2	2	72.48

bold = residuals > 7

c = correct
c1 = rotated 90°
c2 = rotated 180°
c3 = rotated 270°
c4 = correct but inverted
c5 = inverted, rotated 90°
c6 = inverted, rotated 180°
c7 = inverted, rotated 270°

Adapted from Kitchin (1996)

8.7 Convergent Validity of Measures

As described in this chapter, there are many ways to assess cognitive maps. Therefore an important issue is whether different methods have *convergent validity*. Convergent validity means that different ways of assessing the same variable (e.g., an individual's estimates of distances in a familiar environment) should all result in the same findings for that individual. However, in cognitive map research this is not always the case. For example, Montello (1991a) compared the distance estimates gained from five different tests designed to measure cognitive distance. The tests were psychophysical ratio scaling, psychophysical interval/ordinal scaling, mapping, reproduction, and route choice. Montello found that the results obtained from these tests differed in several ways. Not only did the distance estimates vary with each measure, but other factors (related to scale translation, ratio calculations, and the degree of non-independence between estimates) also varied.

Other researchers have also found a lack of convergence when using several measures to investigate the same aspect of cognitive maps. Bryant (1984) compared two pointing and two mapping tasks and found that there was little correspondence between the measures. For example, whether a participant pointed to the right or left of a location in the environment did not correspond to whether the same participant placed the location to the right or left of its real-world position on the mapping task.

Kitchin (1996a) compared the results of 13 different tests designed to measure aspects of configurational knowledge. Kitchin found little consistency between the accuracy of participants' spatial products either in comparison with the real world, or in comparison with their peers. For example, it was quite possible for participants to do well in a spatial cued response test but do poorly in a recognition test. Kitchin found other differences were due to the amount of cued information provided. In the spatial cue condition, participants were asked to locate towns and cities when many cues, such as a coastline or a road network, were provided. In the locational cue condition, participants were given a set of specific places to locate. Spatial cueing resulted in more accurate performance because participants were provided with a spatial framework. In contrast, locational cueing introduced random error, because participants were required to locate places with which they had different degrees of familiarity (see Kitchin and Fotheringham, 1997).

These studies indicate that different tests designed to measure the same knowledge can produce different results. Newcombe (1997) gave an example of this with reference to the development of configurational knowledge. In early studies by Kosslyn et al. (1974), children and adults were asked to learn the layout of objects placed on the floor of a large room. The objects were placed in four quadrants that were defined by barriers, some of which were transparent. After learning the layout, they were asked to rank order the distance between the objects, by considering one specific object and then estimating which other object in the layout was closest, then the next closest, and so on. Rank orderings were made between all pairs of objects and then multidimensional scaling was used to gain an insight into each participant's cognitive map. Kosslyn *et al.* found that children, but not adults, exaggerated distances between objects separated by transparent barriers. They argued that children exaggerated such distances because children, unlike adults, were influenced by the travel time between objects. In other words, the children's cognitive maps were affected by the functional distance, rather than the actual distance between objects in the environment.

Newcombe and Liben (1982) tested participants in the same learning task as Kosslyn *et al.* (1974), but used a different measure for distance estimation. After participants had learnt the layout they were shown one object that was placed at the end of a line, and a second object was moved along the line until participants said that they were the same distance apart as in the layout they had learnt. Using this technique, Newcombe and Liben found that children did not overestimate distances between objects separated by the transparent barriers, and they argued that there was no evidence that children's cognitive maps were based on functional distance. In this example, the methods used (rank ordering, or placing objects on a line) had resulted in different findings, and these led to different inferences about the structure of children's cognitive maps.

Different methods may place different demands on participants, and as Allen *et al.* (1989) pointed out, the skills needed to carry out a task may be specific to that task, and may have developed independently. In addition, if participants are aware of more than one strategy for carrying out a task, the one that an individual chooses may depend on that individual's cognitive style (Embretson, 1982; Just and Carpenter, 1985). In other words, inferences about cognitive maps that are based on a single measure should be treated with caution.

8.8 Types of Ecological Validity

Many different environments have been used in the study of cognitive maps. This is inevitable because people live in different environments. Whenever participants' established knowledge is being investigated, it goes without saying that the environment has to be one that is familiar to the participant, and this will depend on where the investigation is being undertaken (e.g., on a specific college campus, or in a particular building or city). Real-world environments are not likely to be ones that can be manipulated experimentally, because it may be impossible to make any alterations or changes to such environments. Only a few rare experiments have included the manipulation of real-world environments. For example, Heft (1979) examined the way that participants learnt a route through a biological reserve that included tracts of wooded and grass land. The route included 22 intersections and participants learnt it under two conditions. Some learnt the route without any changes being made to the natural setting, and some learnt the route after distinctive artificial landmarks (such as road markers, flags, and lawn ornaments) had been placed at each of the intersections. In this way, Heft attempted to manipulate a natural environment. The participants were given a single experience of the route and then they were asked to retrace it from memory. The participants in the condition with the artificial landmarks relied on these as wayfinding aids, but there was no difference in the number of wayfinding errors made in each condition. In other words, participants were likely to incorporate the artificial landmarks into their cognitive maps of the route when such landmarks were available, but participants were equally capable of using natural features when the artificial landmarks were not present. Heft's experiment provides some insights into how people might select landmarks when developing their cognitive maps, however it also demonstrates the limitations of manipulating real environments, because in practice it is only possible to add information to the environment (in this example, the artificial landmarks). This means that conditions cannot be equivalent, because one condition will usually include more information than another condition. In this example, in one condition participants had access to whatever natural landmarks they chose to encode, and in the other condition participants had access to the same natural landmarks and the artificial ones as well.

Researchers who want to consider the effects of different environments on the formation of cognitive maps have usually resorted to either small enclosed environments (like a building) or 'artificial' environments that can be manipulated. In the past the latter have included, for example, films, slide presentations, models, layouts of objects, or paths through rooms (for examples of all these, see Foreman and Gillett, 1997). However, the use of any space other than real ones raises the issue of ecological validity. Most environments used in experiments are likely to be impoverished compared with real-world environments. For instance, the real world is a very rich environment with a large amount of information, most of which may be redundant, but because of its existence people can be selective in which aspects of information they encode. The real world also includes information about distant views and landmarks, and perspective changes due to locomotion that are usually impossible to reflect in any more limited environment or in films.

Several studies have compared the development of cognitive maps in real and simulated environments and have shown that learning is better in real-world contexts. For example, Cornell and Hay (1984) compared how children learnt a route from seeing a series of slides along the route, from watching a film of traveling along the route, and from actually walking it. Children were given one experience of the route, with either the slides, or the film, or by walking it, and then they were asked to retrace it on their own. They had to retrace it in the same medium that they had learnt it (e.g in the film condition, the children were asked to say which way they would turn as they approached a junction). The children's recall of the route was better in the condition when they actually walked it than in either the film or slide conditions. In a similar study, Gale *et al.* (1990a) asked children to learn a route either by walking the route itself, or by watching a film of the route. The children who learnt the route by walking it learnt it more effectively than those who had learnt it from a film, and Gale *et al.* found that children learnt as much from one walk along the route as they did from seeing the film five times. These studies demonstrate that cognitive maps may develop more effectively from experience in real environments than from simulations.

If there are differences in learning the same environment through different media it raises the issue of why this might be the case. As noted above, real environments usually include much more information than simulations and this in itself may account for some of the differences in learning. It is also likely that greater information permits more (or more effective) encoding processes and strategies. As Heft (1979) found, participants in his experiment took advantage of the distinctive landmarks when they were provided. Gale *et al.* (1990a) found that the children in their study who walked the route often noted street names, but these were not legible on the film of the route, and children who walked the route had more opportunity to encode distant views and landmarks off the route itself. If it is the case that people select different information or apply different strategies in real-world environments, then any conclusions about cognitive maps that are drawn from research using simulations can only be extrapolated to real-world performance with caution. Of course, it may be the case that the cognitive processes that people use to encode information from, for example, a series of slides along a route are similar to the processes that they use to encode information from real environments. To establish whether this is the case, more studies are needed that make direct comparisons between cognitive map learning in real and simulated environments.

Given the difficulty of manipulating the real world, most researchers who have manipulated environments have done so in small-scale environments, or using simulations such as films or slides. Nonetheless, the results from these experiments have been extrapolated to the way that people process information in large-scale environments, and this raises the issue of ecological validity. It may be the case that the processes used for learning, for example, the layout of objects on the floor of a room, are the same as the processes for learning, for example, the distribution of buildings in a town, or that learning a route through a computer-simulated city is the same as learning a route through a real city, but only a few studies have been designed to specifically study this.

These studies that have compared learning in different environments have resulted in inconsistent findings. Regian and Yadrick (1994) asked participants to explore the layout of an invented amusement park (on a computer screen) and compared their ability to gain configurational knowledge from this layout with their configurational knowledge of their own college campus. Participants carried out similar tasks (e.g., direction and distance estimations) for both the park and the campus, and Regian and Yadrick found that for some measures (e.g., direction error) performance was similar for both environments. Rossano *et al.* (1999) asked a group of participants to learn a college campus from direct experience and a second group to learn it from a computer-simulated walk through the campus. When the latter group were tested on their wayfinding ability in the actual campus, most of them were able to carry out a wayfinding task without error. On some, but not all, of the measures of configurational knowledge, the group that learnt from the simulation had similar results to the group that learnt from direct experience. Although both the studies by Regian and Yadrick and by Rossano *et al.* found some similarities in learning real and simulated environments, other researchers have not found the same effects. For example, Richardson *et al.* (1999) asked participants to learn a building from direct experience or from a computer simulation and found that the participants who learnt from the simulation had poorer configurational knowledge of the building.

Although researchers are now beginning to compare learning in different environments, there have only been a few studies to date, and several of these studies have only included small numbers of participants (e.g., Regian and Yadrick, 1994; Rossano *et al.*, 1999). Until there are more studies, and more extensive ones, it is not possible to know whether conclusions drawn about participants' performance in simulated environments can be extrapolated to their performance in real environments.

8.9 The Use of Virtual Reality in Cognitive Mapping Research

One way round the quandary of using either the real world, with little opportunity for controlled manipulation, or limited environments, with little ecological validity, is the use of virtual reality. Virtual reality can be used to simulate three-dimensional visual environments so that the user can interact with the simulated world and explore it in real time. The simulation can include sensory feedback to the user, including the illusion of sound from fixed sources irrespective of the user's orientation in the simulation (Wilson, 1997). Most importantly, virtual reality allows the researcher to manipulate the type of environment, and this offers many advantages in investigating different aspects of the cognitive map. Complex environments such as part of a city can be created, as can very simple environments consisting of just a few features on an otherwise empty plain. The latter might not be an environment that is possible to find in the real world, but the simulation of such environments could be important in addressing questions about the development of cognitive maps, and between these two extremes of simple and complex environments any number of intermediary environments can be designed (Wilson, 1997). There would, of course, be no possibility of finding such a range of environments of graded complexity in the real world.

Virtual reality can be used to find out more about specific aspects of cognitive maps. As discussed in Chapter 3, a component in the development of cognitive maps is learning about landmarks, but landmarks have not always been defined clearly, and are difficult to isolate in the real world where any number of potential landmarks are available. But in a virtual reality simulation, landmarks can be added, removed, or changed at will, to examine the effect of such changes on the formation of the cognitive map. For example, Tlauka and Wilson (1994) asked participants to navigate through a simulation of a series of rooms. Progress from one room to another was through one of two doors (a choice of a left or a right door in each room), and the participants' task was to learn the sequence of doors to find a route through all the rooms. In one condition the rooms were empty (except for the two doors), and in another condition each room included a distinctive landmark. Tlauka and Wilson did not find any difference between the two conditions, which suggested that route learning was not dependent on the landmarks. This experiment is like Heft's (1979) study, summarized above, which included the real-life manipulation of landmarks, but unlike Heft's study, the simulation by Tlauka and Wilson meant that they could exclude any other potential landmarks in the environment. Other virtual reality studies have investigated the effects of removing or altering the position of distant landmarks in a scene on route learning (e.g., Jacobs et al., 1997), and, again, this type of study would be impossible in a real environment.

It is important to know that cognitive map performance in simulated environments is similar to performance in real environments. There is some evidence that learning in simulated environments generates the same effects as learning in real ones. For example, Tlauka and Wilson (1996) asked participants to explore a simulated environment consisting of a building and, outside the building, eight features. One-half of the participants in this experiment were able to learn the simulated environment by freely navigating between features, and one-half were presented with a static bird's-eye view of the environment. The participants in the navigation condition developed a cognitive map of the features that was not biased to any orientation, but the participants who had learnt the bird's-eye view encoded the environment in the specific orientation that it was presented. This result parallels the way in which people learn real environments from direct exploration or from maps (e.g., Levine et al., 1982) and suggests that learning from simulations may be similar to learning in the real world.

Other studies have demonstrated that participants can transfer information learnt from simulations to real-world environments. Wilson et al. (1997) asked some participants to learn an actual building, and others to learn a simulation of the building, in both cases by freely navigating round the building or navigating through the simulation. All the participants were given a pointing task in the actual building and asked to point to features that were not directly visible.

Participants who had developed a cognitive map of the building from the simulation were as good at this task as those who had explored the actual building. In other words, they were able to transfer information learnt from the simulation to the real environment. Other researchers have found similar transfer effects (Wilson, 1997).

The studies summarized above suggest some parallels in the way that a cognitive map can be developed from a simulation and from real-life experience, but as yet there are few such studies, and they have not always found such clear results (Peruch et al., 2000). To establish the ecological validity of virtual reality simulations, more experiments will be needed that make direct comparisons between performance in a real environment and performance in a simulation of the same environment. Nonetheless, virtual reality simulations offer an important way to investigate cognitive maps because of the ease with which they can be manipulated.

Virtual reality simulations are also important because they will provide the opportunity to study cognitive mapping through brain imaging such as Positron Emission Tomography (PET) and functional Magnetic Resonance Imagery (fMRI). These techniques can be used to find out which areas of the brain are functioning during specific cognitive processes. However, such techniques require a participant to remain still, and are therefore inappropriate for investigating processes that are activated during interaction with an environment. However, the development of virtual reality means that it will be possible to carry out brain imaging techniques with people who can be viewing and reacting to a simulated environment without themselves moving, and this offers the potential for discovering far more about human brain functioning in cognitive map tasks than has been possible before.

There may be some limitations in the use of virtual reality. For example, people may need to be physically active when learning new environments if they are to do so successfully, and Peruch et al. (1995) found that participants who actively chose how to navigate through a virtual environment learnt the environment better than participants who were only shown a predetermined route through that environment. However, other researchers have found that whether or not participants are active while exploring a simulated environment makes little or no difference to how well they learn it (Wilson, 1997). In any case, as simulations become more sophisticated, participants may be able to navigate through environments on motion platforms or on stationary bicycles that will permit a more realistic sense of movement and locomotion (Peruch *et al.*, 2000). In these ways it is very likely that future advances in our understanding of cognitive maps and the way they develop will come out of this new research exploiting all the experimental advantages of simulated environments and locomotion.

8.10 Conclusions

Over the past 40 years a number of different methodologies for examining cognitive maps have been developed. These methods take a number of forms, each used to measure a particular facet of spatial knowledge. Whilst these tests have revealed a great deal about individual and collective cognitive maps, at present we do not know enough about the tests themselves. As we have discussed in this chapter, tests can introduce bias into the findings, with the level of knowledge measured as much a function of the medium as individual cognitive maps. This raises concerns about the validity of the findings from studies that might have used tests that introduced significant variable error. It is essential that more research be conducted on testing the methods used to measure cognitive maps and other aspects of ecological validity, such as using laboratory measures to indicate cognitive mapping in real-world environments. One useful strategy that can be adopted is to use multiple testing procedures, cross-comparing results from tests designed to measure similar aspects of cognitive maps. Adopting more robust research procedures is, however, only one aspect of strengthening cognitive mapping research. As we have already noted, there is a need to develop sophisticated and integrated conceptual models to guide future research. In the next chapter we develop one such model.

CHAPTER 9

A Model for Future Research

Any research concerning cognitive maps should be philosophically, theoretically, and methodologically sound and these three should be strongly related (Downs, 1970). This is best achieved when the research is carried out within a model that provides an underlying theory with a guiding base of ideas and linked hypotheses. Developing such a model comprises two practices: developing a theory or integrating several existing ones, and adopting a research strategy. In Chapter 2, the models put forward by a number of researchers were summarized, and in this chapter, a new model is proposed. The aim of this model is to show how geographical and psychological theory and practice can be combined more effectively to provide a framework for future cognitive mapping research. Given the shifting philosophical underpinnings of geographical research, we devote the latter part of this chapter to issues relating to the integration of theory from behavioral geography and environmental psychology.

9.1 Providing a Theoretical Base for Cognitive Mapping Research

... we operate on two levels, both as model builders concerned with a particular aspect of our subject and as students of our entire subject. For some, there is but one level: their intellectual curiosity has shrunk to the size of a specialty. Many though are still concerned about this unsettling distinction and about the ways in which different points of view may be composed into a more comprehensive kind of understanding (Papageorgiou, 1982: p. 346).

Golledge et al. (1985) argued that, in many cases, cognitive mapping theories represent general positions rather than formal models, and that empirical studies are not often tied explicitly to formal models. Such a position leaves cognitive mapping research open to criticism. As Allen (1985) has noted, there has been no shortage of empirical studies, but these have examined hypotheses that are either too limited to be of general applicability, or too general to have been meaningful hypotheses in the first place. He blamed this situation on the lack of theoretical constructs used to provide the conceptual link between theories and testable hypotheses. Similarly, Lloyd (1982) noted that geographical research concerning cognitive mapping has been seriously hampered by the lack of theoretical structures within which meaningful research could be based and empirical findings judged. Liben (1988) further argued that researchers have been too ready to accept conclusions based upon early 'shotgun' empirical studies, which were then used as the foundation blocks for future research. It is argued that, at present, theories suffer because they are often too specific (e.g., about structure, form, or learning strategy) to relate to cognitive mapping in general, or too vague (environment–behavior interaction schemata) to give rise to testable hypotheses.

One possible avenue to strengthening the theoretical bases of cognitive mapping research is to integrate theory, methodology, and practice from the principal disciplines of geography and psychology. Our contention is that greater cross-disciplinary collaboration is important for the development of cognitive mapping research. Researchers in different disciplines have much to offer one another in terms of ideas, theory, and methodologies. We should appreciate that each discipline approaches cognitive mapping with certain preconceived notions and that collaboration will force many to re-evaluate their positions. It is suggested that if cognitive mapping research is to continue advancing at the current rate, and gain wider recognition within its parent disciplines, a sound theoretical framework should exist that unites the multidisciplinary base. This means that investigators have to seek out and develop appropriate integrative frameworks for study (Gärling *et al.*, 1991b).

Evans and Gärling (1991) argued that the integration of paradigms (e.g., environmental psychology and behavioral geography) is a fruitful venture because it forces a more synthetic analysis that may reveal points of convergence and divergence among topics of scholarly inquiry. They argued that integration might help to illuminate correct and incorrect models and hypotheses, and suggested the integration of research from environmental cognition, cognitive maps, environmental assessment, and environmental decision making. As Hanson argued:

> only through the process of communication among divergent points of view, will any semblance of convergence ever be achieved or maintained; through discourse the bits and pieces can be fitted into larger structures, and some

degree of order emerges from the mess ... At the heart of this process of change is communication (1983: p. 35).

There is little doubt that geographers and psychologists can learn from one another. Where psychologists offer geographers a path into understanding the mechanisms of knowledge development and cognition, geographers can offer psychologists unique insights into the natural and built environment, analyzing behavior patterns, and providing complex spatial and cartographic analyses of externalized knowledge. Lunt (1994) argued that psychologists could also learn much from the recent transformations within geography, both in terms of theoretical positions and methodological advances. He explained that geography has been rethinking the role of everyday life and personal identity in contemporary study with a move to social theory and cultural studies, and a move away from positivism, so that it has become more reactive to the wider social, cultural, and economic context in which behavior occurs.

For collaborative research to develop, an integrative framework needs to be formulated that can unite the ideas and theories from both psychology and geography. Hart and Conn (1991) contended that researchers fear developing such an integrative framework because it cannot be established easily using the traditional tenets of good theory-building through experimental research design. Russ and Schenkman (1980) argued, however, that such integrations form the basis of advancing scientific progress, and that scientific advancement is dependent upon quick, untested exchanges, ideas, and hypotheses, which can later be formalized and tested. But as Gärling et al. (1991b) cautioned, the basis and process of integration must be carefully established before any systematic collaboration is undertaken, to stop the misuse and abuse of theory and methodology.

Both environmental psychology and behavioral geography are products of the intellectual currents of the 1960s (Gold, 1980) and consequently share a number of characteristics. Both deal with the environment defined and ordered through human actions and, as such, both include people as an integral part of every problem. In addition, both are multidisciplinary in outlook (Gold, 1980). Furthermore, as Spencer and Blades (1986) noted, researchers in the two fields share interests in a range of issues, although joint research remains rare. The disciplines also share research techniques and are attempting to apply their research to the same types of applications. For example, work can be found in both disciplines relating to environmental cognition, environmental assessment, and environmental behavior (see Kitchin *et al.*, 1997b).

A key difference, on the other hand, lies in their respective relationships to their parent disciplines. Behavioral geography represented a challenge to the 'peopleless' geographies of spatial science and the excesses of the quantitative revolution, with the main impetus being the dissatisfaction with the stereotyped, mechanistic, and deterministic nature of many of the quantitative models being developed, and a realization that not everyone behaved in a spatially rational manner. Environmental psychology, in contrast, was a self-conscious attempt to apply psychology to new contexts and as such sought to study behavioral processes in real-world settings (Gold, 1980). As a result, environmental psychology has been assimilated into mainstream psychology, but behavioral geography is still seen as seeking such assimilation, despite many pieces of research adopting behavioral approaches and characteristics (Golledge and Stimson, 1997; Sell, 1994).

The most notable difference between geography and psychology is the scale of analysis. Psychologists tend to adopt a comparative and developmental approach using individual data and are concerned with the underlying processes of cognition of the environment and its phenomena (Spencer and Blades, 1986). As such, psychologists tend to concentrate manageable, small-scale spaces and environments. Geographers, in contrast, are more interested in people's behavior in the macro-environment, so that rather than asking the 'how' questions often asked by psychologists, they are more interested in 'what', 'where', and 'why' questions, and the reasons for the resultant location or behavior patterns, especially in real-world situations. Lately however, geographers have become more interested in these 'how' questions and have started to tackle them, explicitly integrating psychological theory into their studies (e.g., Golledge *et al.*, 1985; Lloyd, 1989a).

Indeed, on the basis of reviews of both disciplines (see Gold, 1980; Golledge, 1981; Saarinen *et al.*, 1984; Aitken *et al.*, 1989 for behavioral geography: see Craik, 1970; Proshansky and O'Hanlon, 1977; Stokols and Altman, 1987 for environmental psychology), there seems to be little problem with integrating the two subject areas (Kitchin, 1993) especially if a multi-data collection, multi-analysis approach is adopted that incorporates research techniques preferred by researchers in both disciplines. The philosophical underpinnings of environmental psychology and behavioral geography generally seem compatible and many of the ideas and research techniques that exist in both subject areas overlap (see Section 9.3 for full discussion).

The evidence for this compatibility comes from the growing frequency of collaboration. For example, there have been a number of edited books and journals with cross-disciplinary authorship and contributors (e.g., Gärling and Evans, 1991; Gärling and Golledge, 1993; Portugali, 1996; Freundschuh and Montello, 1995; Jackson and Kitchin, 1998; Golledge, 1999; and Kitchin and Freundschuh, 2000). In addition, several meetings have had the aim of bringing researchers from different disciplines together (e.g., at the Cognitive Mapping Symposium (Fort Worth, April 1997) over 60 geography, psychology, cartography, and computer/information science researchers presented papers and explored possible research futures), and the National Center for Geographic Information Analysis (NCGIA) has sponsored a number of multidisciplinary workshop meetings on issues relating to cognitive mapping. Therefore, it seems to be an appropriate time to put forward a more integrated conceptual model of cognitive mapping.

9.2 A Proposed Integrated Model of Cognitive Mapping

As described in earlier chapters, models of cognitive mapping have often been oversimplified and have not explicitly detailed the relationships and processes of communication between elements. In addition, contemporary cognitive mapping research tends to be fragmented (Portugali and Haken, 1992) and focuses on specific aspects of environment–behavior research. To gain better insights into the whole process of spatial thought and behavior it is necessary to draw disparate theories together into a more coherent whole. Hence, the conceptual schema outlined here is an attempt to provide a consistent framework for empirical research, drawing upon theories from both geography and psychology. The model described here is slightly different to the original version published in Kitchin (1996d).

The model rests on five premises. First, an individual is a decision maker, actively making conscious decisions, setting goals, and performing tasks which he/she then uses to respond to and guide behavior in the environment to achieve those goals. The goals are constantly changing based upon the information that is continuously acquired. Here, there is a constant interplay between perception and cognition. Second, behavior is a function of both the real and subjective worlds. Consequently, sometimes individual reactions are deterministic, in that one's options become limited and constrained. Such limitations can be imposed by environmental factors (for example, there may be only one safe route down a mountain); economic factors, such as the cost of travel; social factors, such as employment; or by other constraints, such as the built environment or time limitations. However, though these constraints are recognized, most of the time individuals have the capacity to use and process the information received from the environment to construct self-made decisions. Third, an individual is an active perceiver. He/she is a discriminating and active selector of real-world information, using past experiences and present beliefs to filter out the information required. An individual does not just passively receive information and react to this, but selects what is thought to be important and processes that information in the light of previous encounters and future expectations. Fourth, the whole system is dynamic and embedded. Information is constantly recycled and reprocessed, with many problems and scenarios being processed in parallel. The whole cycle linking thought and behavior is thus in a constant state of flux. Fifth, thought is both internalized and externalized (as with inter-representational networks, see Chapter 2), with previous actions changing the environment into which future actions are based.

Six main theories are drawn upon to form the basis of the conceptual schema: Golledge's (1991) cognitive counterparts theory; McNamara's (1986) partial hierarchical theory; Golledge's (1978) anchor-point theory; Paivio's (1979) dual coding theory; Tuan's (1975) schemata 'gate-keepers' theory; as well as the assumption that working memory constructs spatial mental models.

The overall schema proposed (Figure 9.1) is divided into three sections, all of which are linked and entwined. Like Neisser's (1976) schema, these sections are seen as being embedded rather than successive. There is no start and end point and, although portrayed as stages in a successive order, sub-units can be running in parallel to each other rather than waiting for information from another section.

The first section is the 'real world' and represents the environment with which individuals are interacting. Unlike Kirk's (1963) or Gold's (1980) proposals, a behavioral environment is not portrayed in the model, although it is suggested that such an environment is constructed within the working memory, based on a combination of the 'real-world' information and information from long term memory. The 'real-world' has been divided into two sources of information: primary (or environmental) interaction and secondary (or social interaction). These represent the factors with which

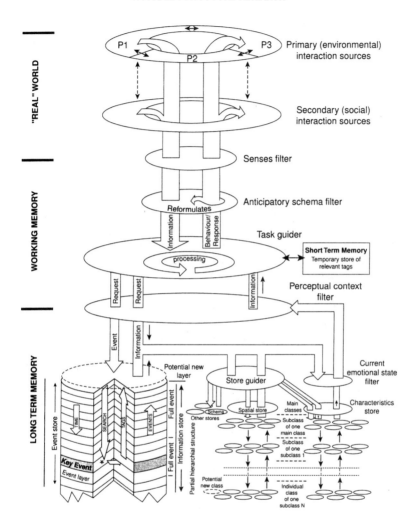

Figure 9.1: A proposed conceptual schema of cognitive mapping
Adapted from Kitchin (1996d)

individuals interact and which influence the development of the cognitive map, and form the information on which individuals base their spatial choices and decisions. The parts representing environmental and social interaction are shown as two different entities but there is interaction between the two, indicated by the broken arrows.

The second section, which is divided into six parts, is the working memory and this illustrates the process of thinking (both conscious and unconscious). First, there is a senses filter, which represents all five main senses as well as secondary senses such as balance and coordination. Each sense differs in its capacity to measure and report a current situation and, consequently, the information reaching the brain will differ depending on the particular scenario. Second, there is the anticipatory schema. This was proposed by Neisser (1976) and has the role of actively selecting received information and directing behavior to influence the information gathered. It is through this mechanism that an individual stops being a passive recipient of information and instead becomes active and discriminatory. The anticipatory schema is constantly being reformulated as new situations arise and goals are altered. Third, the task guider is responsible for making decisions based upon the information received from both the 'real world' and long term memory. It directs the thought process and controls the responses, and is equivalent to Charness' (1985) problem space. It makes decisions on the basis of constructed spatial mental models which vary in form and which are context-dependent. Fourth, there is the short term memory store, which acts as a temporary storage of information just processed that is deemed relevant for the current or forthcoming situation. Relevant information itself is not stored but a relevant memory tag is retained, avoiding subsequent searches of long term memory by providing an exact address. The fifth part of the working memory is the perceptual context filter. This is in effect the anticipatory schema between working and long term memory. It uses a current context or situation to influence the requests from, and the information received by, the task guider. The sixth part of working memory is the current emotional state filter, which works in partnership with the perceptual context. This represents the effect of the personality and character upon the decision-making process. It includes factors such as beliefs, needs, emotions, values, and personality, preferences, and desires, all of which influence decisions.

The third section of the proposed schema is the long term memory and illustrates how we store and access our knowledge. It is divided into two main parts, the first being an event store containing records of situations within a time framework. Each layer represents a situation and is placed within the context of a series of related situations with certain layers relating to key situations. As new situations arise they are added to the event store. The second part of the long term memory is an information store, which is partially hierarchical in structure and is controlled by the store guider. The store guider divides the requests into their constituent parts and directs them to the information they are seeking. If a piece of information is new then it is added to the information store.

The model is based upon the assumption that memory consists of a system of pointers linking a set of partially hierarchical network stores. These stores are accessed using schemata. The store guider and event store provide quick access to the information store by interpreting the tags and directing requests to the relevant information, like the relationship of an index to a book. Each piece of knowledge is tagged with a memory tag and a set of pointers to relevant information (Figure 9.2). For example, in the spatial store, information concerning landmarks may be given the memory tag A, monuments Aa, statues Aaa, and an individual statue $Aaa1$. Each individual statue has a set of pointer tags which tell the store guider where information concerning this individual class are located within the event or location store. The store classes pointed to consist of all the information relevant to that individual class and can include information such as distances or relative position concepts such as near/far.

There is no start and end point for the schema but to describe the process it is easiest to start with the input of new data from the 'real world'. Such information was gathered using instructions from the task guider on the basis of the previous situation. The information from the 'real world' first passes through the senses filter and the anticipatory schema before reaching the task guider. Before processing the data, the task guider needs to determine what the information consists of, and assess the situation. To do this, it simultaneously passes a request to the event and information store. Because the information is new it has not yet been tagged and both the event store and the information stores are capable of giving the information its first tags. The event store is a situation schema that is time indexed and which tries to find a similar scenario that will provide memory tags of information connected with that scenario that will aid the decision-making process. Schema are based on the notion that because we have limited abilities to process the perceptual world, we rely on automated ways of processing everyday data. Lloyd (1994) described them as prototypes, which act as skeleton keys to unlock, or identify, similar objects or information.

In the information store, the store guider passes any untagged information to the schema store to determine its general nature. The store guider then uses the tags from the event store and the schema store to investigate the information store to which the tag corresponds. If the tag and, hence, the information is new and unique

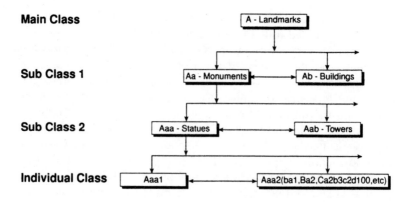

Main Class	Subclasses	Individual Tags
B-Roads	a - A roads	1 - Gower Road 2 - County Road
C-Districts	a - Continent b - Country c - County / State d - Town	2 - Europe 3 - Wales 2 - West Glam. 100 - Swansea
D-Affective components	a - Good feelings	1 - Happiness

Figure 9.2: A partial hierarchical model showing the memory tagging with associated pointers
Source: Kitchin (1996d)

then the store guide creates a new class, thereby producing a new schema class. If at any time in the future this schema is again encountered, and there is additional information to supplement the schema and the information to which it points, the memory tags are updated and transferred to an appropriate store. Every situation is added to the event store with significant events tagged as key events. After a time, other event layers fade and in effect become 'forgotten'.

The information from the stores is passed back to the task guider through the current emotional and perceptual context filters. The task guider can then either investigate further the pointers associated with a tag, search for more information, or make a decision based upon the information so far retrieved. Any tags that are deemed to be relevant for the current situation can be stored for immediate or future use. By further processing of the tags it is possible to anticipate future outcomes by using the gained knowledge to construct scenarios. The task guider uses the information returned from the long term memory store to construct either analog or propositional constructs (a spatial mental model). Once the task guider has processed enough information, a decision can be taken which affects the behavior or response to the situation: thought is externalized. This response also updates the anticipatory schema. It is possible, though, just to think about a scenario without interacting with the 'real world'. In this case, the task guider sets, and then investigates, a scenario without input from or output to the 'real world' (as in the ability to think, imagine, and daydream). The whole system is dynamic and embedded so that the task guider is constantly dealing with information and situations. It does not receive a piece of information and pass this onto the long term memory and wait for a response, rather it is constantly receiving information from the 'real world' and the long term memory so that many operations are being processed simultaneously. Because this model works on the basis of pointers and tags linking all processes of spatial thought and behavior within a dynamic and embedded system, it would be possible to simulate its operation as a connectionist neural network model.

As the proposed model brings together a number of theories to produce a more coherent whole, it raises questions about the relationships between findings in different research areas. These questions can become the focus of future research to help formulate a more complete picture of spatial thought and behavior. Indeed, one useful avenue of research will be to test whether the various components of the model are correct and whether they link in the ways proposed. Here, intervention strategies can be used, comparing and contrasting how expected and unexpected information are processed, for example, to test the role of anticipatory schemata and task guider. Another strategy is to design, as Lloyd (1997) proposed, experiments comparing neural network simulations with the performances of human subjects, and a series of these experiments could be developed to test different aspects of the model. Such neural networks would be limited for practical and computational reasons in that they are likely to be confined to the simulation of cognitive maps of secondary sources. They would therefore need to be complemented by experiments in which participants complete tasks in real-world environments. These experiments would, preferably, be longitudinal studies that would allow the learning process to be examined in detail and would allow the testing of whether the proposed structures, such as the event store, exist and how they might work.

Such comprehensive studies, where detailed individual profiles are constructed over time, do not as yet exist. Indeed, despite their general acceptance, evidence for most of the theories we integrate into our model is lacking, and based on a limited number of empirical studies. These studies often differ across participant backgrounds, environment, scale, and the measures used. As a consequence, although there is some evidence to support the theories we utilize in our model, the evidence is limited. For example, in our model we hypothesize a partial hierarchical structure, but we are still unsure about the encoding of temporal aspects in this structure, how different knowledge structures fit within this hierarchy, how imagery and propositions are stored within the hierarchy, or how aspatial attributive information is stored. The links between these sub-areas (e.g., learning, form, and structure) are still underdeveloped and we know little about the processes that link thought with behavior, and their relationship in different contexts. In addition, the relevance of the proposed schema to different populations (e.g., people with visual impairments) and to different developmental periods poses a number of questions.

For these questions to be answered, and the utility of the model tested, an effective research strategy which adopts elements from both geography and psychology needs to be adopted. Self *et al.* (1992) suggested that cognitive mapping researchers should adopt a research strategy which involves the coupling of passive laboratory exercises with active field exercises to form a multi-data collection, multi-analysis approach. Such an approach is crucial because, as noted in previous chapters, the convergent validation of current methodologies is weak. Holohan and Dubrowolsky (1978) suggested that using a combination of naturalistic and laboratory tasks would permit researchers to investigate whether tests of spatial knowledge actually underlie spatial behavior, and such a combination is recommended here as the strategy to underlie integrative research.

9.3 Critically Appraising an Integrated Approach

The problems and criticisms that an integrated approach might attract can be anticipated through a critical appraisal of behavioral geography. As explained above, behavioral geography is largely considered to have been marginalized and less assimilated into mainstream geography (rightly or wrongly) than environmental psychology has been into psychology. This is because environmental psychology represents an application of psychology to studying environment and behavior, whereas behavioral geography was a challenge to the way in which geography studied the world. Because cognitive mapping research by geographers is traditionally framed within a behavioral approach, it has been subject to the criticisms of behavioralism. If geographers are to once again return to a concerted engagement with psychology, as experienced during the early 1970s, then the concerns of doubters and critics need to be addressed. To many psychologists this section may seem redundant, but given the intended multidisciplinary audience we feel it is important for geographers to feel that a re-engagement with environmental and social psychology is timely and philosophically sound.

As noted above, behavioral geography is based upon the belief that the explanatory powers and understanding of geographers can be increased by incorporating behavioral variables, along with others, within a decision-making framework that seeks to comprehend and find reasons for overt spatial behavior, rather than describing the spatial manifestations of behavior itself (Golledge, 1981). It is argued that superficial descriptions of the natural, human, or built environments are not enough and for both an understanding and explanation of geographic phenomena an insight into 'why' questions is needed so that investigations become process-driven (Golledge and Rushton, 1984). The approach to these questions can be divided into two major branches of behavioral geography: scientific–positivist and phenomenological–humanist, but both are united in believing that 'we must understand the ways in which human beings come to understand the geographical world in which they live' and that 'such understanding is best approached from the level of the individual human being' (Downs, 1981).

Behavioral geography has, however, been described by Cloke *et al.* (1991) as a forgotten element of human geography and Gold (1992) has commented that behavioral geography is no longer presented as an approach with a major future in human geography. Gold (1992) identified three reasons why behavioral geography has not been fully embraced by the geographic fraternity (especially in the UK). First, due to structural changes in the late 1960s and early 1970s, young behavioral geographers failed to secure posts and thus a critical mass failed to develop. Second, as social issues came to the fore during the 1970s, behavioral geography was perceived to be inappropriate for examining them. Third, the philosophical bases of behavioral geography were heavily criticized by other researchers from different traditions. Interestingly, Wakabayashi (1996) notes the same pattern in relation to Japan.

Both humanists and structuralists criticized behavioral geography for its positivistic allegiances. They argued that instead of offering a viable alternative to the positivistic, quantitative revolution, behavioral geography has just shifted emphasis so that many of the criticisms of positivism still apply. Cox (1981) argued that the emergence of behavioral geography was emphatically evolutionary rather than revolutionary. Both groups criticized behavioral geography for over-emphasizing empiricism and methodology at the expense of worthwhile issues and philosophical content (Gold, 1992). Cullen (1976) argued that behavioral geographers blindly borrowed from the scientific paradigm, which then determined the nature of the problems to be investigated, so that the independent–dependent variable format was overused. Cullen suggested that the ubiquity of this framework was also its principal failing because it was almost wholly lacking in content, explained nothing, and generated no testable hypotheses when using behavioral variables. Such an approach also precluded the use of a whole range of techniques in the study of human spatial behavior, some of which could prove very fruitful (Cullen, 1976). He suggested studying mental processes at an individual level.

Ley, a humanistic geographer, further argued that the allegiance or 'appendage' to the scientific paradigm led to a preoccupation with measurement, operational definitions, and highly formalized methodology so that 'subjectivity has been confined to the strait-jacket of logical positivism' (1981: p. 211). Humanists disputed the dichotomy between subject/object and between fact/value and argued that research which accepted these dichotomies would only provide clues to everyday life, failing to 'conceive of life in its wholeness or for that matter of individuals in their wholeness' (Eyles, 1989: p. 111). Humanists argued that the subject and object could not be separated because of the intervening consciousness which imposes its own interpretations upon the objective world and thus affects behavior (Cox, 1981). Subject/object, fact/value become infused and inseparable and need to be investigated as such, so that the methods used by behavioral geographers are invalid, as they assume that the investigator and investigated have the same meanings.

Moreover, it was argued that behavioral geography ignored the contours of experience and reduced individuals to crude automatons (Thrift, 1981), systematically detached from the social contexts of their actions (Ley, 1981). It is in these contexts of a social world that actions originate and have their meaning and Ley (1981) argued that an understanding of such actions cannot proceed in separation from the social contexts to which they are bound. He argued that behavioral geography adopts a naturalist stance which sees no essential discontinuity between people and nature and gives human consciousness little theoretical status. Consciousness is thus seen as a product of external factors and this has behaviorist connotations. Consciousness, however, is seen as being fundamental to humanist approaches.

Further criticism focused upon the adoption of psychological theory and practices. Brookfield (1989) argued that the principal reason for the lack of popularity with behavioralism lay in its close links to cognition and its associated problems of measurement, analysis, and generalization. His solution was to study decision making in a broad sense, focusing upon individuals subjected to a variety of constraints in time and space (Walmsley and Lewis, 1993). Bunting and Guelke (1979) came to a similar conclusion when they suggested that it was best to observe behavior and infer mental processes rather than examine these processes and look for their manifestations in behavior.

Walmsley and Lewis (1993) argued that because of the difficulties in relating form, or cognition, with process, or behavior, behavioral geographers must be aware of the dangers of psychologism, that is, the fallacy of explaining social phenomena purely in terms of the mental characteristics of individuals. By concentrating upon the individual, behavioral geography is susceptible to the trap of building models inductively, beginning at the level of the individual, so that outcomes can only be treated as the sum of parts (Greenburg, 1984). This is particularly important because one of the main criticisms of behavioral geography has been its one-dimensional look at environmental behavior at the expense of economic, political, and social considerations. Gold argued that this attempt 'to straitjacket *all* areas within a strictly psychological paradigm' (1992: p. 240) is one of the fundamental reasons that led to disillusion concerning behavioral geography. It was argued that spatial behavior is not simply a function of cognitive map knowledge, but a whole range of influences and constraints that should be examined in context, and that the behavioral geographer must focus upon the multi-faceted situation in which behavior occurs and the way in which meaning is ascribed to both situation and resulting behavior (Walmsley and Lewis, 1993).

Many criticisms during the 1970s and early 1980s expressed concern for the lack of theory, poor research, and its applied worth. Most notable amongst these were Cullen (1976) and Bunting and Guelke (1979). Both argued that behavioral geography had done little more than observe rather than explain or understand behavior. Indeed, Golledge, a main proponent of behavioral work, has himself noted that early behavioral work was conceptually rich but operationally poor (Golledge and Stimson, 1987), stating that new and more powerful theories proved to be more elusive than expected (Cox and Golledge, 1981).

However, criticisms like those made by Cox and Golledge (1981) have been influential on behavioral geography so that there is now less emphasis on an individual as an isolated decision maker and more emphasis on the individual as part of a 'web' of social constraint. Indeed, recent advocates of the behavioral approach within both geography (Walmsley and Lewis, 1993) and environmental psychology (Canter, 1988) have acknowledged the importance of a more socially-constituted behavioral perspective, which, while focusing on the individual, recognizes the importance of the social and cultural context in which behavior occurs. The evolution in behavioral approaches is due, in part, to its increased psychological sophistication. Further integration will strengthen the bases of research by providing a united theoretical and empirical framework for research, avoiding some of the inconsistencies that led to widespread criticism of behavioral geography. Integration will further strengthen the psychological sophistication of geographical research and provide sophisticated spatial analysis and knowledge of the geographic environment to psychological research.

9.4 Conclusions

It has been argued in this chapter that previous models of environment–behavior interaction are over simplistic and have led to few testable hypotheses, despite the shift from an interactional to a transactional approach during the 1980s. It is suggested that a fruitful route to future research is through the integration of theory and practice from the parent disciplines of geography and psychology. A model has been described that aims to advance transactionalism through the inclusion of the underlying mental processes that govern spatial thought and behavior. The model combined five contemporary cognitive mapping theories from both geography and psychology. It is argued that this model can provide a possible theoretical framework for future research by providing a more holistic and complete account of environment–behavior interaction, linking cognition and human agency, and including environmental, societal, and cultural contexts. In addition, it raises questions about how we acquire, learn, think about, and store data relating to the everyday geographic environment. The model illustrates that geographic and psychological theory can be successfully integrated and it is suggested that the best method to test the questions raised is through a multi-data collection and multi-analysis strategy.

CHAPTER 10

Future Research

This book is a summary of some of the existing research related to cognitive maps and an attempt to merge the theory, practice, and conclusions of researchers from a variety of disciplines that have studied how we think about geographic space. Although there have been many investigations of cognitive maps, compared to the research into other psychological processes, spatial cognition has been underresearched and some specific topics examined have received little attention. As we have noted throughout the book, among those topics that have received more attention there have been divergent findings and theories. Indeed, as we have illustrated, there is still a long way to go before we fully understand how we come to know, learn, and process spatial information at the geographic scale. In this final chapter we consider a number of issues (in no particular order) that need further attention and which, if addressed, will more fully reveal cognitive maps and the processes of cognitive mapping.

10.1   Agenda for Future Research

10.1.1   The development of collaborative research programs

As outlined in the previous chapter, despite edited collections, cognitive mapping is characterized by its diversity and fragmentation with a need for more communication and integration of ideas both within and, in particular, between disciplines. There are signs that collaborative links are once again starting to be forged between geography, psychology, and other relevant disciplines and these links should be encouraged and fostered. This collaboration may encourage a re-evaluation of ideas and the exploration of alternative propositions. There is little doubt that researchers trained in different disciplines can learn from one another. For example, psychologists can offer geographers a path into understanding the mechanisms of knowledge development and cognition, and geographers can offer psychologists insights into the natural and built environment, and provide methods for the spatial and cartographic analyses of cognitive maps.

In particular, one link that has been particularly under-explored is that to neuropsychology. Although there is a large body of neuropsychological literature concerning the brain bases used during cognition, there has been little attempt to marry it to research by cognitive, developmental, and environmental psychologists and geographers. There will be important insights to be gained from linking the neuropsychological evidence and cognitive mapping abilities, and the development of connectionist models of neural networks offers one way forward. More importantly, the rapid development of brain imaging techniques now provides the best opportunity to investigate cognitive processes, and the use of virtual reality simulations offers the potential of using imaging techniques while participants undertake cognitive mapping tasks in simulated environments.

10.1.2 *Integrate specific theories into a larger whole*

There is a need to integrate specific theories of cognitive mapping into a larger understanding of the whole cognitive mapping process. At present, most holistic models of the cognitive mapping process are simplistic, and fail to detail the specific processes underlying the links between components. By failing to synthesize different specific theories into a larger whole we have only gained a partial understanding of cognitive mapping. The model presented in the previous chapter was an attempt to produce a more coherent model of the whole cognitive mapping process. Other models (e.g., connectionist ones and IRNs) also hold promise and need to be explored further.

10.1.3 *Dynamic, not static, models of interacting with space*

As both Heft (1996) and Sholl (1996) have argued, future models of cognitive mapping also need to be dynamic and not static, to acknowledge that spatial thought usually occurs while we are mobile and interacting with an ever-changing environment. As such, there is a need for future studies to explore the relationship between perception and cognition during navigation, because we do not navigate solely on the basis of cognition, but through a process of interfacing between perception of objects in the environment and cognition of macro-spatial relations. When mobile we encounter *and* interact with static and moving objects, which we have to avoid and plan new routes around. As a consequence, our travel plan is constantly being updated and we often radically change plans as a result of chance encounters and opportunities. In particular, the role of vision and the recovery of the invariant structure from optical flow needs to be assessed and its importance compared to information obtained from kinesthetic, haptic, and auditory senses. At present, much cognitive mapping research does not evaluate knowledge when mobile but at static points of rest (e.g., sitting at a desk drawing a sketch map). To what extent this reflects knowledge when mobile is unknown, but it probably reduces the extent to which (Gibsonian) perception is noted as an important process. More naturalistic studies of actual behavior, coupled with cognitive testing, may provide answers to these issues.

10.1.4 Methodological validity

As argued in Chapter 8, there is a need to understand more about the methodologies of data collection and analysis used to assess cognitive maps. Most of the tasks have not been subjected to tests of validity and reliability. This is in marked contrast to many other established areas of cognitive research (e.g., intelligence testing) where there is, appropriately, much emphasis on the reliability and validity of the measures used to test people. Researchers of cognitive maps have used a large number of measures, but have rarely considered the validity of these, and this weakens the whole area of research because there is a danger that findings and conclusions may be based on tests with little validity. Assessing reliability and validity is straightforward, if unexciting, but is important so that the results from cognitive mapping tasks can be accepted without doubts about the value of those tasks.

Many tests still introduce significant amounts of methodological bias. In many cases the nature of any biases has not yet been assessed. In the main, we know that methodological biases are introduced through spatial or locational cueing. In cases of spatial cueing, a participant is provided with a frame onto which they 'hang' their knowledge. In the cases of locational cueing, participants are either allowed to choose what knowledge to reveal or are forced to answer questions about places they know little about, thus reducing their overall score even though they may be competent wayfinders. Further problems can arise by using unsuitable methods of analysis. In particular, strategies of aggregation need to be used with caution because they can remove significant levels of individual error, thus inflating a group's overall score. Although such specific effects have been noted there is still a need to explore the nature of all tests and the specific and contextual biases that are introduced through their use. Two particular avenues that need to be explored further are the combined use of naturalistic and laboratory-based tests, especially as a device for validating laboratory-based results with real-world behavior, and an assessment of qualitative methodologies for eliciting spatial data.

10.1.5   Continued evaluation of current theories

The diversity of current ideas and theories need to be more formalized, and further experimentation should lead to a convergence in evidence, helping us to reject some hypotheses and concentrate attention towards more deserving theories. This process is apparent for one or two aspects of cognitive map research. For example, in recent years several studies have helped to formalize the theories relating to knowledge structure, and here the evidence now indicates that spatial knowledge is organized in a hierarchical manner. But other aspects of cognitive maps need similar clarification, for example to distinguish between competing theories relating to forms of knowledge or learning strategies.

10.1.6   Specific mechanics of spatial learning

While there has been a great deal of research concerning how we learn new environments, our understanding is still sketchy. Much of the evidence suggests that when learning environments from direct experience we anchor knowledge to specific places with some places gaining more salience, and that knowledge progresses from landmark and route knowledge to configurational knowledge. Recent studies, however, have questioned the basis of this progression and the alternative theories of parallel learning need to be assessed (see Chapter 4), and more emphasis placed on the types of learning strategies that can be used in new environments (Chapter 3). What we do not know yet is how the environment might influence the choice of strategy. Learning may be partially dependent upon the type and differentiation of environment, with landmark-based learning predominating in some areas and route-based in others. Learning strategies may also be a function of the mode of experience (e.g., walking or driving), and they may vary significantly with educational or cultural background (see Chapter 3).

There is also a need for further research into the effects of learning from different mediums. We know that knowledge gained from many secondary sources (e.g., maps) differs from that gained by direct experience, but we do not know whether knowledge gained from different secondary sources differs. For example, how does information gained from maps, three-dimensional models, verbal and written narratives, video, slides, computer games, virtual reality simulations, and in-car navigation systems differ. Further research is needed to establish the nature of knowledge gained from each type of representation, their differences, and their relative merits as forms of spatial communication.

10.1.7   Integration of types of knowledge

In the main, studies have sought to understand how we learn or know an environment, charting knowledge progression. Researchers have tended to concentrate on singular routes or areas, and as a result we know little about how we integrate together experiences from multiple routes. Our movements rarely consist of single static, independent journeys. Instead we travel across an area using a variety of pathways that cross and overlap. Our cognition of a whole area, and the ability to infer short-cuts, directions, and crow-flight distances, is dependent upon our ability to integrate this knowledge together. Several studies, such as those by Gale *et al.* (1990b), Montello and Pick (1993) and Jackson (1996), have begun to address the question of how we integrate experiences of two, three, or more routes into a coherent whole. This question considers the important issue of how people progress from route knowledge to configurational knowledge and it might be thought to be central to an understanding of cognitive maps. But as yet very few researchers have considered this aspect of cognitive map development, and even fewer have investigated it in real environments.

We also have little understanding about how information from different representations is integrated together. We gain spatial knowledge from a variety of primary experiences (e.g., walking, traveling in a car, flying over an area) and secondary sources (e.g., maps, television, narrative descriptions) and it seems unlikely that primary and secondary experiences remain separate cognitive representations. Instead, information from various sources is likely to be integrated together, and there is a need to determine the processes that allow such integration. For example, do people combine configurational knowledge learnt from maps with route information learnt from direct experience, and if so, how do they achieve this?

10.1.8   Development across the lifespan

There has been a decline in the influence of traditional theories like Piaget's for describing children's developing cognitive maps. To some extent this decline has been compensated for by the more recent research into the cognitive processes and the wayfinding strategies that children use. This latter research offers the opportunity to link cognitive map research more firmly to general theories of cognitive development and place the research in a better theoretical context than before. However, there are still very few studies of children's cognitive strategies and therefore we know little about how these change and develop over time. Further research into these would be useful, especially if stronger links were made between the development of cognitive maps and the development of other cognitive skills.

Some researchers (e.g., Hart and Conn, 1991) have suggested that longitudinal studies of spatial cognition would complement the cross-sectional designs that are the basis for most research into cognitive map development, and there is no doubt that in this, as in other areas of cognitive development, well designed longitudinal studies would be an ideal research approach, though the difficulties of carrying out such studies means that they may be not be feasible in practice.

10.1.9   Gender and individual differences

While a number of studies have investigated the effect of gender upon cognitive map knowledge and ability, the results from these studies are conflicting. As a consequence there is a need for studies that explore whether gender differences do exist and, if so, why. As there are some established gender differences in small-scale spatial tasks it would be useful to know more about the relationship, if any, between performance on such tasks and cognitive mapping performance. By the same argument, individual differences have been found on small-scale tasks, but there has been very little consideration of individual differences in cognitive maps. If there are gender or individual differences the identification of these will have both theoretical and educational implications.

10.1.10   Visual impairment

There has been a comparatively large number of studies into the cognitive maps of people with visual impairments. Nonetheless, all the issues that we have raised above with reference to the cognitive maps of people with sight would also apply to the cognitive maps of people with visual impairments. For example, issues such as the integration of information learnt at different times, the use of secondary sources, the cognitive processes underlying performance, wayfinding strategies in the real world, and individual differences are all ones that apply as much to people with visual impairments as to other people. One of the difficulties in interpreting previous research has stemmed from the fact that much of the early work into the spatial and cognitive maps of people with visual impairments took place in small or very restricted environments. However, recent researchers have demonstrated that it is feasible to test people with visual impairments in the real world, and therefore it is to be hoped that future research into the issues summarized above will include research that is carried out in real environments. Only in this way will we gain an accurate impression of the cognitive map abilities of people with visual impairments, and only then will it be possible to draw valid conclusions about the difficulties or limitations experienced by this group. If there are such limitations, further research would be useful in designing effective training programs to contribute to the mobility and orientation skills of people with visual impairments.

10.1.11 Spatial language

It is only comparatively recently that researchers have begun to consider questions concerning how we learn and communicate spatial knowledge through language. There are a small number of studies that have provided illuminating insights into the nature and form of spatial language, and how we process some spatio-linguistic information. For example, it has been established that spatial mental models may play an important role in the encoding and decoding of spatial language, and that there are links to imaginal thinking. However, only a few researchers have examined other aspects of spatio-linguistic information, and there is a need for more investigation into many topics. For example, whether spatial descriptions of different spatial information (e.g., routes *versus* maps) differ, how information learnt from language is combined with other spatial knowledge; how the use of spatial language develops across the lifespan; or whether there are cultural, gender-based, or individual differences in language, style, and form.

10.1.12 Scale

Two particular issues that have been largely ignored are scale effects and time. Several researchers have used studies at table-top, room, and building scale to infer cognition at a larger geographic scale. It is clear that we do experience spaces at different scales, from microspaces of the layout of a room, to the configuration of a building, to the spatial form of a neighborhood, to the matrix of a town, and beyond to regional, country, and continental scales (see Chapter 3).

Some of this knowledge is gained from direct experience and some from secondary sources. What is not clear, however, is how spatial information that is learnt at different scales is encoded and integrated. Many spatial searches and movements cross over scales: for example, when someone is searching for a set of keys he or she might try to remember the specific room in which he or she left them, before narrowing the search to that room. How is the knowledge of the spatial layout of the house integrated with that of a room? How is information in different representations at different scales, such as a map of a region, a narrative description of a town, and experience of a neighborhood, dealt with? These are all questions that it would be useful to address.

10.1.13   Time

Just as we experience spaces at different scales, we live and move through a time–space continuum. Time is important for two reasons. First, time relates to *when*; the specific time in which a place is experienced, and spatial products *are* spatio–temporal products (they are of a specific space in time). Places experienced at different times might lead to different cognitions. At night, when visual stimuli are darkened the effectiveness of spatial cues may be lessened; during rush hour cognitive attention may be stretched and engaged in other tasks such as obstacle avoidance rather than spatial layout. Second, the time of travel—the speed of *mobility*—may lead to different cognitions. For example, driving quickly through an area may provide little time to remember spatial information, but walking slowly may allow time to note the relative locations of objects in the environment. At present, very few studies have considered the interrelationship between space and time in cognitive maps.

10.1.14   Applied Research

Cognitive mapping has been a field of promised real-world applications. Cognitive map research has the potential to help improve planning, geographic education, maps and Geographical Information Systems, navigation and orientation aids, and search-and-rescue strategies. But as yet, cognitive map research has had very little input into such applied areas. The reasons for this center on the perceived lack of potential clients, and the fact that little attempt has been made to develop guidelines for planners and educationalists and others who might benefit from an awareness of the research. It is only recently that this need has started to be addressed, especially in relation to maps and Geographical Information Systems, and navigation and orientation aids. Cognitive theory is now starting to appear in textbooks on map-making (e.g., MacEachren, 1995) and there are now some specific examples of the application of cognitive map research—for example, the development of personal guidance systems for people with visual impairments (Golledge *et al.*, 1996).

10.2 Final Words

The cognition of geographic space is fundamental to our daily living. Without the ability to move in a directed fashion through the environment our lives would be impossible. But despite its central role in daily functioning, cognitive map abilities have been relatively underresearched (especially in comparison with other essential cognitive processes). In this book we have tried to synthesize some of what we currently know concerning how we think about geographic space and the ways in which this underlies spatial behavior and decision and choice making. As outlined above, there are still many questions that need to be answered to fully understand cognitive maps. Central to the construction of this understanding are collaboration between researchers in different disciplines, a strengthening of methodological validity and integrity, and an agenda which promotes the integration of ideas and theory across areas and questions of study. As explained above, there are signs that such an agenda is being adopted and the study of cognitive maps will develop as the importance of this research is increasingly recognized.

References

Abu-Obeid, N. (1998) Abstract and scenographic imagery: The effect of environmental form on wayfinding. *Journal of Environmental Psychology* 18, 159–73.

Aginsky V., Harris, C., Rensink, R. and Beusmans, J. (1997) Two strategies for learning in a route driving simulator. *Journal of Environmental Psychology* 17, 317–31.

Aitken, S.C. (1991) Person–environment theories in contemporary perceptual and behavioral geography 1: personality, attitudinal and spatial choice theories. *Progress in Human Geography* 15, 179–93.

Aitken, S. (1992) Person–environment theories in contemporary perceptual and behavioral geography 1: the influence of ecological, environmental learning, societal/structural, transactional and transformational theories. *Progress in Human Geography* 16, 553–62.

Aitken, S.C. and Bjorkland, E.M. (1988) Transactional and transformational theories in behavioral geography. *Professional Geographer* 40, 54–64.

Aitken, S.C., Cutter, S.L., Foote, K.E. and Sell, J.L. (1989). Environmental perception and behavioral geography. In Wilmott, C. and Gaille, G. (eds), *Geography in America*, London: Merrill, pp. 218–38.

Aitken, S.C. and Prosser, R. (1990) Residents' spatial knowledge of neighborhood continuity and form. *Geographical Analysis* 22, 301–25.

Allen, G. (1981) A developmental perspective on the effects of 'subdividing' macrospatial experience. *Journal Experimental Psychology: Human learning and Memory* 7, 120–32.

Allen, G. (1985) Strengthening weak links in the study of the development of macrospatial cognition. In Cohen, R. (ed.), *The Development of Spatial Cognition*, Hillsdale, NJ: Erlbaum Lawrence, pp. 301–21.

Allen, G.L. (1999) Spatial abilities, cognitive maps, and wayfinding: Bases for individual differences in spatial cognition and behavior. In Golledge, R.G. (ed.), *Wayfinding Behavior, Cognitive Mapping and Other Spatial Processes*, Baltimore: John Hopkins pp. 46–80.

Allen, G.L., Kirasic, K.C. (1996) Predicting environmental learning from spatial abilities: An indirect route. *Intelligence* 22, 327–55.

Allen, G.L., Kirasic, K.C. and Beard, R.L. (1989) Children's expressions of spatial knowledge. *Journal of Experimental Child Psychology* 48, 114–30.

Allen, G.L., Kirasic, K.C., Siegel, A.W. and Herman, J.F. (1979) Developmental issues in cognitive mapping: The selection and utilization of landmarks. *Child Development* 50, 1062–70.

Allen, G., Siegel, A.W. and Rosinski, R.R. (1978) The role of perceptual context in structuring spatial knowledge. *Journal of Experimental Psychology: Human learning and Memory* 4, 617–30.

Altman, I. and Rogoff, B. (1987) World views in psychology: trait, interactional, organismic and transactional perspectives. In Stokols, D. and Altman, I., (eds), *Handbook of Environmental Psychology*, Volume 1, New York: John Wiley and Sons, 1–40.

Anooshian, L.J. and Seibert, P.S. (1996) Diversity within spatial cognition: Memory processes underlying place recognition. *Applied Cognitive Psychology* 10, 281–91.

Anooshian, L.J. and Siegel, A.W. (1985) From cognitive to procedural mapping. In Brainerd, C.J. and Pressley, M. (eds), *Basic Processes in Memory Development: Progress in Cognitive Development Research*. New York: Springer-Verlag, pp. 47–101.

Anooshian, L.J. and Young, D. (1981) Developmental changes in cognitive maps of a similar neighborhood. *Child Development* 52, 341–48.

Antes, J.R., McBridge, R.B. and Collins, J.D. (1988) The effect of a new city traffic route on the cognitive maps of its residents. *Environment and Behavior* 20, 75–91.

Appleyard, D. (1969) Why buildings are known: a predictive tool for architects and planners. *Environment and Behavior*, 2, 131–56.

Appleyard, D. (1970) Styles and methods of structuring a city. *Environment and Behavior* 2, 100–117.

Aubrey, J.B. and Dobbs, A.R. (1990) Age and sex differences in the mental realignment of maps. *Experimental Aging Research 16*, 133–39.

Axia, G., Bremner, J.G., Deluca, P. and Andreasen, G. (1998) Children drawing Europe: The effects of nationality, age and teaching. *British Journal of Developmental Psychology* 16, 423–37.

Axia, G., Peron, E.M. and Baroni, M.R. (1991). Environmental assessment across the life span. In Gärling, T. and Evans, G.W. (eds), *Environment, Cognition and Action—An Integrated Approach*, New York: Oxford University Press, pp. 221–44.

Baird, J.C. (1979) Studies of the cognitive representation of spatial relations I: overview. *Journal of Experimental Psychology: General* 108, 90–1.

Baird, J.C., Merrill, A.A. and Tannenbaum, J. (1979) Studies of the cognitive representation of spatial relations II : A familiar environment. *Journal of Experimental Psychology* 108, 92–8.

Baird, J.C, Wagner, M. and Noma, E. (1982). Impossible cognitive spaces. *Geographical Analysis* 14, 204–16.

Barrash, J. (1994). Age-related decline in route learning ability. *Developmental Neuropsychology* 10, 189–201.

Barrett, M. and Farroni, T. (1996) English and Italian children's knowledge of European geography. *British Journal of Developmental Psychology* 14, 257–73.

Barrett, M. and Short, J. (1992) Images of European people in a group of 5–10 year old English schoolchildren. *British Journal of Developmental Psychology*, 10, 319–28.

Beatty, W. and Troster, A. (1987) Gender differences in geographical knowledge. *Sex Roles*, 16, 565–89.

Beck, R.J. and Wood, D. (1976a) Comparative developmental analysis of individual and aggregated cognitive maps of London. In Moore, G.T. and Golledge, R.G. (eds), *Environmental Knowing*, Stroudsberg, PA: Dowden, Hutchinson and Ross, pp. 173–84.

Beck, R.J. and Wood, D. (1976b) Cognitive transformations from urban geographic fields to mental maps. *Environment and Behavior* 8, 199–238.

Berry, J.W. (1971) Ecological and cultural factors in spatial perceptual development. *Canadian Journal of Behavioral Sciences*, 3, 324–336.

Bettis, N.C. (1974) *An Assessment of the Geographical Knowledge and Understanding of Fifth-grade Students in Michigan*. Doctoral dissertation, Michigan State University.

Biel, A. (1982) Children's spatial representation of their neighborhood: A step towards a general spatial competence. *Journal of Environmental Psychology* 2, 193–200.

Bigelow, A. (1991) Spatial mapping of familiar locations in blind children. *Journal of Visual Impairment and Blindness* 85, 113–17.

Bigelow, A.E. (1996) Blind and sighted children's spatial knowledge of their home environments. *International Journal of Behavioral Development* 19, 797–816.

Blades, M. (1990) The reliability of data collected from sketch maps. *Journal of Environmental Psychology* 10, 327–39.

Blades, M. (1991a) Wayfinding theory and research: The need for a new approach. In Mark, D.M. and Frank, A.U. (eds), *Cognitive and Linguistic Aspects of Geographic Space*, Dordrecht: Kluwer, pp. 137–165.

Blades, M. (1991b) The development of the abilities required to understand spatial representations. In Mark, D.M. and Frank, A.U. (eds), *Cognitive and Linguistic Aspects of Geographic Space*, Dordrecht: Kluwer, pp. 81–115.

Blades, M. (1997) Research paradigms for investigating children's wayfinding. In Foreman, N. and Gillett, R. (eds), *Handbook of Spatial Research Paradigms and Methodologies, Volume 1*, Hillsdale, NJ: Erlbaum, pp.103–29.

Blades, M. and Banham, J. (1990) Children's memory in an environmental learning task. *Journal of Environmental Education and Information*, 9, 119–31.

Blades, M., Blaut, J., Davizeh, Z., Elguea, S., Sowden, S., Soni, D., Spencer, C., Stea, D., Surajpauli, R. and Uttal, D. (1998) A cross-cultural study of young children's mapping abilities. *Transactions of the Institute of British Geographers* 23, 269–77.

Blades, M. and Medlicott, L. (1992) The development of children's ability to give directions from maps. *Journal of Environmental Psychology* 12, 175–85.

Blades, M. and Spencer, C. (1994) The development of children's ability to use spatial representations. *Advances in Child Development and Behavior* 25, 157–99.

Blades, M, Ungar, S. and Spencer, C. (1999) Map using by adults with visual impairments. *Professional Geographer* 51, 539–53.

Blaut, J.M. (1987) Notes towards a theory of mapping behavior. *Children's Environments Quarters*, 4, 27–34.

Blaut, J.M. (1991) Natural mapping. *Transactions of the Institute of British Geographers* 16, 55–74.

Blaut, J.M. (1997) The mapping abilities of young children. Children can. *Annals of the Association of American Geographers* 87, 152–58.

Bloch, H. and Morange, F. (1997) Organizing gestures in external space: Orienting and reaching. In Foreman, N. and Gillett, R. (eds), *Handbook of Spatial Research Paradigms and Methodologies, Volume 1*, Hove, Sussex: Psychology Press.

Blough, P. and Slavin, L. (1987) Reaction-time assessments of gender differences in visual–spatial performance. *Perceptuion and Psychophysics* 1, 276–81.

Bonsall, P.W. (1992) The influence of route guidance advice on route choice in urban networks. *Transportation* 19, 1–23.

Boyle, M.J. and Robinson, M.E. (1979) Cognitive mapping and understanding. In Herbert, D.T. and Johnston, R.J. (eds), *Geography and the Urban Environment: Progress in Research and Applications* 2, London: Wiley, pp. 59–82.

Brambring, M. (1982) Language and geographic orientation for the blind. In Jarvella, R.J. and Klein, W. (eds), *Speech, Place and Action: Studies in Deixis and Related Topics*, Chichester: Wiley, pp. 203–18.

Brantingham, P.J. and Brantingham, P.L. (1981) Notes on the geometry of crime. In Brantingham, P. and Brantingham, P.L. (eds), *Environmental Criminology*. Beverly Hills, California: Sage, pp. 27–54.

Bratfisch, D. (1969) A further study of the relation between subjective distance and emotional involvement. *Acta Psychologica* 29, 244–55.

Bremner, J.G. and Andreasen, G. (1999) Young children's ability to use maps and models to find ways in novel spaces. *British Journal of Developmental Psychology* 16, 197–218.

Brewer, W.F. and Treyens, J.C. (1981) The role of schemata in memory for places. *Cognitive Psychology* 13, 207–30.

Briggs, R. (1973a) Urban distance cognition. In Downs, R.M. and Stea, D. (eds), *Image and Environment*, Chicago: Aldine, pp. 361–88.

Briggs, R. (1973b) On the relationship between cognitive and objective distance. In Preisner, W.F.E. (ed.), *Environmental Design Research* 2, Stroudsberg, PA: Dowden, Hutchinson and Ross, pp. 186–192.

Briggs, R. (1976) Methodologies for the measurement of cognitive distance. In Moore, G.T and Golledge, R.G. (eds), *Environmental Knowing*, Stroudsberg, PA: Dowden, Hutchinson and Ross, pp. 325–34.

Brookfield, H.C. (1989) The behavioral environment: how, what for and whose? In Boal, F.W. and Livingstone, D.N. (eds) *The Behavioral Environment* London: Routledge, pp. 311–28.

Brown, M.A. and Broadway. M.J. (1981) The cognitive maps of adolescents: confusion about inter-town distance. *Professional Geographer* 33, 315–25.

Bryant, K.J. (1984) Methodological convergence as an issue within environmental cognition research, *Journal of Environmental Psychology* 4, 43–60.

Bunting, T. and Guelke, L. (1979) Behavioral and perception geography: a critical appraisal. *Annals of the Association of American Geographers*, 69, 448–62.

Burnett, P. and Briggs, R. (1975) *Distance cognition in intra-urban movement.* Paper presented at the Conference of Association of American Geographers, Carbondale, Illinois.

Burroughs, W. and Sadalla, E. (1979) Asymmetries in distance cognition. *Geographical Analysis* 11, 414–21.

Butler, D.L, Acquino, A.L, Hissong, A.A. and Scott, P.A. (1993) Wayfinding by newcomers in a complex building. *Human Factors*, 35, 159–73.

Buttenfield, B.P. (1986) Comparing distortion on sketch maps and MDS configurations. *Professional Geographer*, 38, 238–46.

Byrne, R.W. and Salter, E. (1983) Distances and directions in cognitive maps of the blind. *Canadian Journal of Psychology*, 37, 293–9.

Cadwallader, M.T. (1973) A methodological examination of cognitive distance. In Preisner, W.F.E. (ed.), *Environmental Design Research* 2, Stroudsberg, PA: Dowden, Hutchinson and Ross, pp. 193–199.

Cadwallader, M.T. (1976) Cognitive distance in intra-urban space. In Moore, G.T. and Golledge, R.G. (eds), *Environmental Knowing*, Stroudsberg, PA: Dowden, Hutchinson and Ross, pp. 316–324.

Cadwallader, M.T. (1979) Problems in cognitive distance and their implications to cognitive mapping. *Environment and Behavior* 11, 559–76.

Cammack, R. and Lloyd, R. (1993) *Connected space: Regional neural networks*. Paper presented at the Annual Meeting of the Association of American Geographers, Atlanta, Georgia.

Canter, D. (1977) *The Psychology of Place*, London: Architectural Press.

Canter, D. (1988) Environmental (social) psychology: an emerging synthesis. In Canter, D. (ed.) *Environmental Social Psychology*, Munich: Kluwer.

Canter, D. and Larkin, P. (1993) The Environmental Range of Serial Rapists. *Journal of Environmental Psychology*, 13, 63–69.

Carpman, J., Grant, M. and Simmons, D. (1985) Hospital design and wayfinding: a video simulation study. *Environment and Behavior* 17, 296–314.

Casey, S.M. (1978) Cognitive mapping by the blind. *Journal of Visual Impairment and Blindness* 72, 297–301.

Chalmers, D. and Knight, R. (1985) The reliability of ratings of familiarity of environmental stimuli: a generalizability analysis. *Environmental and Behavior* 17, 223–38.

Charness, N. (1985) Aging and problem-solving performance. In Charness, N. (ed.), *Aging and Human Performance*, London: Wiley, 225–259.

Chiarello, C., McMohan, M. and Schaefer, K. (1989) Visual cerebral lateralization over phases of the menstrual cycle: A preliminary investigation. *Brain and Cognition* 11, 18–36.

Clark-Carter, D.D., Heyes, A.D. and Howarth, C.I. (1986) The efficiency and walking speed of visually impaired pedestrians. *Ergonomics* 29, 779–89.

Cloke, P., Philo, C. and Sadler, D. (1991) *Approaching Human Geography*. London: Paul Chapman.

Cohen, R., Baldwin, L.M. and Sherman, R.C. (1978) Cognitive maps of a naturalistic setting. *Child Development*, 49, 1216–18.

Conning, A.M. and Byrne, B. (1984) Pointing to preschool children's spatial competence: a study in natural settings. *Journal of Environmental Psychology* 4, 165–75.

Cornell, E.H. and Hay, D.H. (1984) Children's acquisition of a route via different media. *Environment and Behavior* 16, 627–41.

Cornell, E.H., Heth, C.D. and Broda, L.S. (1989) Children's wayfinding: Response to instructions to use environmental landmarks. *Developmental Psychology* 25, 755–64.

Cornell, E.H., Heth, C.D. and Rowat, W.L. (1992) Wayfinding by children and adults: Response to instructions to use look-back and retrace strategies. *Developmental Psychology* 28, 328–36.

Cornell, E.H., Heth, C.D. and Skoczylas, M.J.. (1999) The nature and use of route expectancies following incidental learning. *Journal of Environmental Psychology* 19, 209–30.

Cornell, E.H., Heth, C.D., and Alberts, D.M. (1994) Place recognition and wayfinding by children and adults. *Memory and Cognition* 22, 633–43.

Coshall, J.T. (1985) Urban consumer's cognitions of distance. *Geografiska Annaler* 67B, 107–19.

Couclelis, H. (1996) Verbal directions for way-finding: Space, cognition and language. In Portugali, J. (ed.) *The Construction of Cognitive Maps*, Dordrecht: Kluwer, pp. 13–153.

Couclelis, H. and Gale, N. (1986) Space and spaces. *Geographica Annaler B* 68, 1–12.

Couclelis, H., Golledge, R.G., Gale, N. and Tobler, W. (1987) Exploring the anchor-point hypothesis of spatial cognition. *Journal of Environmental Psychology* 7, 99–122.

Cousins, J.H., Siegel, A.W. and Maxwell, S.E. (1983) Way finding and cognitive mapping in large scale environments: a test of a development model. *Journal of Experimental Child Psychology* 35, 1–20.

Cox, K.R. (1981) Bourgeois thought and the behavioral geography debate. In Cox, K.R. and Golledge, R.G. (eds), *Behavioral Problems in Geography Revisited*, Northwestern University Press, pp. 256–79.

Cox, K.R. and Colledge, R.G. (eds), (1981) Behavioral Problems in Geography Revisited, Northwestern University Press.

Cox, K.R. and Zannaras, G. (1973) Designative perceptions of macro-spaces: Concepts, a methodology, and applications. In Downs, R.M. and Stea, D. (eds), *Image and Environment*, Chicago: Aldine, pp. 162–78.

Craik, K.H. (1970) Environmental psychology. In Newcomb, T.M. (ed.), *New Directions in Psychology* 4, New York: Holt, Rinehart and Winston.

Cullen, I. (1976) Human geography, regional science, and the study of individual behavior. *Environment and Planning A* 8, 397–409.

Curtis, L.E., Siegel, A.W. and Furlong, N.E. (1981) Developmental differences in cognitive mapping: Configurational knowledge of familiar large-scale environments. *Journal of Experimental Child Psychology* 31, 456–69.

Dabbs, J., Chang, E-Lee, Strong, R. and Milun, R. (1998) Spatial ability, navigation strategy, and geographic knowledge among men and women. *Evolution and Human Behavior* 19, 89–98.

Darvizeh, Z. and Spencer, C. (1984) How do children learn novel routes? The importance of landmarks in the child's retracing routes through the large scale environment. *Journal of Environmental Education and Information* 3, 97–105.

Day, R.A. (1976) Urban distance cognition: review and contribution. *Australian Geographer* 13, 193–200.

DeLoache, J.S., Miller, K.F. and Rosengren, K.S. (1997) The credible shrinking room: Very young children's performance with symbolic and non-symbolic relations. *Psychological Science* 8, 308–13.

Denis, M. (1997) The description of routes. A cognitive approach to the production of spatial discourse. *Current Psychology of Cognition* 16, 409–58.

Denis, M., Pazzaglia, F., Cornoldi, C., and Bertolo, L. (1999) Spatial discourse and navigation: An analysis of route directions in the city of Venice. *Applied Cognitive Psychology* 13, 145–74.

Denis, M. and Zimmer, M. (1992) Analog properties of cognitive maps constructed from verbal descriptions. *Psychological Research* 54, 286–98.

Devlin, A. (1976) The 'small town' cognitive map: adjusting to a new environment. In Moore, G.T. and Golledge, R.G., (eds), *Environmental Knowing*, Stroudsberg, PA: Dowden, Hutchinson and Ross, 58–66.

Devlin, A.S. and Bernstein, J. (1995) Interactive wayfindings: Use of cues by men and women. *Journal of Environmental Psychology* 15, 23–38.

Dijkink, G. and Elbers, E. (1981) The development of geographic representation in children. *Tijdschrift voor Economische en Sociale Geografie* 72, 2–16.

Dodds, A.G., Howarth, C.I. and Carter, D.C. (1982) The mental maps of the blind. *Journal of Visual Impairment and Blindness* 76, 5–12.

Downs, R.M. (1970) Geographic space perception: past approaches and future prospects. *Progress in Geography* 2, 65–108.

Downs, R.M. (1981) Maps and mappings as metaphors for spatial representation. In Liben, L.S., Patterson, A. and Newcombe, N. (eds), *Spatial Representation and Behavior Across the Life Span*, NY: Academic, pp. 143–66.

Downs, R.M. (1985) The representation of space: Its development in children and in cartography. In Cohen, R. (ed.), *The Development of Spatial Cognition*, Hillsdale, NJ: Erlbaum Lawrence, pp. 323–45.

Downs, R.M. and Stea, D. (1973a) Theory. In Downs, R.M. and Stea, D. (eds), *Image and Environment*, Chicago: Aldine, pp. 1–7.

Downs, R.M. and Stea, D. (1973b) Cognitive maps and spatial behavior: process and products. In Downs, R.M. and Stea, D. (eds), *Image and Environment*, Chicago: Aldine, pp. 8–26.

Downs, R.M. and Stea, D. (1977) *Maps in Minds: Reflections on Cognitive Mapping*. New York: Harper and Row.

Ebdon, D. (1985). *Statistics in Geography*, Oxford: Blackwell.

Eddy, J.K. and Glass, A.L. (1981) Reading and listening to high and low reading sentences. *Journal of Verbal Learning and Verbal Behavior* 20, 333–45.

Edwards, G. (1991) Spatial knowledge for image understanding. In Mark, D.M. and Frank, A.U. (eds), *Cognitive and Linguistic Aspects of Geographic Space*. Dordrecht: Kluwer, pp. 35–44.

Embretson, S.E. (1982) Improving the measurements of spaitial aptitude by dynamic testing. *Intelligence* 11, 353–355.

Espinosa, M.A., Ungar, S., Ochaita, E., Blades, M. and Spencer, C. (1998) Comparing methods for introducing blind and visually impaired people to unfamiliar urban environments. *Journal of Environmental Psychology* 18, 277–87.

Evans, G.W. and Gärling, T. (1991) Environment, cognition, and action: The need for integration. In Gärling, T. and Evans, G.W. (eds), *Environment, Cognition and Action—An Integrated Approach*, New York: Oxford University Press, pp. 3–13.

Evans, G.W., Marrero, D.G. and Butler, P.A. (1982) Environmental learning and cognitive mapping. *Environment and Behavior* 13, 83–104.

Evans, G.W., Fellows, J., Zorn, M. and Doty, K. (1980) Cognitive mapping and architecture. *Journal of Applied Psychology* 65, 474–8.

Evans, G.W. and Pezdek, K. (1980) Cognitive mapping: knowledge of real-world distance and location information. *Journal of Experimental Psychology: Human Learning and Memory* 6, 13–24.

Evans, G.W., Skorpanich, M.A., Gärling, T., Bryant, K., and Bresolin, B. (1984) The effects of pathway configuration, landmarks, and stress on environmental cognition. *Journal of Environmental Psychology* 4, 323–35.

Eyles, J. (1989) The geography of everyday life. In Gregory, D. and Walford, R. (eds), *Horizons in Human Geography*, London: Macmillan, pp. 102–17.

Farah, M.J. (1988) The neuropsychology of mental imagery: converging evidence from brain-damaged and normal subjects. In Stiles-Davis, J., Kritchevsky, M. and Bellugi, U. (eds), *Spatial Cognition: Brain Bases and Development*, Hillsdale, NJ: Lawrence Erlbaum Associates, pp. 33–56.

Feingold, A. (1988) Cognitive gender differences are disappearing. *American Psychologist* 43, 95–103.

Feldman, A. and Acredolo, L. (1979) The effect of active vs passive exploration on memory for spatial location in children. *Child Development* 50, 698–704.

Ferguson, E.L. and Hegarty, M. (1994) Properties of cognitive maps constructed from texts. *Memory and Cognition* 22, 455–73.

Fletcher, J.F. (1980) Spatial representations in blind children, 1: development compared to sighted children. *Journal of Visual Impairment and Blindness* 74, 381–85.

Foley, J.E. and Cohen, A.J. (1984a) Working mental representations of the environment. *Environment and Behavior* 16, 713–29.

Foos, P.W. (1980) Constructing cognitive maps from sentences. *Journal of Experimental Psychology: Human Learning and Memory* 6, 25–38.

Foreman, N. and Gillett, R., (eds), (1997) *A Handbook of Spatial Research Paradigms and Methodologies. Volume 1*, Hove, Sussex: Psychology Press.

Foreman, N., Foreman, D., Cummings, A., and Owens, S. (1990) Locomotion, active choice and spatial memory in children. *Journal of General Psychology* 117, 215–32.

Foulke, E. (1983) Spatial ability and the limitations of perceptual systems. In H.L. Pick and Acredolo, A.J. (eds), *Spatial Orientation: Theory, Research and Application*, New York: Plenum, pp. 125–141.

Franklin, N. and Tversky, B. (1990) Searching imagined environments. *Journal of Experimental Psychology: General* 119, 63–76

Franklin, N., Tversky, B. and Coon, V. (1992) Switching points of view in spatial mental models. *Memory and Cognition* 20, 507–18.

Freundschuh, S.M. (1991) The effect of the pattern of the environment on spatial knowledge acquisition. In Mark, D.M. and Franks, A.U. (eds) *Cognitive and Linguistic Aspects of Geographic Space*, Dordrecht: Kluwer, pp. 167–83.

Freundschuh, S.M. (2000) Micro- and macro-scale environments. In Kitchin, R. and Freundschuh, S.M. (eds) Cognitive Mapping: Past, Present and Future. Routledge, London. pp. 125–146.

Freundschuh, S.M. and Egenhofer, M. (1997) Human conceptions of spaces: Implications for GIS. *Transactions in GIS* 2, 361–75.

Freundschuh, S.M. and Kitchin, R.M. (eds) (1999) Cognitive Mapping. *Professional Geographer*, 51: 507–561.

Freundschuh, S.M. and Montello, D. (eds) (1995) *Geographical Systems*, Special Issue on Spatial Cognitive Models, 2.

Gale, N. (1982) Some applications of computer cartography to the study of cognitive configurations. *Professional Geographer* 34, 313–21.

Gale, N., Golledge, R.G., Pellegrino, J.W. and Doherty, S. (1990a) The acquisition and integration of neighborhood route knowledge. *Journal of Environmental Psychology* 10, 3–25.

Gale, N., Golledge, R.G., Halperin, W.C. and Couclelis, H. (1990b). Exploring spatial familiarity. *Professional Geographer* 43, 299–313.

Gallistel, C.R. (1993) *The Organization of Learning. Second edition*. Cambridge, MA: MIT Press.

Gärling, T., Book, A. and Lindberg, E. (1985) Adults' memory representations of the spatial properties of their everyday physical environment. In Cohen, R. (ed.), *The Development of Spatial Cognition*, Hillsdale, NJ: Erlbaum Lawrence, pp. 141–84.

Gärling, T., Book, A. and Lindberg, E. (1986a) Spatial orientation and wayfinding in the designed environment. *Journal of Architectural Planning Research* 3, 55–64.

Gärling, T., Book, A., Lindberg, E. and Arce, C. (1991a) Evidence of a response-bias explanation of non-Euclidean cognitive maps. *Professional Geographer* 43, 143–9.

Gärling, T. and Evans, G.W (eds), (1991) *Environment, Cognition and Action—An Integrated Approach*, New York: Oxford University Press.

Gärling, T. and Golledge, R.G. (1989) Environmental perception and cognition. In Zube, E. and Moore, G.T. (eds), *Advances in Environmental Behavior and Design* 2, New York: Plenum, pp. 203–236.

Gärling, T. and Golledge, R.G. (eds), (1993a) *Behavior and Environment: Psychological and Geographical Approaches*, London: North Holland.

Gärling, T. and Golledge, R.G. (2000) The role of cognitive maps in spatial decision making: Implications of the past for the future. In Kitchin, R. and Freundschuh, S.M. (eds), *Cognitive mapping: Past, present and future*, London: Routledge, pp. 46–65.

Gärling, T., Lindberg, E., Carreiras, M. and Book, A. (1986b) Reference systems in cognitive maps. *Journal of Environmental Psychology* 6, 1–18.

Gärling, T., Book, A., Lindberg, E. and Nilsson, T. (1981) Memory for the spatial layout of the everyday physical environment: Factors affecting rate of acquisition. *Journal of Environmental Psychology* 1, 263–77.

Gärling, T., Lindberg, E. and Mantyla, T. (1983) Orientation in buildings: effects of familiarity, visual access, and orientation aids. *Journal of Applied Psychology* 68, 177–86.

Gärling, T., Lindberg, E. Torell, G. and Evans, G.W. (1991b) From environmental to ecological cognition. In Gärling, T. and Evans, G.W. (eds), *Environment, Cognition and Action—An integrated Approach*, New York: Oxford University Press, pp. 335–44.

Gärling, T., Selart, M. and Book, A. (1997) Investigating spatial choice and navigation in large-scale environments. In Foreman, N. and Gillett, R., (eds), *A Handbook of Spatial Research Paradigms and Methodologies, Volume 1*, Hove, Sussex: Psychology Press.

Gatrell, A.C. (1983) *Distance and Space: A Geographical Perspective*, London: Clarendon.

Gentry, T.A. and Wakefield, J.A. (1991) Methods for measuring spatial cognition. In Mark, D.M. and Frank, A.U. (eds), *Cognitive and Linguistics Aspects of Geographic Space*, Dordecht: Kluwer, pp. 185–217.

Gibson, J.J. (1979) *The Ecological Approach to Visual Perception*, Boston: Houghton-Mifflin.

Gilhooley, K.J., Wood, M., Kinnear, P.R. and Green, C. (1988) Skill in map reading and memory for maps. *Quarterly Journal of Experimental Psychology* 40A, 87–107.

Gilmartin, P. (1985) The cued spatial response approach to macro-scale cognitive maps. *Canadian Geographer*, 29, 56–9.

Gilmartin, P. and Lloyd, R. (1991) The effects of map projections and map distance on emotional involvement with places. *Cartographic Journal* 28, 145–51.

Gilmartin, P. and Patton, J.C. (1984) Comparing the sexes on spatial abilities: map-use skills. *Annals of the Association of American Geographers* 74, 605–19.

Glicksohn, J. (1992) Subjective time estimation in altered sensory environments. *Environment and Behavior* 25, 634–52.

Glicksohn, J. (1994) Rotation, orientation, and cognitive mapping. *American Journal of Psychology* 107, 39–51.

Golbeck, S.L., Rand, M. and Soundy, C. (1986) Constructing a model of a large-scale space with the space in view: Effects on preschoolers of guidance and cognitive restructuring. *Merrill–Palmer Quarterly* 32, 187–203.

Gold, J.R. (1980). *An Introduction to Behavioral Geography*, Oxford: Blackwell.

Gold, J.R. (1992) Image and environment: the decline of cognitive-behavioralism in human geography and grounds for regeneration. *Geoforum* 23, 239–47.

Golding, J.M., Graesser, A.C. and Hauselt, J. (1996) The process of answering direction-giving questions whan someone is lost on a University campus: The role of pragmatics. *Applied Cognitive Psychology* 10, 23–39.

Golledge, R.G. (1976) Methods and methodological issues in environmental cognition research. In Moore, G.T. and Golledge, R.G. (eds), *Environmental Knowing*, Stroudsberg, PA: Dowden, Hutchinson and Ross, pp. 300–13.

Golledge, R.G. (1977) Environmental cues, cognitive mapping and spatial behavior. In Burke, D. *et al.*, (eds), *Behavior—Environment Research Methods*, Institute for Environmental Studies, Univ. of Wisconsin, pp. 35–46.

Golledge, R.G. (1978) Representing, interpreting and using cognized environments. *Papers and Proceedings of the Regional Science Association* 41, 169–204.

Golledge, R.G. (1981) Misconceptions, misinterpretations, and misrepresentations of behavioral approaches in human geography. *Environment and Planning A* 13, 1315–44.

Golledge, R.G. (1991a) Cognition of physical and built environments. In Gärling, T. and Evans, G.W. (eds), *Environment, Cognition and Action—An Integrated Approach*, New York: Oxford University Press, pp. 35–62.

Golledge, R.G. (1991b) Tactual strip maps as navigational aids. *Journal of Visual Impairment and Blindness* 85, 296–301.

Golledge, R.G. (1992) Place recognition and wayfinding: making sense of space. *Geoforum* 23, 199–214.

Golledge, R.G. (1993a) Geography and the disabled: a survey with special reference to vision impaired and blind populations, *Transactions of the Institute of British Geographers* 18, 63–85.

Golledge, R.G. (1993b) Geographical perspectives on spatial cognition. In Gärling, T. and Golledge, R.G. (eds), *Behavior and Environment: Psychological and Geographical Approaches*. Amsterdam: Elsevier, pp. 16–46.

Golledge, R.G., (ed.) (1999) *Wayfinding Behavior. Cognitive Mapping and Other Spatial Processes*, Baltimore: Johns Hopkins.

Golledge, R.G., Doherty, V.J. and Bell, S.M. (1993) *Survey Versus Route-based Wayfinding in Unfamiliar Environments*. Paper presented at 89th Annual meeting of the Association of American Geographers, 6–10th April, Atlanta, GA.

Golledge, R.G., Gale, N., Pellegrino, J.W. and Doherty, S. (1992) Spatial knowledge acquisition by children: Route learning and relational distances. *Annals of the Association of American Geographers* 82, 223–44.

Golledge, R.G., Gale, N. and Richardson, G.D. (1987) Cognitive maps of cities II: Studies of selected populations. *National Geographical Journal of India*, 33, 1–16.

Golledge, R.G. and Hubert, L.J. (1982) Some comments on non-Euclidean mental maps. *Environment and Planning A* 107–18.

Golledge, R.G., Klatsky, R.L. and Loomis, J.M. (1996) Cognitive mapping and wayfinding by adults without vision. In Portugali, J. (ed.) *The Construction of Cognitive Maps*, Dordrecht: Kluwer, 215–45.

Golledge, R.G and Rushton, G. (1984) A review of analytical behavioral research in geography. In Herbert, D.T. and Johnston, R.J. (eds), *Geography and the Urban Environment* 6, pp. 1–43.

Golledge, R.G., Smith, T.R., Pellegrino, J.W., Doherty, S. and Marshall, S.P. (1985) A conceptual model and empirical analysis of children's acquisition of spatial knowledge. *Journal of Environmental Psychology* 5, 125–52.

Golledge, R.G. and Spector, A.N. (1978) Comprehending the urban environment: theory and practice. *Geographical Analysis* 9, 403–26.

Golledge, R.G. and Stimson, R.J. (1987) *Analytical Behavioral Geography*, London: Croom Helm.

Golledge, R.G. and Stimson, R.J. (1997) *Spatial Behavior: A Geographic Perspective*, New York: Guilford Press.

Golledge, R.G. and Timmermanns, H. (1990) Applications of behavioral research on spatial problems I: Cognition. *Progress in Human Geography* 14, 57–99.

Goodchild, B. (1974) Class differences in environmental perception: An exploratory study. *Urban Studies*, 11, 157–69.

Goodey, B. (1971) *Perception of the environment*. Centre for Urban and Regional Studies, University of Birmingham.

Gopal, S. (1996) Neural network models of cognitive maps. In J. Portugali (ed.) *The Construction of Cognitive Maps*, Dordrecht: Kluwer, pp. 69–85.

Gopal, S. and Smith, T.R. (1990) Human wayfinding in an urban environment: A performance analysis of a computational process model. *Environment and Planning A* 22, 169–91.

Gould, P. (1975) Acquiring spatial information. *Economic Geography* 51, 87–99.

Gould, P. and White, R. (1974) *Mental Maps*, New York: Penguin.

Greene, S. (1992) City shape—Communicating and evaluating community design. *Journal of the American Planning Association* 58, 177–89.

Greenburg, D. (1984) Whodunit? Structure and subjectivity in behavioral geography. In Saarinen, T.F., Seamon, D. and Sell, J.L. (eds), *Environmental Perception and Behavior: An Inventory and Prospect*, Research paper 209, Department of Geography, University of Chicago, pp. 191–208.

Griffin, P. (1948) Topological Orientation. In Boring, E.G. *et al.*, (eds), *Foundations in Psychology*. New York: John Wiley, pp. 380–6.

Guth, R. (1990) Space saving statistics: An introduction to constant error, variable error, and absolute error. *Peabody Journal of Education* 67, 110–20.

Haken, H. and Portugali, J. (1996) Synergetics, inter-representational networks and cognitive maps. In Portugali, J. (ed.) *The Construction of Cognitive Maps*. Dordrecht: Kluwer, pp. 45–67.

Hampson, E. (1995) Spatial cognition in humans: Possible modulation by androgens and estrogens. *Journal of Psychiatry and Neuroscience* 20, 397–404.

Hanley, G.L. and Levine, M. (1983) Spatial problem solving: the integration of independently learned cognitive maps. *Memory and Cognition* 11, 415–22.

Hanson, S. (1983) The world is not a stone garden. *Geographical Analysis* 15, 33–35.

Hanyu, K. and Itsukushima, Y. (1995) Cognitive distance of stairways. Distance, traversal time, and walking time estimations. *Environment and Behavior* 27, 579–91.

Hardwick, D.A., McIntyre, C.W. and Pick, H.L. (1976) The content and manipulation of cognitive maps in children and adults. *Monographs of the Society for Research in Child Development* 41, 1–55.

Harman, E.J. and Betak, J.F. (1976) Behavioral geography, multidimensional scaling and the mind. In Golledge, R.G. and Rushton, G. (eds), *Spatial Choice and Spatial Behavior*. Columbus, OH: Ohio State University Press, pp. 3–22.

Harris, M. (1979) *Cultural Materialism*, New York: Vintage.

Harris, L.J. (1981) Sex related differences in spatial ability. In Liben, L.S., Patterson, A. and Newcombe, N. (eds), *Spatial Representation and Behavior Across the Life Span*, New York: Academic, pp. 83–125.

Hart, R. (1979) *Children's Experience of Place*, New York: Irvington.

Hart, R. (1981) Children's representation of the landscape: lessons and questions from a field study. In Liben, L., Patterson, A.H. and Newcombe, N. (eds), *Spatial Representation Across the Life Span*, New York: Academic, pp. 195–236.

Hart, R. and Berzok, M.A. (1983) A problem oriented perspective on children's representation of the environment. In Potegal, M. (eds), *The Neural and Development Bases of Spatial Orientation*, New York, Academic.

Hart, R.A. and Conn, M.K. (1991) Developmental perspectives on decision making and action in environments. In Gärling, T. and Evans, G.W. (eds), *Environment, Cognition and Action—An integrated approach*, New York: Plenum, pp. 277–94.

Hart, R.A. and Moore, G. (1973) The development of spatial cognition: a review. In Downs, R.M. and Stea, D. (eds), *Image and Environment*, Chicago: Aldine, pp. 246–88.

Hasher, L. and Zachs, R.T. (1979) Automatic and effortful processes in memory. *Journal of Experimental Psychology: General* 108, 356–88.

Hazen, N.L. (1983) Spatial orientation: A comparative approach. In Pick, L. and Acredolo, L.J. (eds), *Spatial Orientation: Theory, Research and Application.* New York: Plenum, pp. 3–37.

Hazen, N.L., Lockman, J.J and Pick, H.L. (1978) The development of children's representations of large scale environments. *Child Development* 49, 623–36.

Heft, H. (1979) The role of enviromental features in route-learning: Two exploratory studies of wayfinding. *Environmental Psychology and Nonverbal Behavior* 3, 172–85.

Heft, H. (1983) Wayfinding as the perception of information over time. *Population and Environment: Behavioral and Social Issues* 6, 133–50.

Heft, H. (1996) The ecological approach to navigation: A Gibsonian perspective. In Portugali, J. (eds), *The Construction of Cognitive Maps.* Dordrecht: Kluwer, pp. 105–32.

Herman, J.F. (1980) Children's cognitive maps of large-scale spaces: effects of exploration, direction and repeated expcrience. *Journal of Experimental Child Psychology* 29, 126–43.

Herman, J.F. and Coyne, A.C. (1980) Mental manipulation of spatial information in young and elderly adults. *Developmental Psychology* 16, 537–38.

Herman, J.F. and Klein, R.V. (1985) The effect of travel on children's distance estimation. *British Journal of Developmental Psychology* 3, 353–61.

Herman, J.F., Roth, S. Miranda, C. and Getz, M. (1985) Children's memory for spatial locations: the influence of recall perspective and type of environment. *Journal of Experimental Child Psychology*, 34, 257–273.

Herman, J.F. and Siegel, A.W. (1978) The development of cognitive mapping of large-scale environment. *Journal of Experimental Child Psychology* 26, 389–406.

Herman, J.D.F., Kail, R.V. and Siegel, A.W. (1979) Cognitive maps of a college campus: A new look at freshman orientation. *Bulletin of the Psychonomic Society* 13, 183–86.

Hernandez, D. (1991) Relative representation of spatial knowledge: The 2-D case. In Mark, D.M. and Frank, A.U. (eds), *Cognitive and Linguistics Aspects of Geographic Space*, Dordrecht: Kluwer, pp. 373–85.

Heth, C.D. and Cornell, E.H. (1998) Characteristics of travel by persons lost in Albertan wilderness areas. *Journal of Environmental Psychology* 18, 223–35.

Heth, C.D., Cornell, E.H. and Alberts, D.M. (1997) Differential use of landmarks by 8- and 12-year-old children during route reversal navigation. *Journal of Environmental Psychology* 17, 199–213.

Hewe, G. (1971) Personal communication to J. Blaut. Cited in Stea, D. (1976) Notes on a spatial fugue., in Moore, G.T. and Golledge, R.G. (eds), *Environmental Knowing*, Stroudsberg, PA: Dowden, Hutchinson and Ross.

Hill, E.W., Rieser, J.J., Hill, M., Halpin, J. and Halpin, R. (1993) How persons with visual impairments explore novel spaces: strategies of good and poor performers. *Journal of Visual Impairment and Blindness* 87, 295–301.

Hillman, M., Adams, J. and Whitelegg, J. (1990) *One False Move ... A Study of Children's Independent Mobility*. London: Policy Studies Institute.

Hintzman, D.L., O'Dell, S. and Arndt, D.R. (1981) Orientation in cognitive maps. *Cognitive Psychology* 13, 149–206.

Hirtle, S.C. and Mascolo, M.F. (1986) The effect of semantic clustering on the memory of spatial locations. *Journal of Experimental Psychology: Learning, Memory and Cognition* 12, 181–9.

Hirtle, S.C. and Jonides, J. (1985) Evidence of hierarchies in cognitive maps. *Memory and Cognition* 13, 208–17.

Holding, C.S. and Holding, D.H. (1989) Acquisition of route network knowledge by males and females. *Journal of General Psychology* 116, 29–41.

Holohan, C.J. and Dubrowolsky, M.B. (1978) Cognitive and behavioral correlates of the spatial environment. *Environment and Behavior* 10, 317–33.

Hollyfield, R.L. and Foulke, E. (1983) The spatial cognition of blind pedestrians. *Journal of Visual Impairment and Blindness* 77, 205–10.

Howard, J.H. and Kerst, S.M. (1981) Memory and perception of cartographic information for familiar and unfamiliar environments. *Human Factors* 23, 495–504.

Hughes, F.P. (1999) *Children, Play, and Development*, Third Edition. Boston: Allyn and Bacon.

Hull, C.L. (1943) *Principles of Behavior*, New York: Appleton.

Humphreys, J.S. (1990) Place learning and spatial cognition: a longitudinal study of urban newcomers. *Tijdschrift Voor Econmicshe en Sociale Geografie* 81, 364–80.

Huttenlocher, J. and Newcombe, N. (1984) The child's representation of information about location. In Sophian, C. (ed.), *The Origin of Cognitive Skills*, Hillsdale, NJ: Erlbaum. pp. 81–111.

Ittleson, W.H. (1973) Environment perception and contemporary perceptual theory. In Ittleson, W.H. (ed.), *Environment and Cognition*, New York: Seminar. pp. 1–19.

Jackson, P.G. (1996) How will route guidance information affect cognitive maps? *Journal of Navigation* 49, 178–86.

Jackson, P.J. (1999) *The Effects of Route Guidance Information upon Travellers' Wayfinding and Navigation Ability*. Unpublished PhD thesis, Imperial College of Science, Technology and Medicine, London.

Jackson, P.J. and Kitchin, R.M. (1998) Editorial: Applying cognitive mapping. *Journal of Environmental Psychology* 18, 219–21.

Jacobs, W.J., Laurance, H.E. and Thomas, K.G.F. (1997) Place learning in virtual space I: Acquisition, overshadowing, and transfer. *Learning and Motivation* 28, 521–41.

Jacobson, R.D. (1998) Cognitive mapping without sight: Four preliminary studies of spatial learning *Journal of Environmental Psychology* 18, 289–306.

Jacobson, R.D. and Kitchin, R.M. (1997) Geographical information systems and people with visual impairments or blindness: Exploring the potential to education, orientation and navigation. *Transactions in GIS* 2, 315–32.

Jacobson, R.D., Kitchin, R.M., Gärling, T., Golledge, R. and Blades, M. (1998) Learning a complex urban route without sight: Comparing naturalistic versus laboratory measures. *Proceedings of Mind III: Spatial Cognition Conference*. Dublin City University.

Joshi, M.S., MacLean, M. and Carter, W. (1999) Children's journey to school: Spatial skills, knowledge and perceptions of the environment. *British Journal of Developmental Psychology* 17, 125–39.

Juurma, J. (1973) Transportation in mental spatial manipulation: A theoretical analysis. *American Foundation for the Blind Research Bulletin*, 26, 87–143.

Juurmaa, J. and Lehtinen-Railo, S. (1994) Visual experience and access to spatial knowledge. *Journal of Visual Impairment and Blindness* 88, 157–70.

Just, M.A. and Carpenter, P.A. (1985) Cognitive coordinate systems: Accounts of mental rotation and individual differences in spatial ability. *Psychological Review* 92, 137–72.

Kahl, H.B., Herman, J.F. and Klein, C.A. (1984) Distance distortions in cognitive maps: an examination of the information storage model. *Journal of Experimental Child Psychology*, 38, 134–46.

Kaplan, S. (1973) Cognitive maps in perception and thought. In Downs, R.M. and Stea, D. (eds), *Image and Environment*, Chicago: Aldine, pp. 63–78.

Kaplan, S. (1976) Adaptation, structure and knowledge. In Moore, G.T. and Golledge, R.G. (eds), *Environmental Knowing*, Stroudsberg, PA: Dowden, Hutchinson and Ross, pp. 32–45.

Kirasic, K.C. (1991) Spatial cognition and behavior in young and elderly adults: Implications for learning new environments. *Psychology and Aging* 6, 10–18.

Kirasic, K.C., Allen, G. and Haggerty, D. (1992) Age-related differences in adults' macrospatial cognitive processes. *Experimental Aging Research* 18, 33–39.

Kirasic, K.C., Allen, G. and Siegel, A.W. (1984) Expression of configurational knowledge of large-scale environments: student's performance of cognitive tasks. *Environment and Behavior* 16, 687–712.

Kirk, W. (1963) Problems of geography. *Geography* 48, 357–71.

Kitchin, R.M. (1990) *A study of children's cognitive distance and direction estimates in West Wirral schools*. Unpublished undergraduate dissertation, University of Lancaster.

Kitchin, R.M. (1992) *The Application of GIS to Spatial Cognitive Studies: SCAMS—A Preliminary System. A Study to Investigate Methods of Data Collection and Analysis* Unpublished MSc thesis, University of Leicester.

Kitchin, R.M. (1993) Bringing psychology and geography closer. *Journal of Environmental Psychology* 13, 183–86.

Kitchin, R.M. (1994) Cognitive maps: what are they and why study them? *Journal of Environmental Psychology* 14, 1–19.

Kitchin, R.M. (1995) Increasing the validity and integrity of cognitive mapping research: an investigation of configurational knowledge. Doctoral dissertation, University of Wales, Swansea.

Kitchin, R.M. (1996a) Methodological convergence in cognitive mapping research: investigating configurational knowledge. *Journal of Environmental Psychology*, 16, 163–185.

Kitchin, R.M. (1996b) Exploring approaches to computer cartography and spatial analysis in cognitive mapping research: CMAP and MiniGASP prototype packages. *Cartographic Journal* 33, 51–5.

Kitchin, R.M. (1996c) Are there sex differences in geographic knowledge and understanding? *The Geographical Journal* 162, 273–86.

Kitchin, R.M. (1996d) Increasing the integrity of cognitive mapping research: appraising conceptual schemata of environment–behavior interaction. *Progress in Human Geography* 20, 56–84.

Kitchin, R.M. (1997) Exploring spatial thought. *Environment and Behavior* 29, 123–56.

Kitchin, R.M., Blades, M. and Golledge, R.G. (1997a) Understanding spatial concepts at the geographic scale without the use of vision. *Progress in Human Geography* 21, 225–42.

Kitchin, R.M., Blades, M. and Golledge, R.G. (1997b) Relations between psychology and geography. *Environment and Behavior* 29, 554–73.

Kitchin, R.M. and Fotheringham, A.S. (1997) Aggregation issues in cognitive mapping research. *Professional Geographer* 49, 269–80.

Kitchin, R. and Freundschuh, S., (eds), (in press) *Cognitive Mapping. Past, Present, and Future*, London: Routledge.

Kitchin, R.M. and Jacobson, R.D. (1997) Techniques to collect and analyze the cognitive map knowledge of persons with visual impairment or blindness: issues of validity. *Journal of Visual Impairment and Blindness*, 91, 393–400.

Kitchin, R.M., Jacobson, R.D., Golledge, R.G. and Blades, M. (1998) Belfast without sight: Exploring geographies of blindness. *Irish Geographer* 31, 34–46.

Kitchin, R.M. and Tate, N. (1999) *Conducting Research in Human Geography: Theory, Methodology and Practice*, Harlow: Longman.

Klatzky, R.L., Golledge, R.G., Loomis, J.M., Cicinelli, J.G. and Pellegrino, J.W. (1994) Performance of blind and sighted in spatial tasks. *Journal of Visual Impairment and Blindness* 89, 70–82.

Klein, W. (1982) Local deixis in route directions. In Jarvella, R.J. and Klein, W., (eds), *Speech, Place and Action: Studies in Deixis and Related Topics*, Chichester: Wiley, pp. 161–82.

Kosslyn, S.M., Ball, T.M. and Reiser, B.J. (1978) Visual images preserve metric spatial information: Evidence from studies of image scanning. *Journal of Experimental Psychology: Human Perception and Performance* 4, 47–60.

Kosslyn, S.M., Pick, H.L. and Farriello, C.P. (1974) Cognitive maps in children and men. *Child Development*, 45, 707–16.

Kosslyn, S.M. and Pomerantz, J.R. (1977) Imagery, propositions and the form of the internal representations. *Cognitive Psychology*, 9, 52–76.

Kozlowski, L.T. and Bryant, K.J. (1977) Sense of direction, spatial orientation, and cognitive maps. *Journal of Experimental Psychology: Human Perception and Performance* 3, 590–598.

Kuipers, B. (1978) Modelling spatial knowledge. *Cognitive Science* 2, 129–53.

Kuipers, B. (1982) The 'map in the head' metaphor. *Environment and Behavior* 14, 202–20.

Kulhavy, R.W., Stock, W.A. and Kealy, W. (1993) How geographic maps increase recall of instructional text. *Educational Technology Research and Development* 41, 47–62.

Kulhavy, R.W. and Stock, W.A. (1996) How cognitive maps are learned and remembered. *Annals of the Association of American Geographers* 86, 123–45.

Kulhavy, R.W., Stock, W.A., Peterson, E., Pridemore, R. and Klein, J.D. (1992) Using maps to retrieve text: A test of conjoint retention. *Contemporary Educational Psychology* 17, 56–70.

Landau, B. and Jackendoff, R. (1993) 'What' and 'where' in spatial language and spatial cognition. *Behavioral and Brain Sciences* 16, 217–65.

Langer, J. (1969) *Theories of Development*, New York: Holt, Rinehart and Winston.

Lawton, C.A. (1994) Gender differences in wayfinding strategies: Relationship to spatial ability and spatial anxiety. *Sex Roles* 30, 765–79.

Lawton, C.A. (1996) Strategies for indoor wayfinding: The role of orientation. *Journal of Environmental Psychology* 16, 137–45.

Lee, T. (1968) Urban neighborhood as a social–spatial schema. *Human Relations* 21, 241–62.

Lee, Y. and Schmidt, C.G. (1988) Evolution of urban spatial cognition: patterns of change in Guangzhou, China. *Environment and Planning A*, 20, 339–51.

Leiser, D. (1987) The changing relations between relations between representations and cognitive structures in the development of a cognitive map. *New Ideas in Psychology* 5, 95–110.

Leiser, D. and Zilbershatz, A. (1989) The traveler: A computational model of network learning. *Environment and Behavior* 21, 435–63.

Levine, M., Jankovic, I., and Palij, M. (1982) Principles of spatial problem solving. *Journal of Experimental Psychology: General* 111, 157–71.

Levine, M., Marchon, I. and Hanley, G. (1984) The placement and misplacement of you-are-here maps. *Environment and Behavior* 16, 139–57.

Ley, D. (1981) Behavioral geography and the philosophies of meaning. In Cox, K.R. and Golledge, R.G. (eds), *Behavioral Problems in Geography Revisited*, Northwestern University Press, pp. 209–30.

Liben, L.S. (1981) Spatial representation and behavior: multiple perspectives. In Liben, L., Patterson, A.M. and Newcombe, N. (eds), *Spatial Representation and Behavior Across the Life Span*, New York: Academic.

Liben, L.S. (1988) Conceptual issues in the development of spatial cognition. In Stiles-Davis, J., Kritchevsky, M. and Bellugi, U., (eds), *Spatial Cognition: Brain Bases and Development*, Hillsdale, NJ: Lawrence Erlbaum Associates, pp. 167–94.

Liben, L.S. (1991) Environmental cognition through direct and representational experiences: A life-span perspective. In Gärling, T. and Evans, G.W. (eds), *Environment, Cognition and Action—An Integrated Approach*, New York: Plenum, pp. 245–76.

Liben, L.S. (1997) Children's understanding of spatial representations of place: mapping the methodological landscape. In Foreman, N. and Gillett, R. (eds), *Handbook of Spatial Research Paradigms and Methodologies. Volume 1*, Hillsdale, NJ: Erlbaum. pp. 41–83.

Liben, L.S. and Downs, R. (1997) Can-ism and Can'tianism: A straw child. *Annals of the Association of American Geographers* 87, 159–67.

Lieblich, I. and Arbib, M.A. (1982) Multiple representations of space underlying behavior and associated commentaries. *The Behavioral and Brain Sciences* 5(4), 627–60.

Linn, M.C. and Petersen, A.C. (1985) Emergence and characterization of sex differences in spatial ability: A meta-analysis. *Child Development* 56, 1479–98.

Lipman, P.D. (1991) Age and exposure differences in acquisition of route information. *Psychology and Aging 6*, 128–33.

Lloyd, R. (1976) Cognition, preference, and behavior in space: an examination of the structural linkages. *Economic Geography*, 52, 241–53.

Lloyd, R. (1982) A look at images. *Annals of the Association of American Geographers* 72, 532–48.

Lloyd, R. (1989a) Cognitive maps: encoding and decoding information. *Annals of the Association of American Geographers* 79, 101–24.

Lloyd, R. (1989b) The estimation of distance and direction from cognitive maps. *The American Cartographer* 16, 109–22.

Lloyd, R. (1993) Cognitive processes and cartographic maps. In Gärling, T. and Golledge, R.G. (eds), *Behavior and Environment: Psychological and Geographical Approaches*, London: North Holland, pp. 141–69.

Lloyd, R. (1994) Learning spatial prototypes. *Annals of the Association of American Geographers*, 84, 418–40.

Lloyd, R. (1997) *Spatial Cognition: Geographic Environments*, Dordrecht: Kluwer.

Lloyd, R. and Heivly, C. (1987) Systematic distortions in urban cognitive maps. *Annals of the Association of American Geographers* 77, 191–207.

Loewenstein, J. and Gertner, D. (in press) Spatial mapping in preschoolers: Close comparisons facilitate for mappings. *Journal of Cognition and Development*.

Loomis, J.M., Klatzky, R.L., Golledge, R.G., Cicinelli, J.G., Pellegrino, J.W., and Fry, P.A. (1993) Non-visual navigation by blind and sighted: Assessment of path integration ability. *Journal of Experimental Psychology: General* 122, 73–91.

Lowenthal, D. and Riel, M. (1972) The nature of the perceived and imagined environment. *Environment and Behavior* 4, 189–207.

Lowery, R. A. (1973) A method for analyzing distance concepts of urban residents. In Downs, R.M. and Stea, D. (eds), *Image and Environment*. Chicago: Aldine, pp. 338–60.

Lundberg, V. (1973) Emotional and geographical phenomena in psychophysical research. In Downs, R.M. and Stea, D. (eds), *Image and Environment*, Chicago: Aldine, pp. 332–7.

Lunneborg, C.E. and Lunneborg, P.W. (1984) Contribution of sex-differentiated experiences to spatial and mechanical reasoning abilities. *Perceptual and Motor Skills* 59, 107–13.

Lunt, P. (1994) Rethinking space and place: The transformational cultural geography. *Journal of Environmental Psychology* 14, 315–26.

Lynch, K. (1960). *The Image of the City*. Cambridge, MA: MIT Press.

MacEachren, A.M. (1980) Travel time as the basis of cognitive distance. *Professional Geographer* 38, 30–36.

MacEachren, A.M. (1991) The role of maps in spatial knowledge acquisition. *Cartographic Journal* 28, 152–62.

MacEachren, A.M. (1992) Learning spatial information from maps: Can orientation-specificity be overcome? *Professional Geographer* 44, 431–43.

MacEachren, A.M. (1995) *How Maps Work. Representation, Visualization and Design*, New York: Guilford.

Magana, J.R., Evans, G.W. and Romney, A.K. (1981) Scaling techniques in the analysis of environmental cognition data. *Professional Geographer* 33, 294–301.

Magliano, J.P., Cohen, R., Allen, G. and Rodrigue, J.R. (1995) The impact of a wayfinder's goal on learning a new environment: Different types of spatial knowledge as goals. *Journal of Environmental Psychology* 15, 65–75.

Maki, R.H. and Marek, M.N. (1997) Egocentric spatial framework effects from single and multiple points of view. *Memory and Cognition* 25, 677–90.

Mark, D.M. and Gould, M.D. (1991) Interacting with geographic information: A commentary. *Photogrammatic Engineering and Remote Sensing* 57, 1427–30.

Matthews, M.H. (1981) The mental maps of children. *Geography* 65, 169–79.

Matthews, M.H. (1984) Cognitive maps: a comparison of graphic and iconic techniques. *Area* 16, 33–40.

Matthews, M.H. (1985) Young children's representation of the environment: A comparison of techniques. *Journal of Environmental Psychology* 5, 261–78.

Matthews, M.H. (1986) Gender, home range and environmental cognition. *Transactions of the Institute of British Geographers* NS12, 43–56.

Matthews, M.H. (1992) *Making Sense of Place: Children's Characterisation of Place*, Hemel Hempstead: Harvester Wheatsheaf.

May, M., Peruch, P. and Savoyant, A. (1995) Navigating in a virtual environment with map-acquired knowledge: Encoding and alignment effects. *Ecological Psychology* 7, 21–36.

McCalla, G.I., Reid, L. and Schneider, P.F. (1982) Plan creation, plan execution and knowledge acquisition in a dynamic microworld. *International Journal of Man-Machine Studies* 16, 89–112.

McDonald, T.P. and Pellegrino, J.W. (1993) Psychological perspectives on spatial cognition. In Gärling, T. and Golledge, R.G. (eds), *Behavior and Environment: Psychological and Geographical Approaches*, Amsterdam: Elsevier, pp. 47–82.

McGee, M.G. (1983) Spatial abilities: the influence of genetic factors. In

Potegal, M. (ed.), *The Neural and Development Bases of Spatial Orientation*, New York, Academic.

McGuiness, D. and Sparks, J. (1982) Cognitive style and cognitive maps: sex differences in representation of a familiar terrain. *Journal of Mental Imagery* 7, 91–100.

McGuinness, C. (1992) Spatial models in the mind. *Irish Journal of Psychology* 13, 524–35.

McKeever, W.F., Rich, D.A., Deyo, R.A. and Conner, R.L. (1987) Androgens and spatial ability: Failure to find a relationship between testosterone and ability measures. *Bulletin of the Psychonomic Society*, 25, 438–40.

McNamara, T.P. (1986) Mental representation in spatial relations. *Cognitive Psychology* 18, 87–121.

McNamara, T.P., Hardy, J.K. and Hirtle, S.C. (1989) Subjective hierarchies in spatial memory. *Journal of Experimental Psychology: Learning, Memory and Cognition* 15, 271–87.

Medyckyj-Scott, D. and Blades, M. (1992) Human spatial cognition: Its relevance to the design and use of spatial information systems. *Geoforum* 23, 215–26.

Milgram, S. (1973) Introduction. In Ittelson, W.H. (ed.), *Environment and Cognition*, New York: Seminar Press.

Millar, S. (1994) *Understanding and Representing Space: Theory and Evidence from Studies with Blind and Sighted Children*. Oxford: Oxford University Press.

Miller, H.J. (1992) Human wayfinding, environment and behavior relationships and artificial intelligence. *Journal of Planning Literature* 7, 139–52.

Miller, L.K. and Santoni, V. (1986) Sex differences in spatial abilities: strategic and experiential correlates. *Acta Psychologica* 63, 225–35.

Moar, I. and Bower, G. (1983) Inconsistency in spatial knowledge. *Memory and Cognition* 11, 107–13.

Moar, I. and Carlton, L. (1982) Memory for routes. *Quarterly Journal of Experimental Psychology* 34, 381–94.

Moeser, S.D. (1988) Cognitive mapping in a complex building. *Environment and Behavior* 20, 21–49.

Montello, D.R. (1989) The geometry of environmental knowledge. In Frank, A.U., Campari, I. and Formentini, V. (eds), *Theories and Methods of Spatio-Temporal Reasoning in Geographic Space*, New York: Springer-Verlag, pp. 136–152.

Montello, D.R. (1991a) The measurement of cognitive distance: methods and construct validity. *Journal of Environmental Psychology* 11, 101–22.

Montello, D.R. (1991b) Spatial orientation and the angularity of urban routes—A field study. *Environment and Behavior* 23, 47–69.

Montello, D.R. (1993) Scale and multiple psychologies of space. In Frank, A.and Campar, I. (eds), *Spatial Information Theory: A Theoretical Basis for GIS*,

Lecture Notes in Computer Science 716, New York: Springer-Verlag. pp. 312–21.

Montello, D.R. (1998) A new framework for understanding the acquisition of spatial knowledge in large-scale environments. In Golledge, R.G. and Egenhofer, M.J. (eds) *Spatial and Temporal Reasoning in Geographic Information Systems*, New York: Oxford University Press, pp. 143–154.

Montello, D.R., Lovelace, K.L., Golledge, R.G. and Self, C.M. (1999) Sex-related differences and similarities in geographic and environmental spatial abilities. *Annals of the Association of American Geographers*, 515–533.

Montello, D.R. and Pick, H.L. (1993) Integrating knowledge of vertically aligned large-scaled spaces. *Environment and Behavior* 25, 457–84.

Moore, G.T. (1979) Knowing about environmental knowing: The current state of theory and research on environmental cognition. *Environment and Behavior* 11, 33–70.

Moore, G.T. and Golledge, R.G. (1976) Environmental knowing: concepts and theories. In Moore, G.T. and Golledge, R.G. (eds), *Environmental Knowing*, Stroudsberg, PA: Dowden, Hutchinson and Ross, pp. 3–24.

Morrongiello, B.A., Timney, B., Humphrey, G.K., and Anderson, S. (1995) *Journal of Experimental Child Psychology* 59, 211–33.

Muller, J-C. (1982) Non-Euclidean geographic spaces: mapping functional distances. *Geographical Analysis*,14, 189–203.

Murphy, J. (1978) Measures of map accuracy assessment and some early Ulster maps. *Irish Geography* 11, 89–101.

Murray, D. and Spencer, C.P. (1979) The individual differences in the drawing of cognitive maps: the effect of geographical mobility, strength of mental imagery and basic graphic ability. *Transactions of the Institute of British Geographers* NS 4, 385–91.

Naveh-Benjamin, M. (1987) Coding of spatial location information: an automatic process? *Journal of Experimental Psychology: Learning, Memory and Cognition* 13, 595–605.

Naveh-Benjamin, M. (1988) Recognition memory of spatial location information: another failure to support automaticity. *Memory and Cognition* 16, 437–45.

Neisser, U. (1976). *Cognition and Reality*, San Francisco: Freeman.

Nesbitt, R.E. and Wilson, T.D. (1977) Telling more than we can know: verbal reports on mental processes. *Psychological Review* 84, 231–59.

Newcombe, N. (1985) Methods for the study of spatial cognition. In Cohen, R. (ed.), *The Development of Spatial Cognition*, Hillsdale, NJ: Erlbaum Lawrence, pp. 1–12.

Newcombe, N. (1989) The development of spatial perspective taking. *Advances in Child Development and Behavior*, 22, 203–47.

Newcombe, N. (1997) New perspectives on spatial representation: What different tasks tell us about how people remember location. In Foreman, N. and Gillett, R. (eds), *Handbook of Spatial Research Paradigms and Methodologies. Volume 1*. Hillsdale, NJ: Erlbaum, pp. 85–102.

Newcombe, N. and Huttenlocher, J. (1992) Children's early ability to solve perspective taking problems. *Developmental Psychology* 28, 635–43.

Newcombe, N. and Liben, L.S. (1982) Barrier effects in the cognitive maps of children and adults. *Journal of Experimental Child Psychology* 34, 46–58.

Ohta, R.J. (1979) *Spatial Cognition and the Relative Effectiveness of Two Methods of Presenting Information in Young and Elderly Adults*. Unpublished doctoral thesis, University of Southern California, Los Angeles.

Ohta, R.J. and Kirasic, K.C. (1983) Learning about environmental learning in the elderly adult. In Rowles, G. and Ohta, J. (eds), *Aging and Milieu: Environmental Perspectives on Growing Old*, New York: Academic.

Okabe, A., Aoki, K. and Hamamato, W. (1986) Distance and direction judgement in large-scale natural environment—effects of a slope and winding trail. *Environment and Behavior* 18, 755–72.

O'Keefe, J. (1994) Kant and the sea-horse: an essay in the neurophilosophy of space. In Eileen, N., McCarthy, R. and Brewer, W. (eds) *Spatial Representation: Problems in Philosophy and Psychology*, Oxford: Oxford University Press, pp. 43–64.

O'Laughlin, E. and Brubaker, B. (1998) Use of landmarks in cognitive mapping: gender differences in self report vs performance. *Personality and Individual Differences* 24, 595–601.

Orleans, P. (1973) Differential cognition of urban residents: Effects of social scale on mappings. In Downs, R.M. and Stea, D. (eds), *Image and Environment* Chicago: Aldine, pp. 115–30.

Ottosson, T. (1987) Map reading and wayfinding. *Göteborg Studies in Educational Sciences, Volume 65*.

Pacione, M. (1978) Information and morphology in cognitive maps. *Transactions of the Institute of British Geographers*, NS 3, 548–68.

Pacione, M. (1982) Space preferences, location distances, and the dispersal of civil servants from London. *Environment and Planning A*, 323–33.

Pain, R. (1991) Space, sexual violence and social control: integrating geographical and feminist analyses of women's fear of crime. *Progress in Human Geography* 15, 415–31.

Paivio, A. (1979) *Imagery and Verbal Processes*, New York: Holt, Rinehart and Winston.

Paivio, A. (1986) *Mental representations: A dual coding process*, New York: Oxford University Press.

Papageorgio, Y.Y. (1982) Some thoughts about theory in the social sciences. *Geographical Analysis* 14, 340–46.

Passini, R. (1992) *Wayfinding in Architecture*, New York: Van Nostrand Reinhold.

Passini, R. and Proulx, G. (1988) Wayfinding without vision: an experiment with congenitally blind people. *Environment and Behavior* 20, 227–52.

Passini, R., Dupré, A., and Langlois, C. (1986) Spatial mobility of the visually handicapped active person: A descriptive study. *Journal of Visual Impairment and Blindness*, 80, 904–7.

Passini, R., Proulx, G. and Rainville, C. (1990) The spatio-cognitive abilities of the visually impaired population. *Environment and Behavior* 22, 91–118.

Passini, R., Rainville, C., Marchand, N. and Joanette, Y. (1995) Wayfinding in dementia of the Alzheimer type: Planning abilities. *Journal of Clinical and Experimental Neuropsychology* 17, 820–32.

Patel, H., Blades, M. and Andrade, J. (1999) Children's incidental recall for colours. *British Journal of Developmental Psychology*, 17, 537–549.

Pearce, P.L. (1981) A study of travellers' perceptions of a section of countryside. *Journal of Environmental Psychology* 1, 141–55.

Perlmutter, M., Metzger, R., Nezworski, T. and Miller, K. (1981) Spatial and temporal memory in 20 and 60 years. *Journal of Gerontology* 36, 59–65.

Peruch, P., Gaunet, F., Thinus-Blanc, C. and Loomis, J. (2000) Using virtual technology to investigate mental spatial representations. In Kitchin, R. and Freundschuh, S. (eds), *Cognitive Mapping. Past, Present, and Future*, London: Routledge, 108–124.

Peruch, P. and Lapin, E.A. (1993) Route knowledge in different spatial frames of reference. *Acta Psychologica* 84, 253–69.

Peruch, P., Vercher, J. and Gauthier, G.M. (1995) Acquisition of spatial knowledge through visual exploration of simulated environments. *Ecological Psychology* 7, 1–20.

Phipps, A.G. (1979) Scaling problems in the cognition of urban distances. *Transactions of the Institute of British Geographers* 4, 94–102.

Piaget, J. and Inhelder, B. (1956) *The Child's Conception of Space*, London: Routledge and Kegan Paul.

Piaget, J., Inhelder, B., and Szeminska, A. (1960) *The Child's Conception of Geometry*, New York: Norton.

Pick, H.L. (1976) Transactional–Constructivist approach to Environmental Knowing: A commentary. In Moore, G.T. and Golledge, R.G. (eds), *Environmental Knowing*, Stroudsberg, PA: Dowden, Hutchinson and Ross, pp. 185–8.

Pinheiro, J.Q. (1998) Determinants of cognitive maps of the world as expressed in sketch maps. *Journal of Environmental Psychology* 18, 321–39.

Pocock, D.C.D. (1972) The city in the mind: A review of mental maps in urban areas. *Scottish Geographical Magazine* 88, 116–24.

Pocock, D.C.D. (1973) Environmental perception: process and product. *Tijdschrift Voor Econmische en Social Geografie* 64, 251–7.

Pocock, D.C.D. (1976) Some characteristics of mental maps An empirical study. *Transactions of the Institute of British Geographers* NS 1, 493–512.

Portugali, J. (ed.), (1996) *The Construction of Cognitive Maps.* Dordrecht: Kluwer.

Portugali, J. (1996) Inter-representation networks and cognitive mapping. In Portugali, J. (ed.) *The Construction of Cognitive Maps.* Dordrecht: Kluwer, pp. 11–43.

Portugali, J. and Haken, H. (1992) Synergetics and cognitive maps. *Geoforum* 23, 111–30.

Presson, C.C. and Hazelrigg, M.D. (1984) Building spatial representations through primary and secondary learning. *Journal of Experimental Psychology: Learning, Memory and Cognition* 10, 716–22.

Proshansky, H.M. and O'Hanlan, T. (1977) Environmental psychology: origins and development. In Stokols, D. (ed.), *Perspectives on Environment and Behavior*, New York: Plenum, pp. 101–29.

Pylyshyn, Z.W. (1979) The rate of mental rotation of images: a test of a holistic analogue hypothesis. *Memory and Cognition* 7, 19–28.

Pylyshyn, Z.W. (1981) The imagery debate: Analogue media versus tacit knowledge. *Psychological Review* 88, 16–45.

Regian, J.W. and Yadrick, R.M. (1994) Assessment of configurational knowledge of naturally- and artificially-acquired large-scale space. *Journal of Environmental Psychology* 3, 211–23.

Resnick, S.M., Berenbaum, S.A., Gottesman, I. and Bouchard, T.J. (1986) Early hormonal influences on cognitive functioning in congenital adrenal hyperplasia. *Developmental Psychology* 22, 191–8.

Richardson, A.E., Montello, D.R. and Hegarty, M. (1999) Spatial knowledge acquisition from maps, and from navigation in real and virtual environments. *Memory and Cognition*, 27, 741–750.

Richardson, G.D. (1981a) The appropriateness of using various Minkowskian metrics for representing cognitive configurations. *Environment and Planning A* 13, 475–85.

Richardson, G.D. (1981b) Comparing two cognitive mapping methodologies. *Area* 16, 325–31.

Rieser, J.J., Lockman, J.L. and Pick, H.L. (1980) The role of visual experience in knowledge of a spatial layout. *Perception and Psychophysics* 28, 185–90.

Rieser, J.J., Guth, D.A. and Hill, E.W. (1986) Sensitivity to perspective structure while walking without vision. *Perception* 15, 173–88.

Rieser, J.J., Hill, E.W., Taylor, C.R., Bradfield, A. and Rosen, S. (1992) Visual experience, visual field size, and the development of nonvisual sensitivity to the spatial structure of outdoor neighborhoods explored by walking. *Journal of Experimental Psychology: General* 121, 210–21.

Robinson, M.E. (1974) Cloze procedure and spatial comprehension test. *Area* 9, 137–42.

Rossano, M.J. and Morrison, T.T. (1996) Learning from maps: General processes and map-structure influences. *Cognition and Instruction* 14, 109–37.

Rossano, M.J. and Warren, D.H. (1989) Misaligned maps lead to predictable errors. *Perception*, 18, 805–16.

Rossano, M.J., Warren, D.H., and Kenan, A. (1995) Orientation specificity: How general is it? *American Journal of Psychology* 108, 359–80.

Rossano, M.J., West, S.O., Robertson, T.J., Wayne, M.C. and Chase, R.B. (1999) The acquisition of route and survey knowledge from computer models. *Journal of Enviromental Psychology* 19, 101–15.

Russ, R.C. and Schenkman, R.I. (1980) Editorial statement: Theory and method and their basis in psychological investigation. *The Journal of Mind and Behavior* 1, 1–7.

Saarinen, T.F., MacCabe, C.L. and Morehouse, B. (1988) *Sketch Maps of the World as Surrogates for World Geographic Knowledge*, Discussion paper 83–3, Department of Geography and Regional Development, Univ. of Arizona, Tucson.

Saarinen, T.F., Parton, M. and Billberg, R. (1996) Relative size of continents on world sketch maps. *Cartographica* 33, 37–47.

Saarinen, T.F., Seamon, D. and Sell, J.L. (eds), (1984) *Environmental Perception and Behavior: An Inventory and Prospect*, Research Paper 209, Department of Geography, University of Chicago.

Sadalla, E.K., Burroughs, W.J. and Staplin, L.J. (1980) Reference points in spatial cognition. *Journal of Experimental Psychology: Human Learning and Memory* 6, 516–28.

Sadalla, E.K. and Staplin, L.J. (1980a) An information storage model for distance cognition. *Environment and Behavior* 12, 183–93.

Saisa, J., Svensson-Gärling, A., Gärling, T., and Lindberg, E. (1986) Intraurban cognitive distance: the relationship between judgements of straight-line distances, travel distances, and travel times. *Geographical Analysis* 18, 167–74.

Salthouse, T.A. (1991) *Theoretical Perspectives on Cognitive Aging*, Hillsdale, NJ: Erlbaum.

Sanders, R.A. and Porter, P.W. (1974) Shape in revealed mental maps. *Annals of the Association of American Geographers* 64, 258–67.

Schmajuk, N.A. and Thieme, A.D. (1992) Purposive behavior and cognitive mapping: a neural network model. *Biological cybernetics* 67, 165–74.

Schmitz, S. (1997) Gender-related strategies in environmental development:

Effects of anxiety on wayfinding in and representation of a three-dimensional maze. *Journal of Environmental Psychology* 17, 215–28.

Self, C.M. and Golledge, R.G. (1994) Sex-related differences in spatial ability: what every geography educator should know. *Journal of Geography* 93, 234–43.

Self, C.M. and Golledge, R.G. (in press) Sex, gender and cognitive mapping. In Kitchin, R. and Freundschuh, S. (eds), *Cognitive Mapping. Past, Present, and Future*, London: Routledge.

Self, C.M., Gopal, S., Golledge, R.G. and Fenstermaker, S. (1992) Gender-related differences in spatial abilities. *Progress in Human Geography* 16, 315–42.

Sell, J. (1994) Editorial. *Newsletter of the Environmental Behavior and Perception Study Group*, Association of American Geographers.

Sell, J.L., Taylor, J.G. and Zube, E.H. (1984) Towards a theoretical framework for landscape perception. In Saarinen, T., Seamon, D. and Sell, J. (eds), *Environmental Perception and Behavior: An Inventory and Prospect*, Research Paper 209, Department of Geography, University of Chicago, pp. 61–84.

Sellal, F., Fontaine, S.F., Van Der Linden, M., Rainville, C. and Labrecque, R. (1996) To be or not to be at home? A neuropsychological approach to delusion for place. *Journal of Clinical and Experimental Neuropsychology* 18, 234–48.

Shemyakin, F. N. (1962) Orientation in Space. In Ananyev, B.G. *et al.*, (eds), *Psychological Science in the U.S.S.R., Vol 1*, Report #62–11083, Office of Technical Services, Washington DC, pp. 186–255.

Sholl, M.J. (1987) Cognitive maps as orienting schemata. *Journal of Experimental Psychology: Learning, Memory and Cognition* 13, 615–28.

Sholl, M.J. (1996) From visual information to cognitive maps. In Portugali, J. (ed.) *The Construction of Cognitive Maps*, Dordrecht: Kluwer, pp. 157–86.

Shute, V.J., Pellegrino, J.W., Hubert, L. and Reynolds, R. (1983) The relationship between androgen levels and human spatial abilities. *Bulletin of the Psychonomic Society* 21, 465–8.

Siegel, A.W. (1977) Finding one's way around the large-scale environment: the development of spatial representation. In McGurk, H. (ed.), *Ecological Factors in Human Development*, Amsterdam: North Holland.

Siegel, A.W. and Schadler, M. (1977) The development of young children's spatial representations of their environment. *Child Development* 48, 388–94.

Siegel, A.W. and White, S. (1975) The development of spatial representation of large-scale environments. In Reese, H. (ed.), *Advances in Child Development and Behavior*, New York, Academic, pp. 9–55.

Smith, T.R., Pellegrino, J.W. and Golledge, R.G. (1982) Computational process modeling of spatial cognition and behavior. *Geographical Analysis* 14, 305–25.

Smyth, M.M. and Kennedy, J.E. (1982) Orientation and spatial representation within multiple frames of reference. *British Journal of Psychology* 73, 527–35.

Spencer, C. and Blades, M. (1986) Pattern and process: A review essay on the relationship between behavioral geography and environmental psychology. *Progress in Human Geography* 10, 230–48.

Spencer, C., Blades, M. and Morsley, K. (1989) *The Child in the Physical Environment*, Chichester: Wiley.

Spencer, C. and Darvizeh, Z. (1983) Young children's place descriptions, maps, and route finding: a comparison of nursery school children in Iran and Britain. *International Journal of Early Childhood* 15, 26–31.

Spencer, C. and Dixon, J. (1983) Mapping the development of feelings about the city: a longitudinal study of new residents' affective maps. *Transactions of the Institute of British Geographers* 8, 373–83.

Staplin, L.J. and Sadalla, E.K. (1981) Distance cognition in urban environments. *Professional Geographer* 33, 302–10.

Stea, D. (1969) The measurement of mental maps: An experimental model for studying conceptual spaces. In Cox, K. and Golledge, R.G. (eds), *Behavioral Problems in Geography*, Evanston, IL: Northwestern Studies in Geography, pp. 228–53.

Stea, D. (1976) Notes on a spatial fugue. In Moore, G.T. and Golledge, R.G. (eds), *Environmental Knowing*, Stroudsberg, PA: Dowden, Hutchinson and Ross.

Stea, D., Blaut, J. and Stephens, J. (1996) Mapping as a cultural universal. In Portugali, J. (ed.) *The Construction of Cognitive Maps*. Dordrecht: Kluwer, pp. 345–60.

Stevens, A. and Coupe, P. (1978) Distortions in judged spatial relations. *Cognitive Psychology* 10, 422–37.

Stock, W.A., Kulhavy, R.W., Peterson, S.E., Hancock, T.E. and Verdi, M.P. (1995) Mental representations of maps and verbal descriptions: Evidence that they may affect text memory differently. *Contemporary Educational Psychology* 20, 237–56.

Stokols, D. and Altman, I. (1987) *Handbook of Environmental Psychology*, Volume 1 and 2, New York: Wiley.

Talmy, L. (1983) How language structures space. In Pick, H.L. and Acredolo, L.P. (eds), *Spatial Orientation: Theory, Research and Application*, New York: Plenum, pp. 225–82.

Taylor, H.A. and Tversky, B. (1992a) Description and depictions of environments. *Memory and Cognition*, 20, 483–96.

Taylor, H.A. and Tversky, B. (1992b) Spatial mental models derived from survey and route descriptions. *Journal of Memory and Language* 31, 261–92.

Thill, J-C. and Sui, D.Z. (1993) Mental maps and fuzziness in space preferences. *Professional Geographer* 45, 264–76.

Thinus-Blanc, C. and Gaunet, F. (1997) Representation of space in blind persons: vision as a spatial sense? *Psychological Bulletin* 121, 20–42.

Thompson, E.G., Harris, L.J. and Mann, I. (1981) Relationships among sex, measures of cognitive complexity, and performance on spatial tasks in college students. *British Journal of Psychology*.

Thorndyke, P.W. (1983) Spatial cognition and reasoning. In Harvey, J. (ed.), *Cognition, Social Behavior and the Environment*, Hillsdale, NJ: Lawrence Erlbaum, pp. 137–49.

Thorndyke, P.W. and Hayes-Roth, B. (1982) Differences in spatial knowledge acquired from maps and navigation. *Cognitive Psychology*, 14, 560–89.

Thorndyke, P.W. and Stasz, C. (1980) Individual differences in procedures for knowledge acquisition from maps and navigation. *Cognitive Psychology* 12, 137–75.

Thrift, N. (1981) Behavioral geography. In Wrigley, N. and Bennett, R. (eds), *Quantitative Geography in Britain*. London: Routledge and Kegan Paul, pp. 352–368.

Timmermans, H.J.P. (1993) Retail environments and spatial shopping behavior. In Gärling, T. and Golledge, R.G. (eds), *Behavior and Environment*, Amsterdam: Elsevier, pp. 342–77.

Tlauka, M. and Wilson, P.N. (1994) The effect of landmarks on route learning in a computer simulated environment. *Journal of Environmental Psychology*, 14, 305–13.

Tlauka, M. and Wilson, P.N. (1996) Orientation-free representations from navigation through a computer-simulated environment. *Environment and Behavior* 28, 647–64.

Tobler, W.R. (1965) Computation of the correspondence of geographic patterns. *Papers and Proceedings of the Regional Science Association* 15, 131–9.

Tobler, W.R. (1976) The geometry of mental maps. In Golledge, R.G. and Rushton, G. (eds), *Spatial Choice and Spatial Behavior*, Columbus, OH: Ohio State University Press, pp. 69–82.

Tobler, W.R. (1978) Comparison of plane forms. *Geographical Analysis* 10, 154–62.

Tolman, E.C. (1948) Cognitive maps in rats and men. *Psychological Review*, 55, 189–208.

Tolman, E.C. and Honzik, C.H. (1930) 'Insight' in rats. *University of California Publications in Psychology* 4, 215–32.

Torrel, G. (1990) The acquisition and development of environmental cognition in children. *Göteborg Psychological Reports. Volume 20.*

Tracey, D. (1987) Toys, spatial ability, and science and mathematics achievement: Are they related? *Sex Roles* 17, 115–38.

Tuan, Yi-Fu. (1975) Images and mental maps. *Annals of the Association of American Geographers* 65, 205–13.

Tversky, B. (1981) Distortions in memory for maps. *Cognitive Psychology* 13, 407–33.

Tversky, B. (2000) Levels and structure of spatial knowledge. In Kitchin, R. and Freundschuh, S. (eds), *Cognitive Mapping. Past, Present, and Future*, London: Routledge, pp. 24–43.

Tversky, B. and Lee, P.U. (1998) How space structures language. In Freska, C., Habel, C. and Wender, K.F. (eds), *Spatial Cognition: An Interdisciplinary Approach to Representation and Processing of Spatial Knowledge*, Berlin: Springer-Verlag. pp. 157–75.

Ungar, S. (2000) Cognitive mapping without visual experience. In Kitchin, R. and Freundschuh, S. (eds), *Cognitive Mapping. Past, Present, and Future*, London: Routledge, pp. 221–248.

Ungar, S., Blades, M. and Spencer, C. (1996) The construction of cognitive maps by children with visual impairments. In Portugali, J. (ed.) *The Construction of Cognitive Maps*, Dordrecht: Kluwer.

Ungar, S., Blades, M. and Spencer, C. (1997) Strategies for knowledge acquisition from cartographic maps by blind and visually impaired adults. *Cartographic Journal* 34, 93–110.

Uttal, D and Tan, L.S. (2000) Cognitive mapping in childhood. In Kitchin, R. and Freundschuh, S. (eds), *Cognitive Mapping: Past, Present, and Future*, London: Routledge, 147–165.

Uttal, D. (2000) Seeing the big picture: map use and the development of spatial cognition. *Developmental Science*, 3, 247–264.

Valentine, G. (1990) Women's fear and the design of public space. *Built Environment* 16, 279–87.

Valentine, G. (1997) 'Oh yes I can' 'Oh no you can't': Children and parents' understandings of kids' competence to negotiate public sapce safely. *Antipode* 29, 65–89.

Vanetti, E.J. and Allen, G.L. (1988) Communicating environmental knowledge—The impact of verbal and spatial abilities on the production and comprehension of route directions. *Environment and Behavior*, 26, 667–82.

Van Vliet, W. (1983) Exploring the fourth environment: An examination of the home range of city and suburban teenagers. *Environment and Behavior* 15, 567–88.

Von Senden, S.M. (1932) *Space and Sight: The Perception of Space and Shape by the Congenitally Blind Before and After Operation*, Glencoe, IL: The Free Press.

Vujakovic, P. and Matthews, M.H. (1994) Contorted, folded, torn: environmental values, cartographic representation and the politics of disability. *Disability and Society* 9, 359–75.

Wakabayashi, Y. (1990) Relative distortions in cognitive maps in Sapporo. *Geographical Review of Japan* 63A, 255–73.

Wakabayashi, Y. (1994) Spatial analysis of cognitive maps. *Geographical Reports of Tokyo Metropolitan University* Number 29.

Wakabayashi, Y. (1996) Behavioral studies on environmental perception by geographers. *Geographical Review of Japan* 63, 83–94.

Walmsley, D.J. (1982) Mass media and spatial awareness. *Tijdschrift Voor Economische en Sociale Geografie* 73, 32–42.

Walmsley, D.J. and Lewis, G. (1993) *People and Environment*, London: Longman.

Walmsley, D.J., Saarinen, T.F. and MacCabe, C.L. (1990) Down under or centre stage? The world images of Australian students. *Australian Geographer* 21, 164–73.

Ward, S.L., Newcombe, N. and Overton, W.F. (1986) Turn left at the church, or three miles north. A study of direction giving and sex differences. *Environment and Behavior* 18, 192–213.

Waterman, S. and Gordan, D. (1984) A quantitative–comparative approach to analysis of distortion in mental maps. *Professional Geographer* 36, 326–37.

West, R.L., Morris, C.W. and Nichol, G.T. (1985) Spatial cognition on nonspatial tasks: Finding spatial knowledge when you're not looking for it. In Cohen, R. (ed.), *The Development of Spatial Cognition*, Hillsdale, NJ: Erlbaum Lawerence, pp. 13–39.

Wiegand, P. (1992) *Places in the Primary School*, London: Falmer.

Wilkness, S.M., Jones, M.G., Kovol, D.L., Gold, P.E. and Manning, C.A. (1997) Age-related differences in an ecologically based study of route learning. *Psychology and Aging* 12, 372–375.

Williamson, J. and McGuinness, C. (1990) The role of schemata in the comprehension of maps. In Gilhooley, K.J., Keane, M.T.G., Logie, R.H., and Erdos, G. (eds), *Lines of Thinking* 2. Chichester: Wiley, 29–40.

Wilson, P.N. (1997) Use of virtual reality computing in spatial learning research. In Foreman, N. and Gillett, R. (eds), *Handbook of Spatial Research Paradigms and Methodologies. Volume 1*, Hillsdale, NJ: Erlbaum, pp. 181–206.

Wilson, P.N., Foreman, N. and Tlauka, M. (1997) Transfer of spatial information from a virtual to a real environment. *Human Factors* 39, 526–31.

Wilton, R. (1979) Knowledge of spatial relations: a specification from information used in making inferences. *Quarterly Journal of Experimental Psychology* 31, 133–46.

Witelson, S.F. and Swallow, J.A. (1988) Neuropsychological study of the development of spatial cognition. In Stiles-Davis, J., Kritchevsky, M. and Bellugi, U. (eds), *Spatial Cognition: Brain Bases and Development*, Hillsdale, NJ: Lawrence Erlbaum Associates, pp. 373–409.

Wood, D. and Beck, R. (1976) Talking with Environmental A: An experimental mapping language. In Moore, G.T. and Golledge, R.G. (eds), *Environmental Knowing*, Stroudsberg, PA: Dowden, Hutchinson and Ross, pp. 351–61.

Wood, D. and Beck, R. (1989) Janine Eber maps London: Individual dimensions of cognitive imagery. *Journal of Environmental Psychology* 9, 1–26.

Wood, D. and Beck, R. (1990) Tour personality: The interdependence of environmental orientation and interpersonal behavior. *Journal of Environmental Psychology* 10, 177–207.

Worchel, P. (1951) Space perception and orientation in the blind. *Psychological Monographs* 65, 1–28.

Wunderlich, D. and Reinelt, R. (1982) How to get there from here. In Jarvella, R.J. and Klein, W. (eds), *Speech, Place and Action: Studies in Deixis and Related Topics*. Chichester: Wiley. pp. 183–202.

Zubin, D. (1989) Oral presentation cited in Mark, D. (ed.), *Languages of Spatial Relations: Researchable Questions and Agenda*. National Centre for Geographical Information and Analysis Report 89–2A.

Index